THE ROAD TO DEAL PIER

The Undiplomatic Memoirs
of a British Diplomat

Kevin J. Lynch

I AM SELF-
PUBLISHING

@iamselfpub
www.iamselfpublishing.com

FOR LEONE, BENNY AND ADELE

Contents

CONTENTS

Preface

This book is about my life in Her Majesty's Diplomatic Service.

A lot of this book is true; on the other hand, some of the facts and incidents have been embellished, whilst the rest of it is completely untrue and utter rubbish. Throughout it all is my personal bias. At times, my memories of the people, places, geographies, cities, and even continents, may be a bit a hazy. That may be due to being sixty years old, or the fact that I was drunk at the time, or in love, or in lust, or lost; or that nowadays I am in partial denial about certain incidents, or more likely, I just liked the way a particular moment looked on the page. And, of course, fitting some thirty-eight years of working for the Foreign and Commonwealth Office (FCO) into a book of this size means that vast tracts have been missed out – some very deliberately so. And other events, stories, embellishments, lies may have been removed from different time frames and put into one single anecdote or tale.

Anyway, all the dishonesty, subterfuge, exaggerations, facts that are not facts, and historical inaccuracies are entirely my own fault. I do not know if there is such a thing as a non-fiction semi-autobiographical book, but here goes. In the event that anyone does object to anything, get a life, and if that does not suffice, sue me. Actually, do not do that, write a letter of complaint and I will do my best to ignore you or appease you. My choice.

Many of my friends (and enemies!) might be a tad disappointed not to find themselves mentioned in the following pages. I can only apologise and say that they have not been forgotten, but had I done so and included their exploits, the book would have been double the size of *War and Peace*. But saying that, they might find a reference to themselves in the Acknowledgements at the end of the book. And no, do not just go and look there whilst in the bookshop. Buy the book!

Author's Notes on Diplomatic Posts and Diplomatic Postings

Most people will have heard of Embassies and perhaps High Commissions. These are the places abroad where our diplomats allegedly work. However, Her Majesty's representation abroad is a bit more complicated than just Embassies and High Commissions. There are other weird and wonderful establishments (alas, not pubs) in which we hide away to earn our salaries. There are more types than you think, and it is not as simple as you think. We could make it simpler, but then the general population might get too much information and we would not want that, would we?

Here, I try to explain these establishments. So, you'll find below the idiot's guide, should you or your family (and I am not implying that any or all of you are idiots – God forbid) ever need to know the differences:

Embassy – headed up by the Ambassador. There's no such entity as an Ambassadress – at least, I never saw that particular title used. Embassies are based in non-Commonwealth countries (with the exception of the USA, most Commonwealth countries are those that we conquered in days long gone).

High Commission (there are no Low Commissions) – headed up by the High Commissioner (no such thing as a High Commissioneress – at least, I never saw that particular title used). High Commissions are usually based in Commonwealth countries (see above).

Note one: Some diplomatic purists will also no doubt point out that the appointments of these Heads of Post are by Her Majesty the Queen, as Head of State, for an Ambassador and by the Prime Minister, as Head of Government, for a High Commissioner. However, as this is the idiot's guide, I am not going to get into all that.

Consulate General – in really big non-Commonwealth countries (think China and the USA), where work in the capital city is covered by the Embassy, there might be other big cities worthy of having British diplomats to cover the work there (think Chicago, Los Angeles, Shanghai, Guangzhou etc.). And these Consulates General are usually headed up by British Diplomats called Consuls General (the singular is Consul General). They are probably called a lot of other things, but let us not digress. Basically, the Consulates General are sub-offices of the Embassy (but some have been known to take on a life of their own and, to the utter annoyance of the Ambassador, do their own thing, disregarding input from the Embassy).

Consulate – a smaller version of a Consulate General, which is normally headed up by a Consul. Denver, on my arrival, was a Consulate and I a Consul. Later, it was upgraded to a Consulate General and me to a Consul General. However, it is now, I believe, a Trade Office – see more below. But I do wish they would make up their minds about Denver.

Deputy High Commission – in really big Commonwealth countries (think India), where work in the capital city is covered by the High Commission, there might be other big cities worthy of having British diplomats to cover the work there (think Mumbai, Calcutta). And believe it or not, these Deputy High Commissions are headed up by (drum roll) a Deputy High Commissioner.

Note Two: Worldwide, these Consulates General, Consulates and Deputy High Commissions are collectively known as subordinate posts. Some have been described not as subordinate posts, but as living hells, hidden gems, the "what on earth are we doing here post?" And some heads of the sovereign posts in the capital cities have called them insubordinate posts. I could not possibly comment.

Note Three: But the matter of Consulate Generals, Consulates and Deputy High Commissions is further confused by Commonwealth Realms. Excluding the UK, there are thirteen but the only ones that have subordinate posts are the big three: New Zealand, Australia and Canada. These posts are in the Commonwealth and have High Commissions (Wellington, Canberra and Ottawa), but their subordinate posts are Consulates General (Auckland and Sydney, to name two in Australasia, and Toronto and Vancouver, to name two in Canada). Do not ask me why. I am trying to keep this simple.

Delegation – for example, the United Kingdom Delegation to the North Atlantic Treaty Organisation UKDEL NATO, which is the subject of Part Two of this book. We have delegations to various international organisations – the Organisation for Economic Co-Operation and Development (surely, economic co-operation is now a contradiction in terms) is another example. These delegations are normally headed up by a very senior diplomat with the title of Permanent Representative, aka the Permrep. I thought that always sounded like some sort of hairdressing salesperson, but that was just me and, for career purposes, I kept it very much to myself. Nothing permanent about it, of course; those senior figures were posted in and out on the same basis as we mere mortals.

Mission – the United Kingdom Mission to the United Nations (UKMIS New York). Exactly the same as a delegation really, but on a mission – not sure what, but there we go.

Representation – the United Kingdom Representation to the European Union (UKRep Brussels). This is exactly the same as a delegation, as far as I could and can see. But it might, post-Brexit, have to change its name.

Trade Office – few and far between, but can be headed up by a British diplomat, as in Al-Khobar (Saudi Arabia), or a local businessperson, as in Denver (the USA, if you did not know). Normally in existence, as the title suggests, for trade.

Overseas Territory – see the chapter on Pitcairn. These are, basically, fourteen overseas territories "managed" by the British government. It is quite a bit more complicated than that – but I want to get on with the book. These territories are probably the last vestiges of the British Empire. I am sure there are more than a few people in London, and dotted around the globe, who wish that some, if not all, of these territories would cut the Imperial umbilical cord and run their own affairs.

Honorary Consulate – similar to a Consulate, but normally headed up by a local businessperson. They are our value for money offices, where we cannot (or do not want to) open up an expensive Consulate. They can deal with local politics and trade and investment, but nowadays mostly deal with, for their sins in previous lives, British nationals in trouble overseas who have lost passports, just got lost, had too much ecstasy, too much local brew, too much any brew and done too much smuggling, to name but a few of the sins of our fellow countrymen and women.

Diplomatic Postings

As with Diplomatic Posts, diplomatic postings are not that simple. The lengths of these postings are dependent on the nature of the host country and, indeed, the British diplomats are in their diplomatic posts courtesy of the host government. That is, any and/or all of our diplomats can be kicked out at pretty short notice – think of recent events in Salisbury and Russia.

But if everything is going to plan, a diplomat can expect to serve four or five years in the "developed" countries in the "developed world". And then, as the so-called development decreases, so too do the lengths of diplomatic postings. So some postings in Africa and Asia will be three or even two years. In war zones (think Iraq and Afghanistan) postings can be as short as six months. Quite right too, for health, safety and sanity reasons; who would want to hang out in those places for too long? A posting to North Korea is twelve months, I believe – probably fifty-one weeks too long.

And then there are Temporary Duties. This is when a particular post needs a particular officer (although I do not think they were too particular when they chose me to do my Temporary Duties) to help for, normally, a quite short period of time. My TDs, as they were called, were Jeddah, Baghdad, Geneva, The Seychelles, Yekaterinburg and the famous (or infamous) Pitcairn Islands.

And finally, being in the FCO in London was known as a "Home Posting".

So here I am, upside down in a ditch, pinned by a converted quad bike. I have a broken arm and the petrol tank has fractured, dripping petrol on the head of the Head of Tourism Department. She is bleeding. So am I. My blood is a mixture of blood and white wine and is gently flowing from a wound in my arm. And it is getting dark here on Pitcairn Island.

How on earth did it come to this?

Part One

And in the Beginning, there was Prison...

October 1976 – January 1981

Chapter One

Jail Time

My hometown is Deal. A gem of a town planted very nicely in the far corner of South-East Kent.

Deal in 1978 was a hardworking, hard drinking, hard playing and well-paid mining community. Those not working down the mine could earn a living from the cross-channel ferries. And still others worked in various walks of life. The townsfolk, no matter what their professions, be they young or middle-aged, all lived for the Friday and Saturday nights down the pub or the delights (I use the term loosely) of Margate or Folkestone.

For myself, I had done short stints on the cross-channel ferries as a deck boy. Not a cabin boy, nor a rent boy, but a deck boy. There are fundamental differences in the three professions. I shall leave it at that. But I did learn some skills (apart from drinking copious amounts of beer); my seamanship skills – a large exaggeration – were to stand me in good stead for later adventures in Senegal and the Pitcairn Islands. But I am getting ahead of myself.

At the tender age of eighteen, I allegedly had a career. I was in Her Majesty's Prison Canterbury. No, not for some heinous crime (although I think some would like to believe that!), but as a young clerk. I had two roles: the Industries clerk, which entailed ensuring that all the inmates had what they needed (within the law) to work in the prison workshops, and the other as the Earnings clerk. This was a powerful role. It got respect, albeit from those who had either lost or sold theirs and were now languishing in the aforementioned HMP Canterbury. But both roles enabled me the freedom (pun intended) to have certain keys and, with my own personal protection, to enter the wings, landings and cells of Hotel Canterbury. In those cells and workshops and on those landings, I had to work and mix with the bad, sad, mad and evil from the underworld from various dark corners of the United Kingdom.

Occasionally, some very wicked and weird men would cross my path – for obvious reasons, I did not try to cross theirs – members of the IRA, Mad Frankie Fraser, and a sociopathic multiple gangland torturer named Ivan, to name but three. These particular felons all had one thing in common; they were all on their way to the English Alcatraz – the lifer prisons on the Isle of Wight.

As the Industries clerk and the earnings clerk, I had 'trustees' working for me. My favourite was Big John. John was a giant of a man (who would have guessed?) incarcerated for importing pornography from Holland. And also, taken into consideration, was the crime of importing fridges from Holland. I'm not sure if the two are linked, but apparently, fridges from Holland needed some sort of duty to be paid prior to being resold in the sunny suburbs of South-East Kent.

I suspect that the pornography also needed some sort of duty to be paid before being resold to those who needed such stuff, rather than enjoying the real fruits of the sunny suburbs of South-East Kent. I later discovered that John had convictions for running brothels in East Croydon. And, of course, now it all fits together – he needed fridges and porn (not necessarily in that order) for his bordellos in Croydon. The Business plan was simple but effective, cold drinks and hot magazines for even hotter women of loose virtue.

John was in his early sixties. He had had a life of crime and now just wanted to do his time (four and a half years) and get back to his brothel, pornography and fridges. In the meantime, he had to balance my books. In essence, this meant that we would be sitting beside each other for hours on end, before computers were invented, totting up the wages for all the inmates toiling in the prison workshops.

Whilst sitting side by side, we would, occasionally, as normal human beings do (or as normal as one can get when an eighteen-year-old boy, just out of grammar school, is sat next to a convicted old lag who has spent more time behind bars than I had been alive), chat about our respective lives. In prison, it is not the done thing to discuss how one gained a custodial sentence. But, as I had access to John's file and John knew that, he was not opposed to chatting about himself. On a slow day, I asked him what had happened and how he had got caught. John explained that, as he was coming through Dover docks with the aforementioned porno/fridge contraband, he was pulled over by a rather rotund Customs officer, who looked like the late great Welsh singer Harry Secombe.

At this point, I changed the conversation and, as normal, we trotted off to the wings and cells and workshops to check with the prison officers in charge of the inmates that our calculations were correct. What you do not want to do in prison is get the inmates' earnings wrong. Some of the inmates, actually most of them, knew that we could make mistakes and were quite forgiving (for felons); but others would make a rather large song and dance (aka a one-man riot) about the whole thing, forgetting that they were actually in prison and lucky to have a job at all. After our checks, John headed off to his 'Peter'. I was quick to learn that Peter was rhyming slang for cell. Peter Pan equals can and you can guess the rest.

I made my way home and had tea with my Mum, brothers and sisters and my Dad – a Customs officer from Dover who had won prizes for looking like Harry Secombe. After the usual Lynch family banter over the dinner table, I asked my Dad about a certain inmate called John. My Dad told me that yes, he had arrested a large man from Croydon who was trying to smuggle pornography and fridges into England. I explained to my Dad that this man was now my trustee and we had a rather middle-class laugh about the whole affair.

The following morning, in my office, I was chatting to John and I explained to him that the customs officer who had found the porn and the fridges was actually my Dad. He came back with the immortal reply, "What type of family do you come from? Here I am, doing a four-and-a-half-year stretch – your Dad put me away and now I'm working for you, his eighteen-year-old son. Really, what type of family are you?!" At this stage, laughing hysterically through comedy or fear, I do not know which, I thought I might not use my limited A-level intellect to explain to John that perhaps my family might have fared better then he himself was actually doing at that precise moment in time!

John was a lovable rogue. But a rogue he was. One day, I came into work and found that I had a new trustee. I asked the prison officers what had happened to John. They said that they had, in the early hours of that morning, raided several cells and found several hundred packets of tobacco (currency in prison in the late Seventies) in John's cell and, not surprisingly for me, numerous pornographic magazines. He had thus been demoted from his position as a trustee and was now on the wing in one of the workshops – the one that was finishing the sewing of Her Britannic Majesty's Diplomatic mail bags – what an omen that was. We had a quick chat, John was transferred elsewhere but, before leaving, he told me that he forgave me and my Dad! How thoughtful.

Another part of my job as the earnings Clerk was to occasionally pay out inmates as they embarked (not for the first or last time) on their weary, dreary road to freedom. This part of the job was normally done early in the morning by the prison officers. But this particular gentleman had won something on appeal – I suspect it may have been his liberty; otherwise, we had made a big mistake. I was called to his cell (with the usual protection of a prison officer) and handed over his honestly gotten gains and bus pass. All I knew about this particular individual was that, over his forty years on the planet, he had spent some seventeen years incarcerated in various establishments dotted around England's green and pleasant land (not that he had seen much of that).

On paying him out and wishing him good luck, he started to wring his hands in a rather Oliver Moody/Fagin style and kindly informed me that he would probably be back in jail soon, simply because he came from a broken home, his parents were dysfunctional (my word not his), he had a non-existent education, he did not have any money, did not have any friends, society was against him, and thus he would not be able to get a job and would very soon return to a life of crime (something he was, to my untrained eye, not very good at). Now, to the casual reader and perhaps to those with a more social nature than I, these are all perfectly sound and reasonable grounds for returning to the confines of Her Majesty's penal institutions.

However, I did feel the need to point out to my new downtrodden acquaintance that perhaps the reason he could not and would not get a job was nothing to do with the societal deprivations he had listed, but more to do with the fact that he had the word 'F***' tattooed, in large letters, in slightly bluish prison-issued ink, right in the middle of his forehead. This obviously (to me, at least) job-detracting fact seemed to take my new acquaintance by surprise. With heartfelt sincerity, he asked me if I could help with the aforementioned large profanity tattooed on his forehead. I told him that, prior to an interview for a job, he should grow a fringe. I then left the cell to go about my usual duties feeling, at least for that day, that I had helped a would-be recidivist on his way to becoming a fully functional upright member of society. I saw him on the exercise yard a month later on his way to Parkhurst – he did not have a fringe.

There were other days when life was not so fulfilling. HM Prison Canterbury could cater for the bad, the sad, the mad and the evil and the other detritus of society. I will not try to categorise Mad Frankie Fraser: the name already gives him away.

He came through Canterbury on his way to Parkhurst. Everywhere he went he was escorted by at least two prison officers. He had a history of violence in and out of the prisons. Everyone took him very seriously. And lo and behold, it was my responsibility to pay him his transfer money. Basically, transfer money is money he might need whilst he was en route to Parkhurst: that is to say, whilst he was temporarily in Canterbury, he could access his earnings/savings, and this he now wished to do. And who was I to argue? I checked and double checked his figures. The wings were closed down and 'ordinary' inmates locked up as we prepared to deal with Mr Fraser. As he was walking along the wing, the inmates started banging their plastic cups on the doors and chanting "Frankie, Frankie." All very unnerving. He then appeared before my desk; or rather he didn't. First up was a six foot two prison officer, a gap, and then another large beefy prison officer. I should say here that Mad Frankie was as broad as he was long – those who knew him called him the 'Poison Dwarf'. But not to his face.

In the absence of Mr Fraser, I jokingly said to the two large prison officers: "You seem to have lost Britain's most violent inmate." At this point, I might explain that I sat on a high stool behind what we would nowadays call a high cocktail table (no bars or protection, save for the prison officers). This was all to give me some sort of authority (which was about to hastily leave the building) when dealing with the inmates. After my attempt at humour, two gnarled very old hands appeared to grip my desk and then proceeded to pull a very large head with a very large neck into my line of sight. His neck was rather interesting (as necks go). It had a rather large scar going from one side to another. A rather bizarre shaving cut, at least, that is what I was hoping.

He looked me straight in the eye and said, "Do not worry, boy. I am still here." At this point, the reader should know that there are prison Rules of Engagement between inmates, prison officers, civilian staff and cowards like myself.

The conversation then continued something like this: I said, "666291257 Fraser, please do not call me boy. You know the rules." He replied, "Thank you, boy. How much money have they transferred from Wandsworth?" I replied, "Please don't call me boy. You can call me sir or Mr Lynch, otherwise, as you well know, I will have to report you to the governor and you may lose seven days parole." He replied, "Listen, boy. I have lost 1,223 days parole in the last twenty-two years. I am not sure that losing another seven days is going to dramatically change my life or indeed my life sentence." He laughed, a sinister laugh, as he saw the irony of his command of the English language – or, at least, the meaning of his life. Prison officers were now on edge: I was just about to respond when 666291257 Fraser said, "OK,

Mr Lynch, how much have I got?" How nice, he had called me Mr. I replied that he had £3.69. Of course, I should have guessed what was going to happen next. He immediately disagreed and threatened to start a riot.

Then, he laughed again and calmed down as I – with heart in mouth, bowels bursting and cohorts of prison officers descending onto the wing – went through the figures with him (but not near him). And then he eventually decided that he would not start a one-man riot. He told me that I was a nice boy (I had now given up on the disciplinary loss of parole and just wanted to get home alive) and that he was happy with the figures. He then continued by saying that he did not want to buy anything from the canteen. All in all, it was an exercise designed to test how far he could annoy the Establishment.

He was escorted back to his cell and was, in the next twenty-four to forty-eight hours, on his way to Parkhurst. Surprisingly, I never heard from him again (no Christmas cards, birthday cards or death threats – all in all, good news, it has to be said). Years later, I did see in the media that he had been released and had written a book. I must read it one day to see if he has paid me the compliment of mentioning me in his reflections, as I have done in mine (if this rubbish ever becomes a book!).

Those of us who are old enough to remember will know that the late sixties and seventies, and beyond, brought us the scourge of IRA bombings on mainland Britain. Some of those perpetrating those awful crimes were caught and locked up (for a very long time), courtesy of Her Majesty. Invariably, they were held in high-security prisons. Canterbury was not a top security prison, but in order to avoid potential assisted prison breaks of members of the IRA, it was (like other prisons) used as a holding/transfer point whilst these characters were moved from one prison to another. The security services were trying to keep one step ahead of the non-incarcerated IRA colleagues, who would, at the drop of a Kalashnikov, try to help their colleagues regain their freedom.

I saw various IRA terrorists passing through HMP Canterbury and, contrary to the diktat of the government of the day – that they were not to be treated any differently from the other inmates, so as not to give them the status of 'political prisoners' – that was not true in the various people I saw. They were treated differently and invariably behaved differently. But the good news was that they would not accept the Queen's shilling – their earnings. And so I did not have to deal with them face to face. With a name like Kevin Lynch, I might have been subject to some interesting questions, aka abuse.

I mention these particular characters because security was very much heightened with armed police discreetly behind every wall, bush and car. The job was now somehow losing its allure, or perhaps self-preservation was coming to the fore, and I was looking for something else (invariably a large drink at the end of each day!). Perhaps divine providence could assist or, by a happy coincidence, the needs of Her Majesty's Diplomatic Service would intervene. At this point, a green form came across my desk. It was entitled, 'Applications to join Her Majesty's Diplomatic Service.'

Chapter Two

Joining the Foreign & Commonwealth Office (FCO)

A quick glance at the form seemed to indicate to me that those diplomatic chappies in the Foreign Office had run out of support staff to support them in whatever endeavours they were engaged in. And at the tender age of nineteen years old, I had absolutely no idea. But thinking about the IRA, Mad Frankie Fraser, Big John and his brothels, and his views of my family, the then-girlfriend in Deal who I did not like and a previous girlfriend in Deal that I did, I decided to chance my arm and duly completed the form and had a stab at joining Her Majesty's Diplomatic Service – much to the merriment of friends and family. No one, except those from Oxford and Cambridge (the Universities, not the towns) got into the Diplomatic Service, let alone someone from the Prison Service. My arguments that the Prison Service was also under the auspices of Her Majesty were met with incredulity (for that, read hysterical laughter) and deaf ears. But I had despatched my form and, like most of the inmates in Hotel Canterbury, could now only sit and wait. Except I could sit and wait where I liked.

Some weeks later, to my surprise and to the utter disbelief of those who had no faith in me – or more accurately a strong belief in the elitism of Her Majesty's Diplomatic Service – I received a letter asking me to come for an interview. Again, the naysayers amongst my friends and family said that I had no chance of getting in and why should I waste my time and money going to London? I actually won that trivial battle because the good old Foreign and Commonwealth Office was going to pay me my train fare and my lunch; so no matter what the outcome was, I had a free day and lunch paid for in London. What was there to lose?

As I now know, nothing was lost; the next thirty-eight years of my life would be travelling the world, meeting wonderful people, delving into new cultures and languages, and making fantastic lifelong friends – but more of that is in the pages to come.

But back to the moment: I was now convinced by those around me that as I had no chance of joining the Foreign Office, so I decided to meet up with an old friend who was studying at the London School of Economics. We agreed to meet in the student bar at twelve o'clock, prior to my interview with the Foreign Office at 2:30pm. Some would say it was not really a good idea to have a few pints before an interview for a job, but at that point, I thought I had nothing to lose. After three pints and nearly getting on the wrong tube, I arrived, chewing an extra strong mint to hide the beer fumes, dead on time for my interview. Without having much time to think, I was ushered into a very grandiose office in which sat three very serious-looking gentlemen behind a very serious-looking desk.

The three pints in the student bar had obviously done their work and I was quite relaxed about the whole affair. But I was not going in blind (maybe blind drunk, some would day). I had done some homework about the Foreign Office. On the way to the interview, I had, for the first time in my life, bought *The Times* newspaper. That was to be a very wise investment. *The Times* had, on that particular day, quite extensive coverage of foreign affairs. That is to say the political affairs of foreign countries, not the affairs with members of the opposite sex from foreign countries.

And soon after the usual opening pleasantries, the panel got down to the nitty-gritty and started to ask me some pertinent questions about – yes, the Foreign Office and foreign countries! The opening gambit was the usual, "Why do you want to join the foreign office?" And, of course, I replied with the standard, formulaic, "I want to travel and see the world." I obviously had thought through the consequences of an answer that was based on no longer wanting to deal with the likes of Mad Frankie Fraser and the IRA. That would not be a wise opening. The three heads in front of me nodded enthusiastically. *A good start*, I thought, and the pressure on my bladder was minimal.

The next few questions were along the lines of everything that I had read in *The Times* that morning – Rhodesia, General Franco, British tourists abroad and the Middle East (which I had learned on the train was not somewhere near Horsham). And at the same time, thought that these people interviewing me had probably collectively read *The Times* and agreed over coffee that this information would be the basis of their day's questioning of potential future diplomats. *Not a bad job*, I thought. Well, not bad for me; I had read the same paper.

Time flew by and, in the interim, the pressure on my bladder had increased somewhat, and I was glad to hear the beginning of the end: "Do you have any questions for us?" Now, I assume that these learned gentlemen were expecting something on the USA, the USSR or the EU. Basically, anything not within the shores of the United Kingdom. Alas, it was not to be – this budding world traveller could only come up with "Could you please tell me the whereabouts of the nearest loo?!"

On the way home, I thought that, in the circumstances, the day had gone well, but for the moment, I was back to the prison. Those that work or have worked, like me – albeit briefly – in Her Majesty's penal establishments, will no doubt have their own quirky and serious stories about those incarcerated behind bricks, bars and barbed wire. I have mentioned a few, but the reality is that way back from October 1976 to March 1978 there were approximately 49,000 inmates in the penal system. Today, as I write, I am reliably informed that there are some 89,000 people incarcerated. Not a good sign. It might be a good idea to get out of the country.

…Which was exactly what I was going to do. I had got the job in Her Majesty's Diplomatic Service.

Chapter Three

Induction into the FCO: Filing, Fun and Pubs

And so at 9:30am on Tuesday 29th of March 1978, I found myself with nineteen other bright young shiny people in a very serious wood-panelled room at 1 Palace Street (now the building opposite Parliament, which houses the overflow of MPs from their law-making chamber).

This was the start of a two-week long induction course, preparing us for the trials and tribulations of working in and for Her Majesty's Diplomatic Service. At the head of a very serious-looking table were the five people who were to be our guides and tutors over the coming two weeks. Thereafter, we would all be sent to our pre-allocated departments. In front of each one of us was our name and the department to which we had been allocated. Every department in the Foreign and Commonwealth Office (FCO) had an acronym. As time went on in the FCO, it seemed to me that everything in the FCO was acronymised – even people. The top diplomatic dog (not an acronym) was the PUS. If ever there was an acronym that needed changing, surely PUS was it. But back to mine…

I did not like the look of mine. It said WAD. But a more detailed examination proved this to be West Africa Department. Around me, colleagues were allocated to other places, such as FED (Far Eastern Department), MVD (Migration and Visa Department), and my particular favourite – SAD (South Asia Department). On and on it went as we were distributed, on paper, to the four corners of the Earth. And, within three years, those of us still with the Foreign Office would be physically distributed to the four corners of the globe. But I get ahead of myself.

Following the standard format of these induction sessions, everyone was asked to introduce themselves and say why they had joined the Diplomatic Service (henceforth, all references to the Foreign and Commonwealth Office, Foreign Office and Her Majesty's Diplomatic Service will be covered by FCO or DS – see the acronyms already mentioned). To a man and a woman, they explained that they wanted to travel. As I was the penultimate in line to speak, I declared that I had just been released from prison after spending eighteen months inside HM Prison Canterbury supervising the sewing of Diplomatic Bags.

When this remark was absorbed and digested by our tutors (that took a while – at this point most of them were dozing off or doing anything other than listening to their new innocent inductees), there was a bit of a panic. Upon seeing some of the shock, horror and fear on the faces of the future of the FCO (albeit at a low level – unbeknownst to us, we were not the 'Fast Stream'), the Chairperson stepped in to explain.

"I should say that Mr Lynch was not an inmate, but was working as a Civil Servant in Canterbury prison. Is that not correct, Kevin?" (For some reason, he suddenly became very informal).

I replied, "Yes, that is the story I've been told and told to stick to it."

There were, once again, some very serious, worried glances and conversations between those on the top table. They were debating whether the FCO's tried and tested policy of recruiting from the green fields of Eton and Harrow had been abolished. It now appeared, as a result of my first (and not to be last) controversial intervention, that this policy had indeed changed and, in a token gesture to the Labour government's prisoner rehabilitation policy, the FCO was accepting recently released prisoners and no one had told them!

Before widespread panic and resignations ensued, I put them out of their misery and said, "OK, I'm only joking; yes, I was a Civil Servant in Canterbury prison." There was much relief all around, but also a lot of scribbling on the top table (not literally on the top table itself, but on the various files thereon). I am sure, to this day, that something untoward had already appeared on my personnel file.

After this short interlude, we were briefed on the current structure of the DS, who was who (David Owen was the Foreign Secretary at the time), and who were the very senior diplomats currently resident in London (with the admonition that if ever we were to come across them, they must be addressed as 'Sir'). The morning went very quickly and we were given ninety minutes for lunch to get to know our surroundings.

The man next to me, the young inestimable Steve Richards, was to become one of my closest friends and today, forty years later, he still is. I will come on to the others in due course. However, at the mention of the lunch break, I pointed out to my new neighbour that

I had noticed a pub very close to our building and asked whether he fancied a pint. He replied, "You're speaking my language."

As I did not know him too well at that point (actually, I did not know him at all at that point), I refrained from pointing out that I was not speaking the same language – I came from Kent and the Queen's English, whilst he came from Lancashire. But putting our linguistic differences to one side, we headed off to the pub, then we went to another pub, and then to a third.

It was a good, sound introduction to our surroundings – we found during the tea break that our colleagues, led by the outlaw Josey Bradley, had gone to Westminster Abbey (as opposed to the Westminster Arms – our third pub), the public part of Parliament, and then had ventured across Westminster bridge for a view of the Thames – all very jolly. Within days, most of our fellow inductees would be joining the 'Hunt the Pub' club as we explored the finer hostelries of London SW1.

Throughout the next two weeks, we all got to know each other rather well; some of us were staying in the same hostels, some of us would be working in the same building together (at that point, in 1978, the FCO had some four or five buildings scattered about in the Westminster village); some of us liked lager and some of us liked bitter. Still, in the end, we were all bound by the same common thread: we had all left home, left behind friends and family, girlfriends and boyfriends, just to seek out new lands and go where no one from our respective hometowns and villages had gone before (apologies to Captain Kirk). All that future travel, fun and adventure (but not much work) would be courtesy of Her Majesty's Diplomatic Service.

The two-week induction course passed quickly. But it became more and more apparent (to me at least) that the training for the work we were about to undertake seemed incredibly mundane, repetitive and would not challenge the people on this particular induction course, most of whom had good A-levels or, whilst not having finished University, had been there for one or two years. In actual fact, with hindsight, we were all pretty smart – but that would soon be drummed out of us.

We were taught how to file papers (punching a hole one inch down and one inch from the left from the top left-hand corner of a piece of A4 paper). Difficult, I know, but we persevered. We were taught how to tie up diplomatic bags. A bit more difficult, but with two or three good A-levels, just about manageable. We were taught how to change combination locks; this was particularly interesting.

If one got it wrong and broke a combination, one's fingers were broken by one's fellow inductees. At one stage, it got to the point that holding drinks was nigh on impossible. It was then that we collectively started to concentrate. Fortunately, FCO management had foreseen this problem (the breaking of locks, not the breaking of bones) and had on hand (pun intended) a specialist locksmith. If and when he could not work out the numerical error, he would patiently take apart the aforementioned combination lock, throw the pieces at the 'combination class', collect the pieces embedded in various skulls and rebuild the lock. We would then, broken (us, not the locks) but unbowed, start the whole process again. No one failed a second time.

Looking back, the main training on the course was not on the course. We support staff would mainly be responsible for messenger duties, coffee and tea making, fetching wine and, if we had been still in the era of coal-fired offices, coal scuttle duties.

Chapter 4

Coups to Carrington and Flats to Friends

And so, sometime in the middle of April 1978, I joined West Africa Department (WAD). There was a short handover period and then I had my desk and a mass of papers to number, punch holes in, tag and put on file (mostly the wrong file) to be forever lost or to be returned to my two bosses for appropriate action.

WAD in those days was divided into two sections – Ghana and Nigeria (the big boy of the West African nations). I was in the Ghana area. I was the Section clerk, also known as the Registry Clerk. And, of course, I did not know at this particular point in my short career that I would be spending some six years in the region later in my career. Had I known that, I might have paid a bit more attention.

Life would have been easy if I had just been filing papers on Ghana. That is, if I had just put bits of paper with Ghana on them in date order (a good use of those A-levels), and attached them to an ever-growing, gargantuan Ghana file. Simple really. But oh no, it was not that simple.

Each country had some twenty to thirty sub-sector subjects, with their own individual files and, alongside Ghana, I had details on the following countries: Guinea, Senegal, Togo, Mali, Guinea Bissau, Upper Volta (now Burkina Faso, but I never found out where Lower Volta was), Mauritania, the Ivory Coast, Sierra Leone, Liberia, The Gambia and Niger. In a nutshell (and some of these countries were completely nuts back in the seventies), there were some fourteen countries with fourteen capitals; some with High Commissions, some with Embassies and most without. That is to say that we did not have diplomatic buildings (the correct word is "representation") in many of these countries. So not much to learn then – twenty-six countries and capitals, most of which I had never heard of before. And to cap it all, the Head of Department (in Whitehall, remember) was the Non-Resident Ambassador to a godforsaken place called Chad. Chad must be in the top ten countries for having a capital city with an unpronounceable name: N'Djamena.

WAD was known as a geographical or political department. Other such departments would be Western Europe Department (WED – a big beast in the political departments) and North America Department (NAD), and so on across the globe. Thus, inside a large building on Whitehall, the FCO had carved up the whole world into basically three letter acronyms (TLAs). If we could no longer impose our will across the world, as we had two hundred years previously, we could now, at least, arrange the various nations, be they recalcitrant or otherwise, into a nice orderly list of TLAs.

These geographical or political departments were thought of – mainly by those in them – as being the best of the best. We were Tsars of foreign policy in these political departments and dealt with bilateral relationships. We dealt with Johnny Foreigner. We told Ministers where these countries were. We told Ministers, and anyone else who would listen, who was in charge of these countries and, occasionally, who was about not to be in charge; we, in WAD at least, tried to predict (with unfailing inaccuracy) which country in the whole of the WAD region would host the next military coup. In 1978, there seemed to be a whole stream of them. Or maybe that was just my imagination. We were the so-called experts on our countries and cultures (I was just filing papers but I thought I should get into the diplomatic groove). We thought a lot about policies and sent long intellectual notes to Ministers detailing our latest thinking on a coup, a particular Head of State, or a particular incident that needed a robust response, or an equally robust statement in Parliament or, more frequently, recommending the lunch menu for dining with a former corporal who had just had a meteoric promotion to Foreign Minister. Mostly, we got these menus right; on other occasions, we backed the wrong side in a coup and ended up not being liked for many years in the future. But it was all good proper diplomatic work.

We were in the political departments so the great unwashed and undiplomatic work of visa sections, trade sections, aid sections, environmental sections, science sections was not for us. Nor was any other section that was not deemed to be directly 'policy or political'. Of course, that has all changed now; the FCO has had to change and modernise. Trade and immigration are integral to our economy. We need to know about and negotiate deals around climate change, science protocols, and trade agreements (which are big at the time of writing, so big, in fact, that there is now a separate department – the International Trade Department).

But I digress (I will do a lot of that). My two bosses in WAD were great people (I have lost all track of one of them and the other is sadly no longer with us). The Head of Section was a bright thirty-year-old graduate female (unusual, to say the least, back then) who had had, if memory serves me correctly, only one overseas posting in Europe somewhere. Her deputy was a fortyish-year-old gentleman who had been overseas on numerous postings. He knew the ropes. He recognised my complete inability to find the office most days, let alone papers on the internal politics of Togo; he did his own filing so that, for the first few months of my tenure, he could retrieve key papers within a reasonable timescale. Early on, my retrieval times were measured in lunar months (occasionally, in a crisis, a lunar day – twenty-four hours and fifty minutes). It was all so confusing – this ex-Grammar schoolboy, with two good A-levels, was incapable of filing papers.

I was to find out later that I was incapable of many of the tedious chores that held the FCO together. Apart from the filing (or lack of filing, in my case), it was good, during the not infrequent mini WAD receptions, to hear the banter about life overseas. Overseas was the reason I had signed up – not to file papers about Timbuktu – but to go to Timbuktu (I nearly got there).

I eventually mastered both the art of filing and (more importantly) finding the papers I had filed. At times, the speed of delivery of papers to senior officials and the Ministerial Private Offices (more of the Private Offices later) was of the essence. At that time in West Africa, the name of the game was not democracy; the idea of democratic, peaceful and fair transfers of power from one government to another seemed to be, to put it bluntly, an idea from the devil. Military coups, normally bloody, were the order of the day.

Once the coups were in progress, or coming to an end, or restarting after a worthless ceasefire, the job of the Section Heads was to get advice to FCO Ministers as soon as they could. The advice was based on telegram reporting from the Embassy or High Commission in the affected capital city/country. And that advice was mainly about whether or not we should recognise the incoming regime. But if we didn't get the papers 'up' quickly, there might have been, and invariably was, another counter-coup and all the work on the present coup was rendered useless. That could not be allowed to happen. Out-of-date information was a big 'No' in the FCO. We prided ourselves on having immediate up-to-date information on the latest events and carefully thought out, calibrated, responses to those events. It was a shame that over the years we missed noticing the revolution in Iran, the Falklands, two Gulf Wars, the collapse of the Soviet Union and VAT moving from 15% to 20%.

But still, we aimed for perfection. At times, that was not possible. To avoid letting anyone know that we in the political departments were less than perfect, we occasionally held off supplying advice to our political masters until the dust had settled, old scores had been settled, the bar bill had been settled and we officials had settled on a sure winner.

An even better wheeze (if memory serves me correctly), in order not to get Her Majesty's Government (HMG) a bad name, was to not officially recognise the latest head of government nutter (probably educated and trained by us). Because, once we did that, our allies and the United Nations would invariably follow suit. And then our new man (always a man way back then) would do something horrible and deplorable – for example, take his erstwhile colleagues, friends and family down to the beach and shoot them. Not a good look. And good old HMG would have a lot of questions to answer. To solve these minor indiscretions, HMG decided to recognise states rather than governments. The thinking being that a state is an entity and incapable of bad things, even if the Head of State of that state is a complete maniac – see Saddam Hussein and Iraq. We know how to get out of a jam.

The FCO had, in those days, messengers, all great people but they somehow managed, with amazing regularity, not to be there when you needed them most – during crises mainly. They were always there for the drinks parties for people leaving and for the Christmas and birthday celebrations. But as I say, not when papers needed to be somewhere else very fast, so fast that people were demanding them an hour before they had been written. Einstein would have had a field day. And so, with messengers missing in action (or, more likely, in the tea-room) with increasing frequency, it was down to us Section Clerks to master the labyrinthine corridors of power and deliver by hand the great informative, world-changing documents to the powerful people that needed to see them.

After a few months in the job, one got to know the other section clerks in the other offices that dealt with other geographical regions, and of course, there were the friends from the induction course and more friends from the FCO bar/club. And so, when one was sent on an urgent errand, this was an ideal way to catch up with one's new friends. With papers in hand, carrying stickers saying 'Immediate' or the top priority 'Flash', it was common practice to pop in and say hello to friends, arrange drinks at the weekend, or try to get a date with a particularly attractive new arrival. Those of us with a bit more common sense tended to deliver our urgent documents as quickly as possible before engaging on a very long, circuitous but socially rewarding route back to our department.

Others decided to do it on their way to delivering their precious papers to those who needed them. I am not saying who was right or wrong, but it was particularly embarrassing when the secretary of some very important person was calling the Head of Department trying to track down a wayward member of staff. Search parties were not unheard of. And indeed, post-mortems about delivery delays were not uncommon. The excuse "I got lost" wore very thin very quickly.

***

Back in the late seventies / early eighties, it seemed as though the FCO did not have nearly enough Section Clerks – which was a bit like Eton not having nearly enough fags (for any American reader, an Eton fag is where a younger boy is expected to act as the personal servant of the older boy or boys. Nothing more than that, I can assure you. Well, I can't really assure you because I did not go to Eton). And so, recruitment drives took place on a quarterly basis to keep up with the paucity of these junior officers (I had better stop using fags). The average age of the new recruits was about twenty and there was an almost fifty-fifty mix of the sexes.

We new recruits ('new entrants,' as we were called – we were probably called other things behind our backs), were expected to spend about thirty months to three years in London in two different departments before being let loose on the unsuspecting world. After thirty months or three years in London, it was deemed that we might, just might, have some idea of Foreign Affairs.

And so it came to pass that, whilst all these young people were being recruited, learning the FCO ropes and awaiting postings overseas, it was inevitable that friendships, love, romances, bust-ups and marriages would happen.

On their arrival in London, people moved into hostels and then moved out of hostels to share rented houses and flats with like-minded colleagues. Payday ensured a regular round of house parties. Waking up with another FCO or Civil Service colleague in some far corner of London – an event that could turn out to be everlasting or, more likely, did not last until the next payday – was the norm. Some, if not most, of these relationships have stood the test of time, and there are kids and grandchildren. Forty years on, I hear friends reminiscing about their first houses, first flats, first drink, first girlfriend or boyfriend; there were the losses of wallets, shoes, socks, virginities, bras, underpants and knickers (not all necessarily in that order). But that is forty years hence and I have a lot to cover, so it's not quite back to the future, but back to the past, April 1979 to be precise. I had to get to my new department.

After twelve months in WAD, and just when I was beginning to learn where every country was (at least on the map) and which capital city belonged to which country, I was moved on. For reasons that still elude me, I was heading for the Foreign Secretary's Private Office – the command and control nerve centre of the FCO. The office of the big cheese, the head honcho, the big kahuna, the Boss, the main (then) man.

At the time of my arrival, the Foreign Secretary was Dr David Owen, a very nice man who was extremely fond of a very fetching windswept photograph of himself that had to be despatched, unerringly, to anyone who wrote and asked for one. He signed every one of them. But that was all to become academic. I was only in that Labour Private Office for a month. No, I was not immediately removed and sent to Siberia (although I did go there some twenty-seven years later). There was an election on 3rd May 1979. Labour were out and the Conservatives under Margaret Thatcher were in.

And so, in very early May, we waited with bated breath to see who the new Foreign Secretary would be.

Lord Carrington was duly appointed. And the FCO, providing its usual Rolls-Royce service, had prepared briefs to cover every country, every overseas territory and every current overseas problem (including Rhodesia – more on that later) and we young clerks with a senior supervisor in the outer Private Office were the first line of our new master's defence. Everyone who wanted to make a name for themselves with the new Foreign Secretary came out of the woodwork and hovered around. The telephones rang non-stop, with calls from both those inside the FCO and from top Ambassadors abroad wanting a quick chat. Our job was to gather a little information from the callers and then pass them on to the relevant department. So, if it was about West Germany (still a country then), we would pass it to WED, if it was about Yugoslavia (still a country then), we would pass it to Eastern European Department, and so on and so forth. Some callers could be very persistent.

One very insistent lady demanded to speak to the Foreign Secretary directly but did not wish to alert me to the subject matter. She even had the temerity to call him 'Peter'. Eventually, she said something like, "I own a Carrington." I replied, "I own a Ford..." And stressed that she still could not converse with the great man and hung up.

My immediate boss, easily within earshot, gently probed me about this conversation and, all of a sudden, went from healthy pink to puce and then to pale. He gently – as gently as a great white shark might approach its wounded prey – asked if I knew the name of Lord Carrington's wife. Silly question, I thought, but hazarded a few guesses – Gill, Sheilah, Carolyn, Marie, Celia, Val, Barbara, – but no, all wrong. The good lady was called Iona (sadly, she is no longer with us). And suddenly, in my soon to be boiled head, a lot of lights came on and bells started ringing. At this moment, one of the Private Secretaries (senior people these Private Secretaries) appeared and asked, "Who in here owns a Ford?" Fortunately, the lovely Carringtons saw the funny side, and once the big bosses had seen the funny side everyone else did. But strange looks abounded for the next few days.

Every important paper (at least in foreign policy terms) comes to the Foreign Secretary. And to get it to him, it comes through his Private Office. This is an office consisting of fast-stream high flyers called Private Secretaries and supporting them, you had us; the slow-stream daydreamers dreaming that one day we would be Ambassadors or High Commissioners. But it was more likely that we would daydream about next Friday night's bash. Much more importantly, there were the delightful Private Office secretaries, the best in the FCO. They typed for the United Kingdom, took dictation at a rate of knots hitherto unknown to the human race; and they too dreamt of being Ambassadors or High Commissioners or, if not that, their consorts. And some thirty-one years in the future, I would be standing on a small man-made airstrip on a small man-made atoll in the middle of the very large South Pacific Ocean, advising my secretarial colleague from Private Office about the pitfalls of Pitcairn. But again, that is for the future. Keep reading, it gets better – honest!

Briefing document upon briefing document arrived in the Private Office. Back in 1979, these briefs were laden with erudite words, obscure quotes and a smattering of Latin, all of which was designed not to enlighten the Foreign Secretary to the problems at hand, but to show him how clever the author thought he, the author, was. But to the chagrin of many, to make a point, Lord Carrington scribbled in the margins next to the erudite "sine qua non" that he did not speak Latin and that, as far as he was aware, Latin was only used in the Vatican. No one used Latin after that. I had studied Latin at school and, if he had asked, I would, of course, have helped out.

Briefing became much more succinct and to the point after that, and still is. Except when senior Ambassadors have an intellectual lapse of memory or aberration and start talking about Dr Pangloss or encomiums or obscure Greek poets. And once one of them starts, they all follow suit, trying to be the best in retrieving from their grey matter, the most enigmatic and impenetrable knowledge acquired and then putting it into, up until that point, a finely crafted piece of work.

But back to Private Office: the key papers came and went, decisions were made, visits were planned and a one-week conference in London at Lancaster House was dedicated to solving Rhodesia. The FCO cast list was (and still is) a Who's Who of the great and good of the FCO. Everyone and anyone involved in the conference except for me, my colleagues and the secretarial staff, went on to much greater things. But such is life.

On the African side, there were such names as Joshua Nkomo, Bishop Muzorewa, Ian Smith and a certain Robert Mugabe (I wonder whatever happened to him).

History shows that the Lancaster House conference did not take one week, but more like, if memory serves me correctly, thirteen weeks. With hindsight, and knowing what we know now about Mugabe, maybe we should still be conferencing to this day. Nevertheless, a historic agreement had been reached, which avoided, it has to be said, a multi-country, multi-tribal bloodbath. And during those hectic weeks, no one would have taken any notice of a team of young men and women cycling on the old butcher-style bikes from the FCO, across St James's Park to Lancaster House. That was us, the clerks from the Private Office – and inside our baskets, we carried everything from the latest telegrams, detailing reactions from the Southern African front-line states and updated briefs to cheese and ham sandwiches and, for one particular individual (who later became one of our top Ambassadors), packets of Benson and Hedges. I think he still owes me some money for at least one packet.

The Rhodesia/Zimbabwe conference was, of course, important, but we could not just dwell on that particular irritant; the Soviets, in their complete lack of wisdom (and to be fair, the West too some years later), had decided to invade Afghanistan. A big mistake. It is not known as the 'Graveyard of Empires' because it is a timid little state that easily acquiesces to outside interference. We, British, had our butts kicked there in the 19th Century, the Soviets would be in and out in ten years and the 'West' – USA and UK – are still tied up there, with no significant gains to speak of, sixteen years after going in. And prior to the big boys entering the Afghan playing field, there had been various internal squabbles (aka internecine massacres) which had left various tribes in the country with not only a bilateral and multilateral hatred of each other, but also, when needed, a collective hatred against Johnny Foreigner when they messed around in their country. Add to this mix the extremely difficult terrain and the fact that every village elder, fearing his neighbour or neighbours, had turned his village into a modern-day Fort Knox and all in all, Afghanistan was, and still is, not a nation to be trifled with.

But the Soviets did trifle. And when in doubt about some international issue or other, what do we, the West, do? We have a conference. And so it came to pass sometime in 1979 or 1980 (I cannot remember), that a conference was held to discuss the Soviet invasion and occupation of Afghanistan. The Soviets were not invited. Some wag suggested that they might take over the meeting. A not unrealistic thought. The conference was in the FCO main building. The great and the good from all parts of the world were invited. Except, of course, we did not invite anybody who did not like us – which was any country who liked the Soviet Union. And so the slightly biased conference began.

During one slow day of the conference, I was by myself, manning the outer Private Office. The rest of the team was out and about supporting the conference delegates and other hangers-on when, in my patch of offices, there was suddenly the ringing of lots of telephones and urgently whispered conversations coming from the main Private Office. And then there came a movement right in front of me: it was one of the Private Secretaries bearing down on me exclaiming, "Kevin, President Carter is on the phone."

I replied inquisitively, "For me?"

As we know from years of evolution, eyes can roll. Well, this particular pair of eyes rolled and rolled and rolled and then glared (this reaction was to happen to me quite often in my life in Her

Majesty's Diplomatic Service). He then intimated – rather abruptly, I thought – that no, as much as we were sure that the most powerful man in the world, who was in charge of a nuclear arsenal and an economy that beat everyone else's hands down, would like to speak with me one day, today was not that day.

The Private Secretary continued that, believe it or not, the President wanted to speak to his Deputy Secretary of State, Warren Christopher. Deputy Secretary Christopher was chairing the Afghan conference and the Private Secretary asked if it was not too much trouble, could I go and get the aforementioned US Deputy Secretary of State and bring him to the Private Office to talk to his boss? After which he gently said, that I and President Carter could have a nice convivial chat if we so wished. I think I spotted some sarcasm here.

I duly collected Secretary Christopher from the conference. To make small talk as I escorted him the short distance to the Private Office to take the call, I asked him how his day was going. He replied, very nicely, I must admit – that Iran was imploding, the Politburo and the really pro-Soviet Warsaw Pact leaders were on edge over the rumblings coming out Poland and the Soviets were in Afghanistan and who knew where they were going to stop. He said that pretty much summed up his day. Noticeably, during a lull in our brisk chat, he did not ask me how my day was going. I am sure he would have been interested in my latest filing techniques.

Apparently, the conversation with the President was constructive, as were the reports coming out of the conference. The Soviet occupation of Afghanistan was to last another ten years. And that conflict alone would mean highly time-sensitive material had to get to the Private Office pretty damn quick.

In the FCO and across Whitehall, there was the pneumatic tube system. This literally was a system of tubes driven either by compressed air or a partial vacuum that could deliver messages very quickly within the FCO or to our government neighbours on Whitehall. It was very much in use during times of crisis, although not always for its core purpose of getting information to the decision makers that needed it. These tubes were only used for very time-sensitive material and would be marked 'Deskby' followed by a twenty-four hour clock time. For example: Deskby 1630 hours. This meant that it had to be in the addressee's hands by 1630 hours at the very latest. Above this Deskby descriptor was the highest priority message 'Flash'. This literally meant a matter of life or death and any particular tube with that label moved fast, very fast.

When 'Flash' tubes were delivered to the Private Office, they came with a cry of 'Flash' so that everyone knew that something very very urgent had arrived and had to be opened – there were special keys for the tubes. During various crises, these tubes would arrive very frequently and it was all hands on deck to open them and get them into the Private Secretaries – stating the obvious – without further ado. And at times of particular excitement, the Private Secretaries would grab spare keys and help. These times could be quite stressful. But we managed. At least, some of us did.

In those dark and distant days, smoking was allowed in the office. Times of very high workloads increased exponentially the consumption of cigarettes. And when the cigarettes were depleted, no one could be spared to go and get replenishment. I, on the other hand, had a very good friend (now happily retired in Rutland) in the tube room. Nothing much in that you say, except that he smoked. And a quick telephone call ensured that those in need of their nicotine fixes got them. They arrived in tubes marked 'Flash'. I think you can guess where this is going.

And so it came to pass, during the height of the Iranian revolution, with students in Tehran storming Western embassies like there was no tomorrow (little did they know then that their tomorrow was not going to be as great as they thought it would be), 'Flash' tubes were coming into the Private Office thick and fast. Everyone was helping, including the Private Secretaries and the great and the good from the Middle East Command. Only a very select few knew that one of those tubes did not carry key telegraphic reports from the region or, indeed, our own embassy in Tehran, but four Rothman cigarettes instead. And that if the wrong person opened up that tube, the wrath of man would fall on somebody – probably me. As luck would have it, the tube was opened by a friend rather than some very senior diplomat (a foe in this particular context!). The cigarettes were then discreetly removed and passed onto those who needed them. Stress levels were lowered and the evacuation of our Embassy authorised.

And so in 1979 and 1980, life in Private Office went on. The Falklands were on the radar, but not as much as the UK contribution to the EC Budget. Margaret Thatcher (I had actually met her at this stage and had managed to make her laugh) was increasingly on the world stage. The special relationship with the USA was with Carter, but Ronald Reagan was in the wings. But that was, and is, the stuff of high diplomacy – so not really what this book is about.

We new novice diplomats were young and had other, much more important things on our minds – unlike Iran, we wanted to have fun with our new found freedom and friends in the big city of London.

Outside of work, life-long FCO friendships had been forged. I had moved out of the hostel in Victoria to a terraced house in Greenwich with a bath in the kitchen and the loo twenty yards down the garden path. To protect one's modesty (fortunately, we were four men sharing the house), the bath in the kitchen had a plastic curtain that could easily be drawn and, at times, withdrawn. It was not unknown for one flatmate to hand his housemate a fried egg sandwich to be consumed whilst bathing. We knew how to live. This life of luxury was not for me and I soon moved on and into a flat in Peckham with Steve Richards from the induction course. We shared a room and our other flatmate was a delightful Scottish lady who generally looked after us.

Weekends in winter consisted of following or playing for the FCO football team and, in the summer, the FCO cricket team. These sports were just an excuse for copious amounts of drinking, dating and generally having a lot of fun. The Civil Service then had its own sports ground at Barnes Bridge, near Chiswick, a magnificent estate housing numerous playing fields and, of course, a very big subsidised bar.

The sportsmen had their followers – men and women – and, on an average Saturday, plenty of refreshments would be had before heading out to big bad central London. But to get to big bad central London, one had to cross Barnes Bridge footbridge. A relatively simple task, one would assume. But no, not for us; one of our intrepid crew insisted that we should not avail ourselves of the safety of the well-tried and trodden footbridge. No, we should not use the footbridge. We should scale the three iron semi-circular suspensions or trusses that held the bridge together and supported its passage across the Thames. His thinking behind this lunacy was that it might stand us in good stead in the event of a posting to a mountainous country. And so, on a regular basis, on a darkened Saturday night, after several pints of beer, the FCO Sherpa group could be found clambering across this Grade II listed bridge. On one side was a ten-foot fall onto the electric rail and on the other a forty-foot fall into the Thames. We all lived and at least one of the group became quite a skilled mountaineer in a mountainous country far away. Another climbed Sydney Harbour Bridge but the majority of the remainder have developed a respectful fear of heights. One Sherpa, even to this day, has an irrational fear of driving over any bridge that is more than ten feet above the water. He spends a lot of time taking very circuitous routes to places quite nearby.

And there were the regular Monday and Thursday nights at the FCO social club in the Curtis Green building – very near to old Scotland Yard. And now I think Scotland Yard has moved back in. If people can remember those nights, they were not there. The drink of choice was Tuborg Gold (a premium strong lager in those days), combined with no food and, inevitably, the night ended with all the verses and all the choruses of *American Pie*. The words still ring in my head to this day. Post-mortems of the previous night's shenanigans would be conducted the following evening – who left with whom, who got locked in the building, who missed their last transport home, and a head count was taken to see who was missing.

This social life (and perhaps the mundane filing) was not everyone's cup of lager or white wine. Twenty to thirty per cent of the various induction groups saved their livers and their sanity by going and doing something completely different. I salute them.

As the months and years passed by, there was always the underlying theme about when friends and lovers would leave the group to go on their first Posting. This invariably meant lots of farewell drinks and trying to spend the much-needed 'transfer grant' (a grant to help officers with start-up costs of their first home overseas) not on drinks and fun, but instead on its original purpose: the purchase of pots, pans, plates and other domestic paraphernalia to help one live alone for the first time in their lives. But the reality was that most of the grant was spent, by the men at least, on entertainment.

I spent longer in London than my colleagues. The Personnel people told me that it was because I was indispensable in Private Office and they were having trouble finding a replacement. I think this was all code; they were thinking, should we unleash this man on an unsuspecting world? Was the world ready? But I was not too perturbed about spending time in London. At that time, life in London was very comfortable. I was living very happily with a delightful lady and sub-letting the box room to a good friend – the cigarette supplier from the tube room. But underneath that veneer was the desire to get abroad.

It was an autumnal day; I knew that because it was autumn 1980. It was pretty quiet in the Private Office. The Secretary of State was on an overseas visit (when that happened, we managed to get some downtime) and my boss called me in for a chat. He had my Posting notification in his hand and told me that in three months' time, I would be heading out to Brussels – to the United Kingdom Delegation to the North Atlantic Treaty Organisation (NATO) – UKDel NATO Brussels, to be short.

Brussels, I thought. Brussels I screamed (inwardly). I live eight miles from Dover, if you could stand on the roof of my Mum and Dad's house, you could probably see Brussels. You could probably even throw a stone at it and not miss. One could not get much nearer to England (we had returned Calais to the French by 1980, if memory serves me correctly). And to cap it all, I had only three months earlier been there on a long weekend FCO football tour. At the time, I thought this place really was not what I would like as a Posting – it was not far enough away, everyone spoke English, there were no wild animals (apart from visiting English football hooligans), there were no really different cuisines and beverages to try, and not many different cultures and customs to discover. The weather was the same. With hindsight, I was wrong. Just not about the culture, food, beverages, hooligans and weather.

People make postings and one needed to make the best of everything – including Brussels and Belgium. I did; at least, I think I did. We shall come to that. And, in the back of my mind, I was saying to myself that I should not forget the tens of thousands of Civil Servants who commuted into London day in and day out, year in and year out, without the possibility of spending a good deal of their career in foreign lands (even if it was Belgium).

I was disappointed, but go to Brussels I would. I told my friends and family. I think my girlfriend was pleased – she did not want me to go far away. And so the next three months were taken up with pre-posting preparations and training (not much for Brussels).

Part Two

Belgium (Brussels – the North Atlantic Treaty Organisation)

January 1981 – December 1983

Chapter 5

War Games and Pretend Politicians

To be honest, as mentioned earlier, I was quite disappointed to be told I was going to Brussels. My other colleagues were heading to New Delhi, East Berlin, Paris (sounds much better than Brussels), Washington, Bangkok, Moscow and many other far-flung and (in my opinion) more exotic places. But people make postings – rather than the countries, cultures or cities – even though these would be a big help. But it is what you, as an individual, make out of the place that counts (OK – no more philosophy). And, of course, I did not know that I would criss-cross the globe over the next three decades and go to more than my fair share of weird, wonderful and exotic places.

Neither did I know that the next three years would be a fun time during which I would make best friends forever (BFFs in modern-day terminology, I believe) and gain a fascinating insight into the Cold War: NATO vs the Warsaw Pact; Good vs Evil; Luke Skywalker vs Darth Vader; Rocky vs Anyone; Stella Artois vs Russian vodka; The British Embassy Football Team vs the USSR Embassy football team (almost the start of the Third World War). And much more.

The job at NATO was boring. The people were great, but the job was mind-numbingly boring. There were six of us in a massive secure registry. One was our Fearless Leader and his job was to try to keep his errant troops – the famous five – under some sort of control. For over two years, he had to do that. He deserves an award. I still see him; I think he has finally got over his need to slowly kill us all and burn our lifeless bodies in the big NATO incinerator meant only for classified waste. I suppose we could have been described as classified waste. But, once again, I digress.

Back to the job. The 1981 – 1983 period, whilst not quite the boiling point of the Cold War, was still pretty hot. The Soviets were in Afghanistan and Poland was precarious. There were proxy capitalist versus proxy communist skirmishes breaking out in Africa and Central America and, if the human race had colonised it, I suspect the moon would have had its fair share of proxy (or poxy) skirmishes.

I am not sure what the Warsaw Pact was doing at this time to resolve or win this titanic global struggle, but NATO HQ in Brussels was producing tens of thousands of documents, of varying classifications, that had to be dealt with in one way or another. Mostly they were put in boxes, never to see the light of day again. But the powers that be demanded that we troglodytes in the Registry should at least be able to retrieve some of them. Others, many others, were despatched to the Foreign Office in London, various Ministry of Defence buildings in London and elsewhere. And then, as if that were not enough dead trees, they were also despatched out to various NATO bases throughout Europe. And, to add to our excitement, lots went to our Embassy in Washington for further distribution, even though the US Delegation to NATO was also sending the exact same documents to Washington for further distribution.

At one end of the registry was the communications office and at the other the strong room (not a room that was physically strong, in that it could win arm-wrestling matches, just a reinforced room for the safe custody of documents). The communications office, known as 'the box' (not very original, I know, but there you go), was where we sent and received our diplomatic telegrams. It was hermetically sealed to prevent dust from getting into the cypher machines. From 0930 – 1730, we had professional communicators who received and despatched telegrams at a great rate of knots. Outside those hours, the telegraphic duties passed to us minions, whose typing skills varied from pretty good (all my colleagues) to me. In my case, it was quicker to walk the information from Brussels to London than to wait for me to finish typing it up and despatch it. If the Soviets had known that I was on communications duty, they would have crossed into West Germany and been at the front gates of NATO HQ before I had finished typing the telegram to the world letting them know that something was afoot.

On one occasion, late on a Saturday night in December 1981, I was called into the box to receive a very important telegram (Poland was under Martial Law). NATO needed to react and the Ambassador and lots of other senior people wanted to see this particular telegram. There was only one minor problem, I was at a 'couple's party'. This basically meant that couples had to go as famous couples – Fred Astaire and Ginger Rogers, Katherine Hepburn and Spencer Tracey, you get my drift. I and my partner had gone as Sonny and Cher, but as is my wont, I went as Cher. Long dress, high heels, make-up and a wig (this became a bit of a theme, years later in Saudi Arabia – I will keep you guessing for now).

And so I went into the office as Cher, opened up the systems, printed out the telegrams (lots of them now) and went out of the box to distribute them into the appropriate pigeonholes. Well, to my surprise, there was a group of eight or ten of the most senior UK diplomatic and military representation waiting to get their hands on the latest news and instructions from London, Washington and Warsaw. I tottered over to the Ambassador and handed over the telegrams, and he quickly took in the necessary information before ordering a meeting at 0800 the following morning. I was waiting to be stood down. Meanwhile, some of the not-so-senior staff were just staring, jaws dropped, mouths wide open, at a person they knew to be (a) me and (b) a man.

The Ambassador turned to me and thanked me for coming in so promptly on a Saturday evening and hoped that I could now quickly rejoin my husband and enjoy whatever we were doing.

Monday morning brought a few strange and quizzical looks but nothing more was said. I was expecting a summons from our security people who, back in the eighties, would have been apoplectic about such cross-dressing. Instead, of course, Poland is now free from the yoke of communism. And Cher's singing and acting career was unblemished. I think I might have helped with the former and Cher's agent never got in touch, so I got away without impacting the latter.

Apart from cross-dressing, one of the highlights of working at NATO was the biennial war games. The big one was called Wintex (short for Winter Exercise – wow, some serious out of the box thinking there to come up with that – an exercise in the Winter called Wintex). This was the big boys' and big girls' version of the game of Risk. The idea was to create a scenario whereby there would be a worldwide escalation of conflicts leading to a possible nuclear war between Blue and Orange forces. Now, let us see if we can work out who was who, the Blue was… NATO and the Orange… was the Soviet Union and its Warsaw pact allies.

If memory serves me correctly, the exercise lasted over a week. Everyone was involved. All the country delegations to NATO were open twenty-four-seven, including weekends – cross-dressing was not mandatory. In the UK, senior civil servants took the roles of senior cabinet ministers, including the Prime Minister. But our political masters were not to be deprived of the fun. Quite often we would take exercise telephone calls from the real Prime Minister, the real Defence Secretary and the real Foreign Secretary (I was once having a convivial chat with him, catching up on things, when someone came on the line and pointed out there was a war on and, whilst the latest Test cricket score from down under was not good, there was a time and place when such a subject would be quite interesting. But not now. The Orange army was advancing towards Bonn and that needed some deep thought.)

I mention such conversations because one of my colleagues had enjoyed some gentle banter with someone he had thought was a senior female civil servant in the Cabinet office. Only later were we all told that Margaret Thatcher was pleased that, even during a time of great crisis, her diplomats abroad remained calm and relaxed with a sense of humour whilst Europe and Western civilisation was on the brink of final extinction. No one, despite repeated pleas from senior management, stepped forward to receive a suitable reward for pleasing the real Prime Minister with their calm, relaxed and funny view of complete extinction.

And so, as hordes of the nasty Soviets and their allies advanced into West Germany, crossed the Finnish border, created mayhem in parts of Africa and generally made a nuisance of themselves, we at NATO prepared our response. All of this was on paper only, please remember; this did not actually happen, as most of us might not be here today.

Our first response was a twenty-four supply of tea, coffee and biscuits; our second response was to designate someone to arrange the Wintex winning party (Blue always won) and then we got around to hosting a conference – we cannot do without there being a good conference to resolve global conflicts. Meanwhile, West Germany and France had fallen – no change there then. It was obvious that we could not put up with this type of behaviour and so we retaliated with a threat of the nuclear option from NATO.

The Soviets stopped, said sorry and went back behind the Iron Curtain and peace and happiness ruled once again in decimated capitalist Western Europe. Now, obviously, this is my very much truncated version of the Third World War. NATO experts might want to add some detail or corrections. And, of course, the winning scenario might not have had the full backing of the Orange side. They probably (and I have no idea whether they did or not) held similar exercises where Blue was the aggressor and lost, and then withdrew back to their side of the Iron curtain and, of course, apologised profusely for their indiscretions. And happiness once again descended on decimated communist Eastern Europe.

NATO was not the only game in town (although it was the only one that played war games). Diplomatically, we were not alone; seven miles down the road was the UK Representation to the European Union. They too had a massive registry. Our fellow troglodytes there were also distributing tens of thousands of European Union documents to anyone remotely interested. Which was probably not a very high number (people interested – not the number of documents, which was probably colossal).

In between these two diplomatic behemoths was the British Embassy accredited to Belgium, dealing with the bilateral relationship between the United Kingdom and Belgium. I am not sure there was a lot to do in this particular Embassy: I think, like the UK in the early seventies, they worked a three-day week. Alongside the Embassy, there was the rather Soviet-sounding Joint Administration Office (in some circles, this would have ensured a group of cannabinoid fiends queuing up on a daily basis to join in the administering of the joint). The JAO, as it was known, was there to administer to the needs and wants of the Embassy and the big boys and girls at NATO and the EU.

Poor little Belgium: a country historically overrun too many times to count. To make her (Belgium) feel better, the European and Western world powers had decided to put two of their biggest institutions right slap bang in their nice little capital city. And so now, in 1981, instead of being overrun by malignant foreign powers, they were overrun by hordes of diplomats, their support staff (me and my colleagues – more of us in a minute), international staff supporting the EU and NATO, and international secretariats supporting the supporting international secretariats. And then there were the NATO and EU administrators, who went about raising property prices and every other price, putting living in Brussels beyond the reach of the average Belgian. I think most of them went to live in Luxembourg and nobody noticed. But I digress.

So, in Brussels in the early eighties, there were from the FCO in London (and occasionally from other postings), the very keen and very senior diplomats and very keen trainee (fast-stream) diplomats, trying to prove themselves to either people more senior in London or to the more senior people in the office next door. And then there was us – the registry staff busy putting documents in boxes and, one must not forget, a plethora of secretaries (all female way back then) typing and taking dictation from anyone above the rank of Second Secretary (below that, you either had to do it yourself or buy the afore-mentioned secretary a drink, lunch or dinner, depending on the length of your piece – do not even go there). And it this latter group of minions upon which, if you will permit me, I shall dwell.

Chapter 6

The Rise of the British Missions

All in all, I am not sure how many of us UK-based support staff there were in Brussels at that time – forty or fifty. It was an even split of male and female, with the average age about twenty-two. Our own flats for everyone who was not married, which was most of us (do not worry; married people had somewhere to live. Houses, I think). All utilities, bar the telephone, were paid for. Allowances were vastly inflated by the international staff administrators. All in all, there were lots of young, very well-educated people, with simple jobs to do and money in their pockets or purses, who were unencumbered by mortgages, family or anything remotely serious in adult life. And all of us in a foreign land – a recipe for a lot of fun and the occasional disaster.

To start with, the three Missions (NATO, EU and the Embassy/ JAO) did not really mix. We worked and played in our own little silos. There was the Embassy bar (the Red Herring Club), NATO had a staff centre and the EU team had the Red Lion. But then, the Spanish, I think, came up with the idea of an inter-Embassy football league. The Embassy teams, about fifteen in all, would also include staff from respective NATO and EU delegations. And so it came to pass that the British Missions football team was formed and this was ably supported by our legions of lady friends and staff, except when the Royal Navy visited Antwerp. Then, for some reason, all the ladies, not us gentlemen, were invited to an evening of onboard cocktails and soirees in the wardrooms.

This cross-mission football team built up a superb sense of camaraderie, solidarity, friendships, romances and a large selection of bar and restaurant bills. Dutifully, every Tuesday night, en masse, all the UK support staff from NATO, the Embassy, JAO and the EU would head for the rain-sodden, cold, damp and marsh-like football ground at the wonderfully named Grobbendonk. I kid you not. It exists and it is still there today. Most readers will know one of its two world-famous inhabitants, the great Herman Van Springel; who can ever forget that moment back in 1968 when he came second in the Tour de France?

We Brits put up a pretty good show every season; but the highlight was the game against the Embassy of the Union of Soviet Socialist Republics – the much-feared USSR, the Soviet Union, the bad guys, the people who wanted to destroy the Western way of life, the team that did not buy its round of beers at the end of the season party because it was not a Communist Party. As the Americans had not entered a team in the soccer league, it was incumbent upon us Brits to defend – on the field of Grobbendonk – the values, beliefs, promiscuity, morals, integrity and spending power of the free world. Our punishment for losing... actually, in my three games, we never lost, so we never found out what would happen if we did – probably a consoling Irish coffee in the Irish pub.

In the other corner, the Soviet team were under instructions that losing to the Brits was not an option. The British represented the corrupt, capitalist, war-mongering, promiscuous and morally bankrupt West; a West that was bent on destroying the great Soviet Socialist experiment. Losing, no doubt, meant the USSR team faced the threat of a spell in a well-known archipelago once described so eloquently by one Aleksandr Solzhenitsyn.

Understandably, with the metaphorical significance of these annual matches, the games almost became the big Romanesque gladiatorial battles of yesteryear, taking place, significantly, not in Rome, but in the heart of the former Western Front.

The arrival of the USSR team was always worth watching. We had cleaned and polished our new cars. We had a fresh kit, clean boots, and our lady supporters had on their best bling. Prior to heading to Antwerp, one pair turned up in their best cocktail dresses, while our adversaries turned up all together in a rundown coach with more minders than players. Their kit had seen better days and some of the players, it appeared, had not been picked for any particular skill other than Neanderthal prizefighting.

The game that most stands out was when, way back in 1983, the Soviets had a submarine stuck in a Norwegian Fjord. Almost from the start of the game, as soon as a Soviet player fell over, we all shouted to the minders on the side, "It's OK, bring on your sub." And then proceeded to fall about in Western capitalist fits of laughter. At first, the USSR minders at first seemed oblivious to our brand of humour, but it did not take long for the head KGB man to work out what was being said. And so, in the second half, football was forgotten by the Sovs and it was replaced by fighting. We did not help matters by still harking on about the sub. But one incident went too far.

Our centre-half, a true gentleman who would not willingly engage in our banter about the submarine, was punched off the ball. Not punched near his ball, but punched when he did not have the ball. We were perplexed; it was only afterwards that he explained he had very quietly learnt one Russian phrase: "Do you want to defect?" And he had been discreetly seeping the idea into his opposite number all game until, instead of a defection, he got a thump for his troubles.

Unfortunately, the referee saw the incident and had to send off the offending Russian centre-half. For those of you not familiar with football, to send someone off, the referee must brandish clearly a red card for everyone to see. And, of course, as soon as we saw that, we started singing and parading by it in a slow goose-step march, changing the words of *The Red Flag* to "We'll keep the red card flying." Did we laugh!

The game deteriorated after that. But we won: British Mission 1:0 USSR Embassy. Even though I say it myself, I scored the goal. Contrary to popular practice, the opposition did not stay for the usual convivial post-match drinks. To be fair, they never did.

As a post-script, there was a rumour that the USSR Embassy had submitted a Diplomatic Note to our Embassy complaining about that particular game. Apparently, it caused much merriment amongst those who saw it. If it still exists, I would like a copy.

As I alluded to earlier, the footie team brought together the various missions and multi-mission events became the order of the weekends and Friday nights. A great tradition was to head off for a day canoeing (even if one did not know how to canoe) and eating (even if one did not know how to eat) and drinking (everyone knew how to drink). Coaches were booked, canoes ordered and drinks cooled. The river Lesse in the Ardennes area of the French-speaking region of Belgium is a vastly underrated river in the middle of Europe. It is calm with a gentle flow, passing through various towns and villages – my favourite is Dinant. Visit Dinant before you dieant.

And so, on the occasional summer Saturday, some twenty to thirty twenty to thirty-year-olds from Her Majesty's Diplomatic Service headed for the Lesse. The idea was a nice day's canoeing followed by a nice long lunch on the banks of the Lesse. Another idea was not to get wet. And another idea was to do as little paddling as possible. To achieve this third idea, the plan was always to sit at the back of the double canoe. For the first few trips, this was easy. As gentlemen, we let the ladies into the canoes first and that meant, for stability purposes, they sat in the front. We sat in the back, drank beer and pretended to paddle. All very pleasant for us menfolk. However, the ladies soon spotted our plans and arranged for spotters from the other canoes to raise the alarm that a certain gentleman was not pulling his weight. Indeed, in my case, I was not pulling anything.

The second idea of the long lunch was easily achievable, as was the idea of not getting wet – if one chose the right canoeing crew. The Lesse is a lazy meandering river (and, at that time, a bit like one of my fellow registry clerks, but time has moved on and there's no need to dwell on him – good lad that he was). One could probably float from A to B without much effort. But towards the dis-embarking luncheon area, there was a small weir. And it was here at the weir (a bit of poetry there) that the Lesse able seafarers fell afoul of the meandering torrents of the Lesse and ended up wet. My own belief, still with me to this day, is that certain young men wanted to get certain young ladies wet in order to help them undress, dry them and, well, probably not dry them (you can guess the rest), and thus deliberately tried to ensure that the canoe overturned. Not a bad ruse, I suppose, but I found dinner and a good bottle of wine a more agreeable way to start the dark arts of seduction. And if that did not work, at least one had enjoyed a good meal and a nice few glasses of wine (often, in my case, a few meant a few too many). Much better than falling in the river, methinks.

There were many other away days. The European train system was then, as is now, both efficient and cheap. Paris was a frequent venue for meeting up with our colleagues from the Embassy and the OECD, especially the OECD. And, talking of Paris, my particular favourite pastime there was a brisk canter through the bars of Place Pigalle, followed by a nice Chateaubriand and an even nicer Chateauneuf-du-Pape (1952) in the even nicer Ile de la Cite in the First Arrondissement of Paris. Not alone, I might add; it would be a bit sad ordering and eating the old Chateaubriand and Chateauneuf by oneself. Jamie B was there to help me. He who once sent back four bottles of wine before our starters – remember, we were about twenty-three or twenty-four years old. Some of the wines were a better vintage than us. We did not go back to that place for a while.

Further down the track (literally) were visits to Nice and Monte Carlo (where I lost the equivalent of five pounds sterling in the casino). In the middle somewhere, were pastries and partying in Vienna, a toga evening in Bonn, port in Portugal, football in Luxembourg (England won 4-0 and still there were English supporters inspired to riot), and (up the track from Brussels) a weekend in the dreaded Amsterdam. Amsterdam deserves a special mention.

Amsterdam; the city of canals, Anne Frank, Van Gough, museums, coffee shops and sex shows. And whilst, of course, the canals, Anne Frank, Van Gogh and the museums are all fascinating, sex shows are a must-see. At least that was the consensus of our intrepid group. And so, after handing over money to a complete stranger in an unknown darkish street, it was with some trepidation that we followed our new-found friend with his newly-found cash down a backstreet, just off the famous red light district. After paying more dues, we were escorted into a seedy auditorium. I was pleased to see other tourists in there – and noted that no one was sitting in the front row. That would have been too much. So I and a significant majority of our group sat in the second row, which effectively became the first row. And without further ado, the show started.

It did not last long, the usual tourist rip-off, but for me at least, the highlight of the entertainment was when, during a particularly difficult on stage manoeuvre between the male and female, an American voice heckled, "I came to see a sex show, not a contortionist act." This elicited the wonderful reply, in a broad cockney accent, "It is all in one, innit, mate?" I laughed and left. And others (bar two) followed.

Other away days were more sobering (these were rare, extremely rare). To the north of Brussels, there is the town of Willebroek, which is nearby to the former Nazi prison of Breendonk. Technically, it was not a concentration camp, but on a smaller scale, it was just as bad and was once described by a World War II veteran who had been there as a 'human abattoir'. A visit here is a reminder of why we have (and probably still need) NATO, for the military protection of many European countries, and the EU to join us together economically so that we do not start fighting each other again. Do not worry; I do not think that Brexit will result in Europe imploding and we will suddenly degenerate into the bad old days of the Austro-Hungarian Empire, the rise of the Third Reich, Franco, rationing and Watney's Red Barrel bitter. At least I hope we don't – I could not bear the thought of another (I only ever had one) pint of Watney's Red Barrel.

Once, while I was furthering my search for culture in the great country of Belgium, I found myself (furthering my search for a great Belgian beer) in the municipality of Uccle, five kilometres from the centre of Brussels. Whilst searching for a certain bar in which my friends waited (I think it was my round!), I came upon a Russian

Orthodox Church – the Church of St Job the Suffering. Working at NATO and defending the Western world against Soviet tyranny, I was curious as to why a 'Russian' orthodox church was here in Uccle. I ventured inside. To cut a long story short, it was built to the memory of Tsar Nicholas the Second (and the many others who died at the hands of the Bolsheviks during the tumultuous Russian Revolution and Civil war). Allegedly, some of the possessions of the last Imperial family of Russia were buried in the wall of the church. These had been found near their first 'burial' site just outside of Yekaterinburg (then Sverdlovsk) in Western Siberia. I thought, at the time, that this was interesting. Little did I know that, some twenty-five years later, I would be posted around the corner (literally) from where the Tsar and his family were cruelly murdered and later on (with then my wife Leone and children Benny and Adele) visit the places where the Bolshevik murderers tried to dispose, forever, of the remains of the last Russian Tsar and his family and four 'servants'.

Of course, apart from work, away days and cultural bits, we young budding diplomats had to undergo training. One of the key parts of diplomacy is the need to develop the skills to handle successfully the diplomatic cocktail parties and receptions.

These skills are not naturally part of our genetic make-up (unless, dear reader, you come from a fine Royal line wherein such skills are instilled from birth). No sir, they had to be learnt. It was normally senior officers who hosted such cocktail parties and receptions. And it was normally senior officers who received invitations to these events. In the diplomatic maelstrom that was Brussels, the cocktail circuit was non-stop, with multiple events and national days almost on every day of the eleven months that made up our working year.

Despite the Ferrero Rocher adverts, cocktail parties are (a) work after working all day long and (b) tedious. I would dare to pronounce that at least about eighty-five per cent of us who knew about cocktail parties and receptions, would say, with hindsight, that if we had had the ability to decline such invitations, we would have done so. Our nicely attired diplomatic selves would never, ever have darkened the doorstep of such receptions and cocktail parties.

The remaining keen and ambitious fifteen per cent liked attending these events, got something from them, talked about them, looked forward to them, wrote about them and generally, later in life, ended up in their own little, well-guarded institutions. Or as high-ranking diplomats. Or maybe both. But, be that as it may, in HM Diplomatic Service one cannot avoid them. However, there are two distinct types.

The first is when someone senior from Her Majesty's Government is hosting and needs the troops (rent-a-mob) to make the venue look full. Invitations are issued with the dire warning that non-attendance will be punishable by more invitations being sent your way. Death or torture might have been preferable.

Upon receipt of such an invitation, the trooper will immediately find out who else has been press-ganged and make early plans for an early escape from the reception to the nearest hostelry away from the revelry of the gin and tonic sipping keenly-ambitious set. Prior to the event, the host will have given, subtly but surely, the following instructions to the sequestered troops:-

(i)   No fraternising with each other – mix with the guests.
(ii)   No leaving early – leave on the command of someone very senior.
(iii)   No excessive drinking.
(iv)   Make small talk; on no account discuss British government policy (hidden agenda – we were too stupid for that).
(v)   Make sure no one is left alone, except if it is a fellow trooper. See (i) above.
(vi)   If you find yourself talking to anyone from the media, politely faint and terminate further engagement.
(vii)   No excessive drinking.
(viii) If you are bored with any particular conversation, stick with it; it means the host is talking to the interesting people.
(ix)   If you find someone interesting to talk to, immediately introduce them to someone more senior than you (everyone) and then depart that interesting group, returning to (viii).
(x)   No excessive drinking.

The troops, on the other hand, had already planned their foolproof early escape (setting off fire alarms was a last resort). And knew, of course, that the only interesting people at these events were themselves. And indeed, not only had foolproof escapes been developed, but also a secret signalling system to get around (iii), (vii) and (x).

The second type of cocktail party invitation was the kind that no one wants to go to. This was the one that someone very senior had deemed that someone very junior should attend in case of the million to one chance that the host might notice that the United Kingdom was not represented. That host then takes offence and sends a Diplomatic Note expressing their displeasure at this perceived slight of their important nation (I kid you not, I have seen one such note). These types of invitations – the ones no one wants to attend – were a little more delicate. Invariably, the trooper was alone. And none of his so-called best friends would do the honour of taking his place.

Experience told us troops that the event would be filled with other low-life staff, some of whom could not speak English or French and had not received orders to refrain from drink excessively. The UK troops knew that escaping was difficult – as the sole representative of the United Kingdom, one would easily be spotted if one disappeared without the usual polite farewells, especially after only partaking of one national drink. They also knew that they would be the only interesting person there. And talking to oneself and introducing yourself to yourself was not really a good career move.

Based on years of experience of such events, a helpful code had been drawn up to handle these particular invitations:-

(i)   Prior to arrival, go somewhere else, nearby and loosen up (code for having a drink).

(ii)   Arrive late so that you walk into a crowded room (early arrival will entail excruciating small talk with a very limited number of guests). Always ensure that you greet the host or hostess, passing on the regards of someone senior (this is the diplomatic equivalent of clocking in).

(iii)   Drink moderately-excessively.

(iv)   Do not, on pain of death or a bad stomach, have more than one of the traditional national drink.

(v)   Do not, on pain of death or a bad stomach, have more than one helping of the traditional national dish.

(vi)   Develop the false wave (this needs practice beforehand). When it is necessary to extricate oneself from a conversation, look past your interlocutor and wave at nobody, pretending that you need to talk to that nobody, and move on.

(vii)   Drink moderately excessively.

(viii) Stay until the point of thoughts of suicide.

(ix)   Ensure that you bid farewell to your host or hostess as you leave, saying that the Ambassadorial lunch invitation is on its way (the diplomatic equivalent of clocking off).

(x)   And always collect a piece of information that you can pass on later to those who forced you to attend. They like that. If that is not possible, make something up.

Armed with this guidance, which I have called 'Diplomatic Cocktail parties for beginners', one should breeze through the minefields that are politely called the 'circuit'. If and when one moves up through the ranks, more sophisticated strategies and moves come into play. But that is for another time.

My three years in Brussels flew by, having put hundreds of thousands of documents in boxes, diplomatic bags, bins and incinerators. Having visited most of Europe, made some great life-long friends, battled the might of the mighty Soviet Union and its Warsaw Pact allies (and won), eaten raw bird brains (another story for another time), discovered that Stella is a beer and not a girl's name, and started a strip poker club, it was time to move on.

The boss called me to his office and told me that I needed to be in Bangladesh by the end of March 2004 (this was the end of November 2003). And that was almost that. There then came the usual round of farewell drinks and dinners and lunches. And my final (only) farewell chat with our Permanent Representative to NATO, the top dog! It all went splendidly. I do not think he noticed that I had just had a particularly long farewell lunch. Until, that is, on leaving his grandiose office, I tripped on his Persian carpet, fell over, knocked over a rubber plant as I righted myself from horizontal to vertical, and (without a backward glance) hurriedly left, slurring the word, "Sorry." I had a ferry to catch. And he had his office to rebuild.

En Route to Bangladesh: Locusts in Batter in Thailand

As if I had not already had enough fun in the last three years, on my way to Bangladesh, I decided to stop off in Bangkok (as Griff Rhys-Jones and the late great Mel Smith said – a city which lives up to its name). A good friend from Brussels was there and she had agreed I could use her Embassy flat as a base. One of the many great advantages of being in the FCO was that one had friends all over the world in nice accommodation and, whether they liked it or not (mostly not in my case), the expectation was at least a bed and a warmish welcome in many exotic parts of the world.

Bangkok was hot and humid, but had nice air-conditioned bars, lots of nice beaches to the South and, for some reason, lots of ladies who had a penchant for removing their clothes (and yours for a fee). Men did it as well, but that was not for me. The Embassy had a well-stocked nice, sophisticated bar, but it was unusual in that everyone kept their clothes on. Not for me, this British culture; I was off exploring. First of all, Soi Cowboy Street had been recommended – less seedy than the other red light districts of Patpong and Nana Plaza (I am talking about 1984 here). In Soi Cowboy, I spent many a Happy Hour on a revolving street bar watching the world go by and fending off various women in various stages of undress. Because of the revolving nature of the bar, I quite often left it only to find my way home blocked by it. And so had to rejoin it, buy another beer, fend off another woman until such a time came that I could alight in the right direction – I once spent a few days trying to get back to my host's house.

On one occasion, I became hugely hungry and ordered what I thought was a bag of chips. The bar staff looked at me rather oddly when I requested salt and vinegar. Once my odd looking fries were adorned with a suitable amount of salt and vinegar, I proceeded, with the gusto of a hungry young man, to tuck into my odd looking chips. It was only later that I found out that I had consumed locusts in batter. Not only that, but I had consumed the whole beast, rather than removing, as normal human beings would have done, the head and limbs. But no harm was done and I headed for the cultural sights of this green and humid land.

Alas, that hunt for culture would not last for long. After a few cultural days looking at temples, markets, klongs (canals), the Grand Palace and the floating market, the 'lads' at the Embassy decided it was time for a boys' night out. At this time, I had also been joined by a very good friend from Brussels, who had flown in from Jeddah, where he was on a full posting and needed a break (or to be more specific, lots of beer).

The boys rounded up the two 'Bangkok Virgins' – a reference to us, the new arrivals, not some scantily clad ladies of the night (who, as I think about it, would probably not be virgins). Our first experience was a death ride on the world famous Bangkok tuk-tuks. Do not do this if you have any fear whatsoever of meeting your maker earlier than planned. Tuk-tuks are controlled by mad Thai drivers who drive their unstable three-wheeled machines at high speed through hugely congested, but fast-moving streets of traffic. The sole purpose of the other road users was not, as you would think, getting from A to B, but their main aim (bad as it was) was to kill or maim the tuk drivers – tourist passengers were collateral damage. Somehow this form of transportation survives to this day. On that particular day (or, to be exact, night), I and my visiting colleague survived. At least, I think we survived, or perhaps I am typing away in Heaven – oh dear, I was hoping for something better. I digress.

Anyway, alive or dead, our guides dragged us into various bars in the area called Patpong wherein, to put it politely, various rude things were happening, not only on stages, but also in every corner of the bars and even (I am not sure, to this day, how I noticed) under the tables.

Patpong seemed to have a fascination with Ping Pong, and not the one that is an Olympic sport. It also seemed to have a fascination for darts, and not the game played in idyllic English pubs. It also seemed to have a fascination for writing your name, but not the way we were taught at school (at least not in my school).

After we had seen enough, we headed back to a more salubrious bar in a more wholesome part of the town. This bar had ladies with clothes on. Much more respectable. As well as clothes, all the ladies had badges with numbers (no names). The idea being that you chose the number, did a deal with the Madam of the house and, literally, bingo. But not for me, this immoral numbers game. I sipped my beer and played dominoes. Alas, this convivial evening came to a premature close when one of the (English) girlfriends tuned up to extradite her man from all the excitement, only to find him in a booth with the badge of a nice Thai lady in one hand and her left boob in the other. I am not sure how that ended up, not well, I expect.

For more Thai culture, I and a few others headed for Pattaya. Pattaya was an R & R for US soldiers from the Vietnam War. You can guess, therefore, how Pattaya developed – Presidential libraries, national parks, museums of Native American history, hotdog stands and family-oriented Disney parks.

In case you have not guessed already, that is not how the original fishing village of Pattaya turned out. It was pretty much Patpong by the sea. During one particular, non-sex-related cultural event, my so-called friends 'volunteered me' to get into the ring with a Thai kickboxer, a man with a very large Samurai sword (which at one point appeared to go right through my neck) and another man with a bag containing two angry snakes – if memory serves me correctly, a spitting cobra and some sort of viper. Summing up, I did not see the kick boxer's high kick that gently parted my hair; I did not notice how the sword got through my throat; or the fact that the snakes had been let out of the bag and gently put on my shoulders, whilst being distracted (me, not the snakes) by the sword in my throat.

All this was far too much excitement and so, after a week or so, I decided that work was beckoning.

Part Three

Bangladesh (Dhaka)

April 1984 – May 1986

Chapter 7

Dhaka: Povertyville

And so, after my rather splendid holiday in Bangkok, I headed north to Bangladesh for Entry Clearance work (visas to the general public). And, oh my Lord, what a shock to the system that country was going to be. Of course, I had done some homework on the geography, population and culture. It all seemed to boil down to the fact that Bangladesh was, in 1984, the poorest and most densely populated country on the planet, with malaria, cholera, diphtheria and enough dysentery to plug three or four deep space black holes. Everyone was desperate to leave. The weather was unbearably humid for nine months of the year and the country and people were regularly tormented with vicious typhoons and rain storms. Their lands and homes were, with alarming frequency, washed away. No wonder they wanted to leave – most of them wanted to go back to the maternal bosom of the former colonial power that is today known as France – no, only wishful thinking. It was, of course, us – the United Kingdom. I found it interesting that their neighbour India (which actually surrounds ninety per cent of Bangladesh) would not help this poor country – something to do with the civil war in 1970 and, before that, the partition of India in 1947.

Dhaka airport in 1984 was hot, humid, chaotic and corrupt. Being English, I queued quietly and diplomatically as all around me lost their heads, passports, children, small bags, big bags and anything that was not nailed down. The immigration queue did not seem to move. Except in reverse. I noticed that I was getting closer to the back – that is, those behind me were being called to the immigration booth whilst I, in my stoic English manner, remained (at this point standing in a swimming pool of sweat) dutifully queuing until it was my turn.

I would probably still be there to this day had a colleague from the High Commission not dragged me to the front, thrust my passport under the nose of the Bangladeshi immigration official – who seemed to be counting wads of money – and loudly claimed, "Immigration Section, British High Commission – no fee!" This seemed to do the trick. Although nowhere had I heard tell of or seen a sign that indicated fees. Fees were due by one and all, it seemed, to enter Bangladesh (how naïve I was).

Within minutes, I was through immigration. I had collected my two suitcases (one for each year of the posting) and was out into a sea of humanity. Most of this humanity was impoverished (and probably still is). Some had severe deformities which, for the purposes of begging, they thrust into my face, armpit, crutch or anywhere else they could; others were just trying to grab me by whatever part of my body was not entangled with a deformed limb (not mine); others were trying to help me with (steal) my luggage, but the High Commission driver was fighting them off with what appeared to be a very much practised skill and a very sharp machete.

Eventually, I was pushed into the car and off we went, avoiding humanity (be they standing, sitting, squatting or lying on the road), rickshaws, rickshaw drivers and carts of all shapes and sizes. Everyone seemed to be very tired, very emaciated and just doing their very best just to survive the day. The journey to the Diplomatic enclaves (or a better word, sanctuaries) of Gulshan and Banani was a complete cultural eye-opener (also known as a severe culture shock). There were beggars at every corner and no traffic lights – there probably had been, but anything of value that could be sold or used in the 'home' was removed. There was very little litter as even that was reused in some way or another. The beggars came in various shapes and sizes (but not large or extra-large, not even medium) and, very sadly, with varying degrees of deformities or missing digits or limbs or both. I sympathetically commented on this terrible state of affairs, but the reply was the enigmatic, "Wait until you see the roly-poly man." I said no more; I did not want to dwell on the subject.

On the way in from the airport, it was easy to see that this was not a country that was quickly going to join the economic powerhouses of other parts of the globe, or any other economic grouping of countries that had a GDP anywhere in the plus zone. The poverty was everywhere. I saw some Bengal women in a small lake (there were lots of those and we were just entering the monsoon season – the country, depending on the severity of the monsoons, was soon going to be one big lake). I was under the impression that these ladies were sowing rice, but my colleague in the car disabused me of that notion: "They are at toilet." I quickly averted my gaze and tried to revolve my mind to my revolving bar in Bangkok – now but a distant memory.

In another small lake, I watched bemused as two men tried their best to catch a duck which had decided to have a rest on his (or her) flight out of Bangladeshi airspace. I am sure that no self-respecting duck would be seen dead in Bangladesh. And probably that is the point: the two men wildly and unsuccessfully splashing about were not in pursuit of the duck for animal husbandry purposes. This duck was their next meal. Or rather not. The duck soon tired of its potential predators, took flight and was on its way to Bombay – where cunningly, it knew that Bombay duck was a fish that was always on the Bombay menus. The duck, therefore, not being a fish, could cunningly live out the rest of his days in one of India's largest cities. Clever really. But again, I digress – I do a lot of that.

Another striking image was of some other women sitting atop of five or six feet high mounds of red house bricks. They were almost hypnotically engaged in breaking these house bricks down into fine powder. I had so many questions to ask my travelling companions, but I decided for the moment just to absorb my bizarre new country, which would be my home and work for the next two years (if I lasted that long!). I simply stared in amazement at Povertyville and took in the whole ambience and atmosphere of the place. Talking of the atmosphere, the car air conditioner had broken; Bangladesh must have one of the highest rates of humidity in the Milky Way. The atmosphere was nearly one hundred per cent humidity; any liquid inside me was pouring out of my pores at a rate many would assume as very unhealthy – but it seemed to be the norm here.

At some point, I remembered that I had envisioned Gulshan and Banani would be some sort of idyllic Club Med in the middle of this impoverished insanity. To be fair, as I travelled around Dhaka and Bangladesh, Gulshan and Banani was an oasis in a desert of deprivation. But as I entered Gulshan and Banani for the very first time, I thought that, if this is what the posh end of Dhaka city looks like, then I was very far from impressed. In fact, I thought I was doomed.

But fate intervened: we were headed straight for the British High Commission Club. Indeed, an oasis from the times of the Raj and a bit Club Medish – but more sophisticated. White uniformed staff (for clarification: the staff were not white, the uniforms were) were at our beck and call. There was the bar, bar stools, a comfortable seating area, the pool (as in hitting ivory balls pool) room, a kitchen, a cinema screen tucked away in the corner and a darts board; and everywhere indoors was fully air-conditioned. Outside was the pool (as in a water-filled swimming pool – not to be confused with the pool room), the tennis court, an area for BBQs, a little-covered area for shade to watch the tennis and drink cold drinks – beer and gin and tonics. All very pleasant.

The usual, very informal, introductions took place. I met my work colleagues (fellow Entry Clearance Officers), the bosses (Entry Clearance Managers), the boss (First Secretary, Immigration) and the Head of Chancery, who some ten years later, would be my Ambassador in Lithuania. A good man, sadly no longer with us. I also met his secretary, a fine lady who was to become my first wife. I did not know that at the time, nor did she, I suspect. I would meet the High Commissioner (and other members of staff) as the first few weeks progressed. But for my first few days (it was a weekend), I met many people and, of course, instantly forgot most of their names. I settled into my little maisonette with my servants (they did not live in the maisonette, they had their own accommodation in the garden somewhere). Servants? Yes! One could do very little in the heat and so servants were essential. And good ones were worth their weight in gold. Others were not. Others got up to all sorts of tricks to either make money or save money. And there were ingenious ideas on how to save money at the expense of High Commission officials. And who could blame them?

There was the curious case of the missing lingerie. A rather attractive wife noticed that her undergarment drawer was slowly but surely being depleted. Her husband had not suddenly become a cross-dresser and the servants denied all knowledge of the whereabouts of the undergarments. However, during a drinks reception at the house of the missing of bras and knickers, someone dropped a drink by a particularly bright table lamp. As the servants rushed around clearing up the glass and wine, the light nicely shone through the synthetic white trousers of the head servant, clearly revealing a rather nice, skimpy, lacy pair of ladies' red knickers. And so the crime of the missing undergarments was duly solved. There was a guilty plea, an admonition issued, the missing garments returned (but for obvious reasons, not reused by their proper owner) and a signed declaration that such behaviour would not reoccur. And so calm returned to that particular household.

I seemed to have lots and lots of servants, but this was apparently the norm. I was a single man, aged twenty-six and capable of looking after myself. At least, I thought I was capable of looking after myself. Many then and now, would firmly disagree. I am, after all, the man who put the electric kettle on the gas and melted the whole contraption, the man who thought mascarpone cheese was macaroni cheese (and so purchased macaroni cheese for tiramisu), and the man who could not find butternut squash in the soft drinks aisle.

Returning to my domestic help. There was a man who opened the house gate during the day and another one who did exactly the same thing during the night. There was a man who cleaned and there was a man who cooked. And there was a gardener. And prior to buying a car, I had my own dedicated rickshaw driver and rickshaw. And, with the exception of my private driver, I was paid very well to cover the meagre salaries of these fine gentlemen.

But soon after meeting the staff and moving in, it was time for work.

Chapter 8

The Dhaka Immigration Section

The Immigration Section was some two miles away from the actual High Commission. Those offices contained the aid section, the political section, the High Commissioner, Deputy High Commissioner, the Head of the Political section and the FCO Registry Clerk. I think there were, in sum total, about ten people.

The Immigration Section, on the other hand, consisted of twenty-three entry clearance officers, three entry clearance managers, the boss (First Secretary), about forty-five support staff (a mixture of partners and Bangladeshi staff), three floors, and an outside waiting room the size of a small church or (as we were in Muslim Bangladesh) a small mosque. These staff numbers perhaps reflected the number of people who wanted to leave, forever, their not-so-beloved homeland. And to do that, they needed entry clearances (visas to you and me). One might logically think that such a big, expensive and expansive section, with numerous staff from the FCO, the Home Office and the Immigration Service (as was), would be considered mightily important in the UK/Bangladesh bilateral relations. But that was not the case.

In my humble opinion, those in the High Commission up the road saw us as the poor relations who had to deal with the great unwashed of this erstwhile member (as part of India) of the British Empire. We were the people who legitimately prevented those who were not entitled to do so from entering and staying in the United Kingdom. And believe me, here in Bangladesh, there were a lot of people who were not entitled to go to our green and pleasant land. But they did not mind paying their fees and taking their chances in conning an Entry Clearance Officer into issuing a visa. And we could all understand why. In the United Kingdom, standards of living, social security, accommodation, salaries, healthcare, were all far superior to those in Bangladesh. For historical reasons (with which I will not bore the dear reader), most of the visa applicants came from the North East corner of the country, an area called Sylhet (an anagram, I quickly noticed, of "The Sly").

Up the road, in the High Commission, stopping people from travelling to the United Kingdom was not good for bilateral relations. And so the Immigration Section was viewed with some disdain. Not that we cared. The different stands taken by the two buildings created an unhealthy working atmosphere. It was probably the same in most big visa posts (Islamabad, Lagos, Accra and New Delhi). And, as I heard over the years, a siege mentality developed in these Immigration Sections (which was quite obvious in Dhaka early on); mixing with the other High Commission sections was not the done thing. I broke that mould by marrying into the political section – something akin to uniting the feuding royal families of a bygone age. We shall come to all of that.

That was all part of the general background to the job. But for now, the bespoke visa training for the job had to start. This was designed to further enlighten me to the not-so-subtle nuances to visa work here in Bangladesh, the earthly heart of humidity. This local training was completely different from the broader training I had received in Terminal Three, Heathrow, only two months earlier. This was different. Very different.

The first point was that there was a never-ending stream of "applicants", those applying for visas. The visas were mostly to settle in certain parts of England. And I say England advisedly here. If my memory serves me correctly, very few wanted to go to Scotland, Wales or Northern Ireland (I have some sympathy for that). And some wanted just to visit (or so they said). But that was another problem, the majority did not come back. Our job was to weed out the false applicants from those perfectly entitled to go and settle or visit the UK. The false applicants we would now call economic migrants. Not a new expression, I hasten to add. Economic migration has been around for many centuries. It is just that in the twentieth century most countries had to have immigration controls. We were no exception. And perhaps because we had coloured a good third of the world red in our colonial days, we had particular problems with our former colonies not doing economically as well as they wished, and thus belatedly wanting a part of the motherland's economic action, its benefits, its healthcare and housing. Other former colonial powers had and do have similar issues, but not, I think, to the degree that we were having in the eighties. Anyway, enough of that – I expect some people will write in and correct me.

Back to a bit of history (my version of it, which is probably totally incorrect). In the sixties, the UK had almost full employment and we asked our former colonies in the Caribbean, West Africa and the Indian sub-continent if they would not mind helping us out doing jobs that we ourselves did not want to do. The answer was a resounding yes. And from Sylhet in Bangladesh came many young single (bear that word in mind – single) men to help us.

Now, fast-forward to 1984 and my training. Over the years, since the middle to late sixties, our Bangladesh friends had been given the right to stay in the United Kingdom, obtain British passports and, thereafter, the right to bring their families into England. But during their initial stay in the UK, some of these single Bangladeshi gentlemen made a collective decision that would start an immigration issue (that I believe is unique to Bangladesh) which would go on to dominate visa work over the following decade and dominate my work for the next two years. It was known as the Sylhet Tax Pattern. STP for short.

Nobody likes to pay taxes. And, indeed, if one can legitimately get tax relief for wives, partners, children, ailments and the like, then go for it. But, of course, there are others (of all walks of life, cultures, nationalities and genders) who when seeing a potential, but illegal, way to pay less tax will go for it. Where am I going with this?

In England in the sixties, one could get tax relief for wives and children (as you can now), even if the family was thousands of miles away in Sylhet. And, of course, the tax authorities in the UK had no way of checking to see if the wife and children really existed. And so, sometime back in the mid-sixties, a Sylheti immigrant spotted the flaw in the system. More money could be taken home in the pay packet, via a higher tax coding, if one claimed for a wife and one, two, three four or five children, even if one did not have the aforementioned dependents. And whoever it was who spotted the flaw told lots and lots of his fellow countrymen.

Now all that would normally be a matter for the taxman, but this deception (some might say theft) generated a massive immigration problem and, thus, the majority of the work of the Entry Clearance Officers (ECOs) was to work out whether the family in front of them was a real family. Were they related, as claimed, to the British husband and entitled to settle in the UK? Or was that family a 'tax' family?

Did they not belong to the British husband, although they were maybe related in some other way, and so were not, therefore, entitled to settle in the UK? Confused?!

I will not go into too much detail, but to resolve who was who (and at this stage polygamous wives, and the children of those polygamous marriages, were allowed to enter the UK – at one interview, I had three wives and fourteen children in front of me), the ECOs, over the years, had developed a 'family tree pro forma' and, for further investigation into the more difficult cases, made visits to the villages of Sylhet – 'Village Visits'. We shall come to those (I bet you cannot wait). But back to the family tree.

The idea of the family tree was to get the details of the nuclear family, maternal and paternal aunts and uncles, and the details of the maternal and paternal grandparents of the children. Following it so far?

Bangladeshi families were, in European terms, big and perhaps people in some cultures would not be expected to know all of the vast majority of the relatives as described in the family tree. I hail from Irish Roman Catholic stock and certainly could not recall this type of detail from my family tree. But that might be down, not to my memory, but mobility. Lots of our parents have moved throughout the United Kingdom and indeed the globe, to find jobs. And we offspring have become detached from our uncles, aunties, cousins, nephews and nieces, and other members of the extended family. Which in some cases, if not all, is not a bad thing.

In the Bangladesh village system (if you are now bored with this bit of the narrative, I would suggest that you now jump forward a few pages to something more suitable to your taste), mobility is not really a part of their lives. The villagers live in compounds within villages, and within these compounds, the houses would, at the rear, be attached by communal kitchens (do not ask about the toilets, you do not want to know) and inter-extended family marriage was the norm. That is marrying one's cousin; in fact, marrying a second or third cousin was normal and perhaps expected. Nothing wrong with that; it is frowned upon in the UK, but not illegal. And did not Queen Victoria marry her cousin Albert?

And so back to the family trees. We, as ECOs, would have expected, because of the very close proximity of the families, anyone over the age of fourteen (we did not interview anyone below that age) to know most of these relatives. And so discrepancies in the family tree, be they names, ages, missing people, or extra people, were worthy of further investigation. And investigate we did.

The common problem was that the gentlemen from the UK would, either for the benefit of their wider family or for money, replace the invented tax family with 'real' people not entitled to enter the United Kingdom. Our job (as glorified family tree detective work) was to work out who was related to whom and thus who could rightly travel to this green and pleasant land and, hopefully, live there happily ever after. Whilst this was going on, it is worth repeating that going to the UK was a way out for them from poverty and disease and it has to be said that a move to the UK could increase life expectancy. As mentioned earlier (if you were paying attention), if we were still unsure about who was related to whom we would go on village visits.

Chapter 9

Village Visits: Fun and Games with the Village People

These village visits were designed to give us visa officers definitive proof that all the visa applicants were related to the alleged British husband and his alleged wife. They were planned with military precision, with the finest intellects of the FCO and the finest minds of Immigration Service – and out of date 1970s maps. And so, with this mass of intellectual brain power, we headed into the villages of North East Bangladesh and, in a nutshell, got lost. A fact that singularly undermined any precision and intellect whatsoever.

The arrival, in the dry season, of four visa officers, two large land rovers, two drivers, two interpreters in the capital of the Sylhet area (Sylhet town), with enough provisions to see Monty through another North Africa campaign, was just enough (unsurprisingly, you might say) to set off the bush telegraph that the immigration team was in town, and would soon arrive in a village near you. Our base was the Sylhet Hiltown Hotel (long gone, I think) – a corruption, in my humble opinion, of Hilton but without the stars. Any stars. If hotels could get negative stars, this one would be minus five on a good day.

On arrival at one's room, we removed all the bedding (what there was of it) and replaced it with our own sleeping bags and pillows. We rented our own fridges and freezers and brought our own food: you really did not want to get stomach problems so far from the High Commission nurse. There was no running hot water. After attending to our arrival, we spent the next seven days visiting villages (when we could find them) and tried to resolve some of our more complex cases.

At times, we would hire boats to get to certain villages. But once in the middle of some unknown tributary of a larger unknown river, recently created by the combination of a typhoon and Himalayan snowmelt, our 'captain' (I use the term very loosely) would stop and double the fare before taking us to the other side. Nice one! We always paid up. On other occasions, we were directed to the wrong village so that the family or families under scrutiny could, shall we say, arrange for the right (that is the wrong) people to get to the right compound in the right village. On one occasion, during an actual interview in a dwelling, a poor boy, was passed through the window with all his worldly possessions, in order to prove to me that he was part of the nuclear family entitled to entry clearance for England. Where he had been living up until that point was anybody's guess – mine was that he had been living with his real family who was not entitled to go to England.

It has to be said that village visits were not to the liking of every ECO. Some colleagues despaired of the complete lack of amenities in the hotel and out in the villages. These colleagues would do their utmost not to go on them. I understood that. To this day, I believe my bladder and bowel control is down to a week in Sylhet without hygienic toilet facilities. A trait that would serve me well some twenty years later in darkest Siberia.

On my second 'village visit', all was not well. Prior to departing Dhaka, I had pulled a hamstring and developed some sort of ear infection, but at the tender age of twenty-seven, with the last vestiges of teenage immortality still in my system, I foolishly headed for Sylhet. And on my second or third day there, things went from bad to worse – after eighteen months of medical-free problems, I was smitten with food poisoning. I was getting worse and my roommate recalled that, during the previous night, he could not sleep because of the horror movie sound effects coming from the loo (and I use the word loo very loosely). Alas, because of my stomach cramps and the need to evacuate whatever I had inside me (it felt like the giant snake from Harry Potter), every time I strained on the loo, that impacted on my hamstring which, in turn, caused me to vocally vent my pain. Randomly vocalising my pain like this unexpectedly moved my jawbone, which aggravated my ear infection, thus causing another random (but different) emission from my vocal cords. And so, for most of the evening and night, my roommate was serenaded to: "Ooh. Ouch. Shit. Aaah!" He is still, he claims, mentally scarred by that night.

Dawn could not come quickly enough – not just for me but for anyone within earshot. And so, to cut a long story short, I did not go out on the village visits planned for that day. After a while, I decided of my own volition to fly back to Dhaka, see the nurse, get fixed, have a shower, get laid, and the world was a much happier place for all that. With one minor glitch. The nurse told me that, in order to check for a serious gut condition called giardia, I needed to take a stool down to the aid-funded cholera lab, where they did tests for all sorts of dysentery, diarrhoea and, in particular, the dreaded giardia. Not having a stool at home, I popped into the High Commission club and borrowed a bar stool – my simple logic being that, with Bangladesh not having the best hygiene facilities in the world, the clinic would be packed and a high stool would put me head and shoulders above the fray for a quick check-up and I would be back at work in no time. I was taken somewhat by surprise when I was asked by the receptionist to hand over my stool – for obvious reasons (at least, reasons obvious to her but not to me), this lady politely declined my attempt to present her with a British High Commission bar stool. After some quizzical conversation, she enquired of me, "Do you know what a stool sample is?" I replied, "Well, at this present moment in time, I am not sure that I do."

Everything was then explained. Suffice to say two things. The first was that I was not going to go through the procedure to get a stool and, secondly, I never ever showed my face in the cholera lab again. I think, to this day, I still have giardia. And a memory that cannot be discarded. But it is not about the giardia.

On the way back to the High Commission, I stopped for petrol. As my car was being filled up, there was a tinny knocking on my off-side wheel hub. I got out to investigate. And there I saw, for the first and last time, the 'roly-poly' man. This poor soul had no arms or legs (allegedly cut off for being an Indian collaborator in the 1971 Bangladesh War of Independence). He made his living by rolling up and down the road with a tin dish in his mouth into which one could put money. He was dressed only in a loincloth. The skin on his torso had become a scar-ridden hard leather-like hide. I gave him some money and rushed into my car. I was pleased to hear later, that every night and most meal times, he was cared for by his fellow citizens. There is a God. And then I thought, if he gets free food and accommodation, what does he spend his money on? He must be loaded! But may Allah bless him wherever he is now.

Chapter 10

Blood Sports in Dhaka

And so, month in and month out, apart from the village visits, we toiled away at deciding who should and who should not go to England. A thankless task at times, but the camaraderie in the immigration section was second to none. We worked together, played together, holidayed together and some married each other. That is, really married one another, hopefully not for tax purposes.

Sports and sporting events were a key part of relaxation from a tough job. There was tennis, squash, volleyball, football, five-a-side football and the Hash House Harriers (HHH). This was nothing to do with Hashish, but a drinking club for those with a running problem, or was it a running club with a drinking problem? I do not remember. I was formally ejected from it for taking out a rather attractive visitor when I should have been drinking/running. In the absence of much in the way of the same-aged opposite sex, I thought that taking out the attractive visitor was not a bad idea. However, do not mess with the protocols of the HHH.

In addition to all this sporting excitement, there was the annual England versus Australia cricket match. Created in the fashion of the Ashes, but it was only a one-day match – winner takes all. The Ashes 'urn' was a grail-shaped cup onto which was glued an empty tin of Foster's lager (an Aussie win) or an empty tin of John Smith's bitter (yes, you've guessed it, for an England win). This sporting extravaganza, which attracted a crowd of hundreds, was not named the Ashes, probably for copyright purposes – or more likely because, apart from the two nations involved, it bore very little resemblance to the great institution that is the Ashes. It was called, and in my view, more fittingly, the 'Dregs'. And one year, it was nearly the end of me.

In 1985, we had lost. I had been out in the hot sun on the boundary most of the day. Cold beer was used for the purposes of rehydration (doctors and nurses and wives and mothers and many others totally unknowledgeable about my constitution will tell you that beer is not a good way to rehydrate – but, like a lot of things, I did not take any notice of this advice). And so, after lots of rehydration exercises,

I headed home to a nice hot shower. Tired, but not emotional, I climbed into the bath – most showers were in the bath in those days – turned on the luxuriant cleansing and refreshing brown water and slipped. I reached quickly for the safety rail attached to the wall. This came away in my hand and I fell sideways but head first into the toilet cistern. This smashed and, as part of a reflex action, I put out my arm to prevent myself from crashing directly onto the floor. In so doing, the broken porcelain from the broken cistern took it upon itself to gouge out a large gash in my left hand.

Naked and dazed, unable to use my left hand, and with a lot of blood and water everywhere, I shouted for my trusty manservant, Abdul. He arrived and, of course, immediately left because his boss was naked. I then managed to contact the newly arrived lady visa officer who was living in the maisonette below mine. Abdul, in his broken English, had alerted her to some sort of problem with the nutty guy upstairs. I, in the meantime, had managed to get a towel around myself and was sitting on the bed surrounded by blood and water – the cistern was overflowing everywhere – which made the whole scene look like something out of a very bloodthirsty horror film. My new neighbour arrived and entered the bedroom. And promptly fainted. Maybe the mixture of my masculine torso and the blood was not to her liking. *This is not good*, I thought, mainly because the blood was still flowing out of me at a rate of knots. Instinct took over and I stepped over my prone colleague (unbeknownst to me, splattering her with blood) and called the High Commission Duty Officer and explained my predicament. I needed help fast. I was pleased to hear the High Commission radio crackle into life as an all-points bulletin was sent out that I needed help and people in the vicinity should assist. And help did arrive pretty promptly.

It was a group of High Commission ladies, who earlier had been playing bridge or canasta, or whatever. They now, on seeing me, the blood, the blood-spattered phone, and the blood-spattered body on my bedroom floor assumed, Cluedo-like, that some healthy shenanigans had become unhealthy shenanigans. Professor Lynch had killed Lady Mustard in the bedroom with the phone. Case closed. Game over.

Fortunately, my prone neighbour recovered from her faint and told the truth and nothing but the truth. And so it came to pass that the Australian nurse arrived to save the night. I was tourniqueted and ferried to the nearest surgery, where a kindly surgeon sewed me back together again. Or rather he did not. When the stitches were removed, my thumb was useless. And, much to my annoyance, I could not hold a drink in my left hand. No good for going to the bar and ordering two pints for you and a friend. This needed to be fixed. Others will say that I have never bought two drinks in my life; but that is another story.

Fortunately, just after the accident, I was due for some leave in Blighty. Appointments were made and a surgeon in St. Thomas's Hospital kindly re-opened (this time without the assistance of a porcelain cistern) my scar and mended the lacerated nerve and tendon that had been missed in Bangladesh. I still have the scars, but my left hand functions as normal. And, as a further footnote, I was later told that it was I who had single-handedly (pun intended) ensured that, across the world, all official accommodation with showers in the baths had to be equipped with non-slip bath mats and securely fastened safety bath rails. I should have got a knighthood for that; people get them for less.

Chapter 11

Visit Bangladesh before the Tourist Comes

The beauty of Bangladesh is that one can easily visit some of the more off-the-beaten-track countries that are in the neighbourhood. This was 1984-1986, remember. Nowadays, most of the world is accessible to very many people; unfortunately, in my opinion, too few take advantage of seeing the far-flung and less sophisticated (if that is the correct terminology) parts our great planet. But then again, maybe they know something that I do not. That is, they do not like mosquitoes, dirty toilets, soiled hotel bedding, dysentery, bad food and a lack of customer service (I have told them that Margate is not that bad anymore). But there might be something in their hang-ups, so neither the well-travelled nor the less well-travelled have the moral high ground.

Back to travelling out of Bangladesh. Eleven hardy souls from the High Commission spent four days in India, seeing the Taj Mahal, riding elephants, paying homage at the grave of the Mahatma, visiting the Red Fort, the Pink City, and Jaipur, and then beating our New Delhi High Commission colleagues at pool and darts. All was well and good, except that I was sick (food poisoning from a five-star hotel) on the Taj Mahal. Or rather near it, to be exact; I don't want to incur, albeit over twenty-five years later, the wrath of the Taj Local Council. I fell off the elephant and sprained my ankle and got lost in Jaipur. I was beginning to wonder if I was cut out for this travelling lark.

On another occasion, four of us headed for a long weekend in the high Kingdom of Nepal. We were more than privileged that, as we flew into Kathmandu, the clouds cleared on the starboard side of the plane to give magnificent views of the most famous of the Himalayan Mountains: K2, Kangchenjunga and the mighty Everest, to name the top three. Savagely beautiful.

This was in contrast to our first visit to Durbar square (now, sadly seriously damaged by the recent earthquake) in Kathmandu. The buildings are (were) magnificent, but the dirt was ubiquitous. And for our enjoyment on our first day, two dogs (to be accurate a dog and a bitch) had decided to enjoy one of nature's oldest urges – the need to procreate in public. Regrettably, for some reason that only vets will be able to explain, the dog could not unhinge himself from his mate and had, in a manoeuvre that I suppose he hoped would help the situation, turned himself around so that now he and his ever-lasting love looked like the Push-Me-Pull-You Llama of Doctor Doolittle fame. The crowd gathering to watch the spectacle of the two beasts trying to separate fell into two groups. The first finding the whole thing funny. The other was in consternation, wondering how to help resolve this public carnal event without being bitten by a possibly rabid bitch or a very angry dog, who had earlier been going about his lawful business until he had been seduced by the canine pheromones of his present companion.

But help was at hand. A fellow European, hearing us speak English, approached our little group and advised (very seriously) that the only way to separate our canine friends was to insert a digit into the bitch's private part and make a quick anti-clockwise movement. Gosh, was it that time already? We made a hasty retreat, had lunch, and headed for the all-seeing Buddha – the prayer wheels, the prayer flags – all of which was much more culturally fulfilling than the morning's entertainment, which had now included a short lesson in canine husbandry.

In the following days, we cycled around Kathmandu and travelled out onto the Kathmandu plain for many miles to get a good view of the mountains. It was cloudy. We marvelled at the stepped fields clinging onto the high-sided hills, and wondered at the strength of both the men and women who brought their wares to the city. They used the simplest of carts, pulled by hand or beasts of burden, and if the cart was full, the surplus went onto their backs.

We visited what I called (or maybe it was someone else) 'Hippy Alley'. This is a street in Kathmandu occupied by ageing hippies who had arrived in their Nirvana in the late sixties and stayed. Cat Stevens (now Yusuf Islam) and his song *Katmandu* has a lot to answer for. Here was a street in the middle of Nepal wherein ageing British, American and European hippies had addled their way through the seventies and half of the eighties. The hair on top of the male heads had gone, and the ladies' long original tresses were now silvery grey. And all of them were adorned with the look-a-like John Lennon gold-rimmed round spectacles. They all smoked weed and were happily oblivious to such things as the Cold War, cold beer and anything else that was even remotely outside their street. They are all probably there to this day, may their God bless them.

And, of course, as was the norm during such visits, we beat the British Embassy Nepal team at pool and darts.

I was to visit Kathmandu for a second time as a diplomatic courier, carrying the diplomatic bag to our Embassy and bringing one back. A one-night stay. At least that was the idea. After delivering the bag to the Embassy, I had a pleasant meal and drinks with an FCO friend and his wife from the 1978-1981 stint in London. I stayed in a nice hotel, apparently owned by the brother of Stan Bowles (a maverick professional and England football player). I never met the brother. Saying that, I have never met Stan Bowles either. Anyway, the following morning, I was told – although I'm not sure how true this is – that there would be no commercial flights in Nepalese airspace for the next few days as the King of Nepal had decided to fly around his Kingdom. Lucky me, I was thinking of a helicopter trip out to Everest Base Camp One, but that was not to be. I was grounded in the city, just in case a flight became available at short notice, and then Her Majesty's Casual Diplomatic Courier could be available, no matter what, to deliver Her Britannic Majesty's diplomatic mail between Nepal and Bangladesh. Whatever that contained – with hindsight, probably not much.

With time on my hands, and being the culture vulture that I am, I explored the front and backstreets of downtown Kathmandu, visited temples, statues, gardens, markets and numerous bars, wherein I impressed the locals with my pool and dart skills. I learnt various useful Nepalese phrases (technically Nepalee, I was informed), such as: "Now it really is your round," "Do you know the way to the British Embassy?" and "I told you I was good at darts."

A few days later, the King decided that he had seen enough of his Kingdom (the feeling was mutual) and landed the royal flight, kindly freeing up the airspace and allowing hundreds of stranded passengers to go on their weary ways as if nothing had happened. And so, after this unscheduled rest from the Bangladeshi family trees, I was back in Dhaka. But more travel beckoned.

Calcutta is only a thirty-minute flight way from Dhaka but, in reality, it is another world. This can be the only place on the planet where people are glad to get back to Dhaka. The sheer density of humanity, the extreme impoverishment against a background of wealth, has to be seen, felt, smelt, touched and breathed to be believed. Three of us journeyed to Calcutta for one long Easter weekend. A crucifixion might have been preferable.

We were lucky: we had money and a decent hotel. We dined at the segregated (one floor for men only, one floor for women only, and one floor for families) third best curry restaurant in India. And thereafter, went into downtown Calcutta, not for us the bars of the five-star hotel(s). We wanted some local action (that was not going to last long). We found one bar on a third floor. Scruffy but local, with local people, local beers and local spirits (the drinks, not ghosts of the Indian Mutiny). After a little while, the locals were not very welcoming – we had beaten them at darts and pool. Lots of people seemed to have Sikh daggers (Kirpans), and not for religious purposes. And so we headed out, but not before I needed to use the loo. I only wanted a pee, but was directed to the other place where I, before really noticing, urinated into a broken toilet bowl which leaked, or rather cascaded, straight onto the street and people three floors below. I zipped up hastily and searched vainly for the sink. I was quickly met by a largish gentleman offering me some sort of rag and, at the same time, sternly directing me to a tap and a brown sink that was once white.

However, taking it all into consideration, the combination of the brown water overflowing from the blocked brown sink and the brown rag, which looked like something from the days of the Great Plague (and probably still had the ability to resurrect the Great Plague and a host of other life-threating ailments), I politely declined these ablutions, paid the man for his trouble and left this august establishment. We headed for the five-star Hilton hotel bar.

The following day was a choice: the famous Tollygunge club to the South of Calcutta or to the Bustees across the Howrah Bridge (spanning the awfully named River Hooghly). The former was renowned for its golf, squash, riding, tennis, billiards, bar and a host of other Raj-like entertainments. The latter was then the most densely populated piece of earth on the planet; full of people, poverty, depravity, squalor, criminality and most other things society should neither see nor tolerate. And as if that were not enough, there were rumours that very young children were put in large curved narrow-necked clay jars and kept in there so that they grew with awful spinal deformities. Why? So that they could then be sent across the Howrah Bridge and beg. Deformed children were apparently better earners.

Well, obviously no contest. The Tollygunge (or 'Tolly' as it was known) was for me. I was outvoted. As we were visiting the largest democracy in the world, I had little choice but to go with the majority of two, so we hailed the best taxi we could. One that would not leak if it rained, or breakdown and demand money for engine repairs. One that had working windows and at least a fan, if not some sort of air-conditioning (not winding down the window – or as happened once, opening the door at thirty miles per hour).

"To the Bustees and do not spare the horses," we gaily (in the old-fashioned sense of the word) addressed our driver. He immediately wanted triple the fare that the hotel had advised us to pay. No problem, to be honest, it was a pittance. And so off we went – admittedly, with some trepidation to, apparently, one of the worst places on earth.

We did not make it. Halfway across the Howrah Bridge, the sea of humanity brought our taxi to a walking pace. That enabled the Great and the Good, but more importantly the Awful and Evil, to notice three Europeans (which basically was a big sign for money) heading towards India's Heart of Darkness. The Great and the Good did not want us to see that Heart. The Awful and Evil were more than happy to bring us into their lair. In this mini-battle of Good versus Evil in the middle of Howrah Bridge, the Great and the Good triumphed. Or rather, the taxi driver said he was not taking us any further and that we could either walk or he would, still for triple the fare, turn around and get us back to civilisation. This time the vote was unanimous. And so we spent the day strolling through the more pleasant parts of Calcutta, learning about its famous and infamous history and generally congratulating ourselves on extracting ourselves from a fate worse than death. But the heat, humidity and ever-pervasive beggars were never far away. Nor was the smell, which became, at times, the stench of overloaded sewers, a lack of drains and the dead. As I say, it would be difficult to find a place that might be worse than the slums of Dhaka. But here it was – only a thirty-minute flight away. Another might be a place called Kaolack in the centre of Senegal, but that is, literally, another chapter in this peripatetic life.

My colleagues had quietly erased from their minds the fact that we could have been, from early on, sipping cold beers on immaculately maintained patios, admiring the magnificent cultured lawns, flora and fauna of one of India's most famous private clubs. But forgetting that for the moment, not even the discovery of a dead body in a pile of rubbish not far from our hotel could deter us from reminiscing about our great escape on the Howrah Bridge. Perhaps it was a bridge too far… but that has already been used elsewhere and, anyway, I need it for later in this book, much later. I personally would, to this day, like to track down our taxi driver and thank him profusely for his decision not to cross the Howrah. Only the real taxi driver can apply, all other approaches will be sent to the Calcutta (now Kolkata) tax office.

On our way back, the Air India plane was quite new, but it had this unnerving sign on the toilet seat cover in the lavatories: 'Please lift.' Not on the actual bit you sit on, and which most men lift up before a pee, but on the cover that, in effect, hides the bottom of the bowl from the next unsuspecting user. It did beg a question; but this being a family and not a faecal book, I shall not dwell on that particular question.

On another holiday (one needed a lot of holidays whilst in Bangladesh – at times even after a holiday), two of us headed to Burma, just prior to the military takeover.

Burma is a fascinating place today and was even more so in 1986, when tourists had not really discovered this pagoda and temple-laden land. But way back then, life was tough and it seemed that the Burmese Kyat (the national currency, pronounced 'chat', at least that is what I was told, and I loved a good chat) was not what officialdom or anyone else wanted – they wanted US dollars, whiskey (Irish or otherwise) and 'Western' cigarettes more than their currency. And so on entering the country and trying to pay for our visas at the customs control with Burmese Kyat, the nice customs officer ignored his own currency, rooted through our bags and took away a half-bottle of whiskey. Two visit visas were then nicely stamped in our passports. And then a taxi to our accommodation was paid for by a packet of Benson and Hedges. I had a colleague in the Embassy. She had a nice bungalow in the Embassy grounds and had kindly offered to put us up, or perhaps put up with us for a few days.

The temples and pagodas of Burma are well-documented elsewhere and I will not bore you with their details. Suffice to say that, even in the most famous one, the Shwedagon temple in what was then Rangoon and is now Yangon, we were asked for whiskey, dollars or Benson and Hedges. If Buddhism had had the equivalent of Jesus, he would have torn them off a strip. As it was, I had Benson and Hedges and exchanged them for local currency (useful for knick-knacks and beers in local bars) at a very beneficial rate of exchange. As a Catholic, I was worried about such behaviour in a religious establishment, but then realised that if I later confessed my sin (if indeed, it was a sin), I would be forgiven.

And so to the touristy bits (rather than money laundering in temples). We were told that there was an original Raffles hotel in downtown Rangoon and so attempted to find it. And find it we did. It was not the Raffles from Singapore, and I am sure that if the Raffles family had been aware of its existence or actually had any link with it whatsoever, they would probably have sued for its demolition. The building was drab and rundown; the only thing actually running in it was a rather emaciated rat looking for the real Raffles hotel – he would have a long journey. We did not stay long.

One can only see so many temples and pagodas (the same applies to Thailand) before screaming, "I have had enough, get me out of here!" For me, that number was about five. And I was fed up with being asked for cigarettes, dollars and whiskey. Do I look like a chain-smoking, rich alcoholic? Maybe I do, or did then. And so we gave up on temples after a while. The Road to Mandalay (really – it is in Burma, now Myanmar) was closed, so that avenue of adventure was similarly closed. We managed to fill our days by playing avoid the temple, avoid the pothole and avoid the street vendors. However, our arrival had coincided with the Embassy's traditional monthly Sunday lunch, where the Ambassador served the staff. Great stuff, except he conveniently forgot that I drink wine and beer like a fish (perhaps he had been forewarned) and my glasses were not replenished as fast I would have liked. But criticising the Ambassadorial waiter in his own home whilst on leave from a neighbouring post might have been a career limiting move.

Fun aside, if you go to Burma, the Taukkyan War Cemetery is not to be missed.

And so that was Burma – not exactly a fulfilling travel guide, but there you go.

Even though I somewhat malign Bangladesh, I should say a bit about internal travel and holidays in Bangladesh itself. I wish I still had the Bangladeshi tourist poster which proudly announced, 'Visit Bangladesh before the tourist comes.'

Internal travel in Bangladesh was only really possible during the 'dry' season, approximately December to March each year. For the other nine months of the year, heat, humidity, typhoons, monsoons, flooding, rivers and bridges were not where they were supposed to be (if they were there at all) and all sorts of other potential natural disasters precluded a pleasant day out or weekend away. But come the dry season and once again the more adventurous of us wanted to flee the diplomatic enclave and the oppressive heat and humanity of the city. There were others who, and I do have the greatest respect for them, had decided that the Indian subcontinent was not for them. Their idea of the perfect posting, or rather how to make the best of this very imperfect posting, was to visit each other in their air-conditioned houses and/or remain as close as possible to the air-conditioned, Raj-style High Commission club.

That lifestyle was not for me and my hardy friends, but our options were limited. I tried a picnic once with a lady friend. As mentioned earlier, the country was then the most densely populated piece of real estate on the planet. Every piece of land was accounted for, except during the monsoon season when land and rivers, sandbanks and paddy fields all either moved, sank or became hillocks, or even disappeared altogether. Land ownership was fraught with problems and savage disputes over who now owned what were not uncommon. With the population density and land ownership a top priority, attempts at picnics inevitably ended up with the picnickers being surrounded, in a friendly manner, by the local landowners, their families, their extended families, friends of the extended families, passers-by, their families and their friends. You get the picture. Not really a comfortable way to pass a couple of hours with the chilled white Chablis, cheese and cucumber sandwiches and four thousand onlookers. And so land for a picnic was a rarity.

Never one to be deterred, on one pristine day, my lady friend and I headed north. After driving some thirty miles, we came across a small, pristine – for want of a better word – meadow. No one was about, but then again, there never was for the first few minutes. Everyone normally appeared as the food and drink had just been laid out for consumption – a bit like the average British BBQ. As we set about our picnic, no one visited us. We had a very pleasant hour or so before some very angry tribal elders descended on us, en masse, from nowhere. They were clearly agitated, shouting at us in one of the Bengali dialects (a bit pointless really, as neither us could understand a word). Eventually, a translator was found and it transpired that we were picnicking on a very sacred spot. Oops! Apologies were unacceptable but the equivalent of £7.59 was. Once the money had been handed over and distributed, we were all friends and they waved us off on our merry way back to the capital.

To avoid such confusion and, to be honest, avoid the people who lived on the land, it was much easier to hire the British High Commission sea truck. This was an old mini-landing craft moored on the Buri Ganga River on the south-west outskirts of Dhaka. It held about eight people comfortably and had a captain, sailor and 'butler'. And so, on any given dry season day, cliques of friends from the High Commission could spend the day on the river, complete with cool boxes brimming with beer, wine and sandwiches. Most of these days were idyllically spent (once we were away from the hullaballoo of the mooring point) in the breeze, chewing the fat, drinking the wine and watching the world's most densely populated and impoverished country pass by from the safety of our Second World War landing craft.

The other marine traffic had to be seen to be believed. Full-blown steamers were packed to the gunnels with their human and non-human cargo while taxi boats plied their trade, dangerously but fearlessly, between them. Other craft were piled seriously high with the ubiquitous red bricks from the red brick factories further up river. Straw boats (well, not actually straw – boats carrying straw) with the straw piled so high that the captain could not see where he was going and relied on his lookout sitting on the prow shouting directions were all OK, if the directions were not drowned out (pun intended) by the cacophony of the world's second busiest waterway (I might have made that up, but you get the atmosphere). Marine accidents were not infrequent. But, overall, a pleasant, relaxing way to spend the day.

Other days were not so idyllic. Sometimes the dark side took over. And I am not talking about the very occasional sudden storm, which would turn the sky black and deposit a metre of rain in sixty minutes before the sun reappeared from having lunch somewhere else in the galaxy. Whereupon he (if the sun is male) would calmly restore order to the day.

No, this was the dark side of too much sun and too much beer and wine. People became possessed and obsessed and wanted to swim. Now, I am not a water specialist, not then, in 1985 or 1986, and not now. But even with a modicum of intelligence, I knew that in the mid-1980s, Bangladesh did not have a proper waste disposal system nor regulated burial rights for dead animals or, it might be said, for humans; factory waste was not regulated and, of course, there did not exist, at the least in the upper reaches of the rivers of the land of the Bangla, a proper sewage system. Long ago, when I had first seen the lakes of Gulshan and Banani, I had hazarded a guess, a long shot I grant you, that most of the above mentioned human and animal detritus ended up in the lakes and rivers of this fertile land. And so, to me at least, diving and swimming in any river (or lake for that matter) that was still in Bangladesh, or had even entered or left Bangladesh at any point in its existence, was not a good idea. Not a good idea at all. Oh no. Let me repeat that and you read it slowly – not a good idea at all.

But swim they did. My colleagues. They dived in. They swam. They pretended they had fun, even when covered in green slime and brown slime (I wonder what that was); even when they were covered in weird skin-sucking aquatic creatures as yet undiscovered by Sir David Attenborough, they continued with the pretence of having fun. Even when splashing about in the dirt brown liquid, whose sole purpose was to destroy all earthly lifeforms but itself, they continued to pretend to have fun. And even when they reboarded the landing craft with a hint of a radioactive glow about their torsos, they still smiled and laughed. They are all dead now. Not really, but they should be. They should leave their bodies to science. They have survived the unsurvivable.

There was one more way of having a break. The Rocket: a steam paddle ship from an era long gone. Vintage Empire and Raj – a steam paddleboat, complete with steam, paddles, and more importantly, First, Second, Third and Hang-on-the Side class. The trip took one away (it was not one way, it took one away, pay attention) from the capital for two nights and three days. And so, one slow afternoon in the Club, four of us plotted to get away from it all, First Class, from Dhaka to Khulna (the third largest city in Bangladesh) and, in the words of Gerry Rafferty, we would "...forget about everything". But our conversation was overheard and there was no way we four musketeers would be allowed to escape without half the High Commission joining in the fun. And so it was that one long weekend, the whole of the First Class deck was hired out by the all-singing, all-dancing, British High Commission troupe. There were about twenty of us, if I remember correctly.

The trip started well. No one was drunk. Then the ship slipped its moorings, the steam belching from its one-hundred-year-old funnel. The paddles started to paddle, we went astern and promptly crashed into a smaller, much smaller boat, ran it over and carried on as if nothing had happened. Technically, this was correct; nothing had happened to Her Majesty's Steamship the Rocket, but somewhere at the bottom of the Buri Ganga lies a small boat and its cargo of many, many red bricks. I am sure that the responsible body, the Dhaka Port Authority, conducted a full enquiry and found that no blame should be attached to either vessel.

And so, after this exciting start, the Captain decided that the best way to go was forward and we moved smoothly into our shipping lane, heading south for Khulna, where we would unload whatever was on board (which, by the look of things, was everything on the planet that could not be nailed down) and then return to our home port.

Kindly, servants allocated our cabins: doubles for everyone. I shared with a dear friend who, later in life, would regret drinking six Coors Light in Denver with me before his flight to San Francisco.

Our holdalls were unpacked and then we set out onto our very own First Class deck, where doubles for everyone was the order of the evening.

Post the pre-dinner drinks, we sat down to a sumptuous curry (what else) and, post the sumptuous curry, it was time to sit around on our open-air deck. Normally at this point, when a bunch of visa staff are huddled together, the conversation is somewhat dominated by the oddest visa applicant and all sorts of funny visa stories. But we were in mixed company. The siege mentality had been breached and we were a mixture from all the sections of the High Commission. But I cannot resist this one visa story that came out on a later adventure.

The winner for the best immigration story was when a Nigerian turned up at Heathrow claiming to be Jesus Christ. Correctly, he said he was born in Bethlehem, his age was 1980 years old and the purpose of his visit was to return the Protestant United Kingdom to a Roman Catholic vassal of the Vatican. The Immigration Officer pointed out to JC that, in fact, he was Kareem Abeo, aged twenty-six, that he was born in Lagos and that he had an illegal job lined up in a fast food outlet and, because of all that, he was going to be returned to Lagos on the next available flight. At that news, the gentleman in question lay on the airport floor, made himself into a crucifix and said, "Father, forgive them, for they know not what they do." Funny, but it does make you think... was it Him?

And so, without immigration stories, a convivial evening on the Rocket continued: we sipped our cool drinks and wondered what the poor people were doing. I did not need to wonder. I knew. I, in a reverse Leonardo de Caprio moment from *Titanic*, had wandered from First Class to Third, via Second (and that was bad enough).

During a lull in the onboard proceedings, I decided to venture below decks. The First Class deck was separated and guarded from the rest of the ship. At first, the kindly First Class guard would not let me pass, but after politely explaining that I was a former sailor (Deck Boy Lynch of Townsend Thoresen fame) and that I had a sincere interest in all manner of waterborne vehicles, he reluctantly let me pass. And so I ventured into the bowels of the ship. Second Class was immediately below us and appeared to be just a deck with densely-packed families sitting around on rugs, the mother preparing the food for her very large and very young family. And then, to the aft of the Second Class Section, was the Third Class. Here was a sea of humanity packed in with the cargo – it looked like bale upon bale of Jute on its way to various corners of the world.

Bodies were standing, sitting and lying everywhere. To my untrained eye, there was no rhyme nor reason to the sitting, standing or prone positions. A bit like one of our budget airlines today. And the stench of humanity having been packed together, day in and day out, as the ship plied its trade, without, I suspect, a good hosing down occasionally, was overwhelming. As I ventured further into the Jute and closer to the aft end of the ship, I noticed people were hanging on to the outside of the ship. They were not stowaways, just your ordinary paying passengers wishing to avoid their fellow human beings. I will not dwell on the toilet facilities; it seemed to me that this aft end gave a new meaning to the term poop deck – technically, in pure nautical terms, the aft deck is the poop deck, but here it took on a whole new meaning, or should that be nuance? And so, curiosity now satisfied as to this part of the ship, I headed back up and decided to have a look at the bridge.

After a brief conversation with the Captain, during which I had promoted myself from Deck Boy to a Third Mate, I was on the bridge. As an interesting aside (and for some, it might not be remotely interesting), bridges on ships came about because of paddle steamers. Simply put, the paddles needed to be inspected at regular intervals and so little houses were built atop them. This, in turn, obstructed the Captain's view of port and starboard (left and right for the uninitiated) and so a bridge was built. There you have it – the history of nautical engineering in one foul swoop.

I spent a pleasant half hour with the Captain. I decided not to ask about the boat that we had steamrollered to the bottom of the river at the start of our journey; *a conversation best avoided*, I thought. He kindly let me steer the ship – but had he known that, for reasons of pure vanity, I did not wear my much-needed spectacles, and so most of the river buoys, banks and boats were all just a blur to me, he might not have so graciously given me the helm. Saying that, crashing into other vessels seemed to be par for the course. Still, we survived and I ventured back to the safe haven of my friends in First Class.

And so, for the next thirty-six hours, we sailed along at a leisurely pace (the name of the ship, The Rocket, was one of the many oxymorons we all come across in life), stopping occasionally to load and unload passengers and cargo. On board, we amused ourselves with playing cards, reading, eating and testing out new cocktails, but most of all, during daylight hours, observing the life and industries of the riverbanks (although, at times, the river was so wide the banks were not visible to the naked eye).

A popular pastime for those living close to the river seemed to be washing the bottoms of their cows and bulls. A noble endeavour if ever there was one, although not a job I would apply for – I am unskilled in such matters. But this particular cottage industry did make me wonder about (or even confirm the idiocy of) the need for my friends on the sea truck to jump into the river. I shall leave it at that.

I had noticed on our deck numerous doors that did not seem to lead anywhere. I am a curious fellow and, of course, being an ex-cross Channel mariner, I decided to see either where these doors went or what was inside them. Most of them were full of cleaning materials, hoses, buckets and the usual paraphernalia that one would expect to find on a paddle steamer ploughing its trade up and down one of the great rivers of the Indian sub-continent. To my surprise, but probably more to the surprise of those involved, on opening one door of one particular cupboard, tucked away aft in the corner, I saw a male and female couple – colleagues from the High Commission – urgently searching for something, I assume. Maybe some cleaning materials. They had neglected to bring with them their respective (and respected) marital partners to help them in this search. As we looked at each other, the male party made the 'shush' sign (one finger hovering vertically over the middle of his lipstick-covered lips) and slowly pulled the door closed. And that was the end of that. I hope they found the cleaning materials they were looking for – it would have been easier, methinks, if they had put the light on. And so ended the Rocket trip – not to the moon or the stars, but to Khulna and back. I will probably never make it (at least not in this body or life) to the moon or the stars, but I have been on a rocket.

During my time in Bangladesh, the staff were expected to 'volunteer' for casual courier trips to deliver and collect diplomatic bags from a neighbouring post. When I arrived, that post was Calcutta and the list of volunteers was short. And it mainly consisted of the more adventurous Entry Clearance Officers – no one from the political or aid sections would demean themselves to being a glorified postman, especially when the Post Office was Calcutta. Soon after my arrival, the causal courier destination was Kathmandu – and the short list got slightly longer. My disbelief is still with me, how could anyone not take up the chance of a fare paid, hotel paid, one day and one night visit to the Mountain Kingdom of Nepal? Even if the experience was not the most enjoyable, at the very least one could say you had been to Nepal. Very strange.

But then another very strange thing happened. For whatever reason, the casual courier run was changed to Bangkok. Wow did that list then get longer. Not only did it get longer but those who had not done the 'dirty work' of Calcutta and Kathmandu now claimed that, as they had not had the benefit of a break from Bangladesh, they should be at the top of the list. And most of these queue jumpers were senior people. And so, hidden from the rest of the world, in one of Her Majesty's Diplomatic Missions in a far-flung corner of a former bit of the British Empire, a small-scale mutiny started (whilst this might have been my first involvement in a mutiny, it was not to be my last. In the distant future, I would be spending five years of my life dealing with the fallout from one that started some 239 years ago on a ship called The Bounty).

Back to the great mutiny of Dhaka, 1985. Those who were due to go to Kathmandu in the coming months were not going to be pushed to the bottom of the list (and in some cases off the list completely). Covert meetings were convened, managers lobbied, rounds not bought, unions consulted, lawyers hired, spouses recruited to the cause, bribes offered and, just for good measure, issuing visas to senior VIP Bangladeshi officials and businessmen and women became a bit of a chore; papers and passports mysteriously could not be found.

The Entry Clearance Managers and a representative from the visa officers convened talks with the Senior Management from the Political and Administrative sections. Now, much as I admire the great intellect of colleagues in the Diplomatic Service (allegedly the elite of the elite) and their ability to analyse information and their knowledge of negotiating techniques, they had not reckoned on tackling a team who, day in and day out for many years, had to deal with people who had used every lie, scam, subterfuge, ruse and deceit to try to obtain visas to enter the UK – be it here in Bangladesh, elsewhere in the world, or at the port of entry. Not only did they have that experience in their armoury but, at times, their decisions had gone as high as the Supreme Court. They had argued many cases there and their record was not that bad. On paper and orally, these guys were good – especially as, in this case, they had the moral high ground.

The talks did not last long, but true to the key definition of diplomacy – everybody comes away with what they wanted – a face-saving solution was found. Or maybe it was a genuine error. During the talks, it suddenly became apparent that an incorrect casual courier list had been distributed. A revised list was drawn up, much more in line with the previous list, except that Kathmandu was replaced with Bangkok. And even more to the point, because I had volunteered to take on a Kathmandu run for a colleague who had no interest in these diplomatic bag runs, I was top of the list and would spend my twenty-eighth birthday in a nice hotel in Thailand. I suddenly remembered where I had I put that VIP passport.

So, a fascinating two years in Bangladesh came to an end. I had travelled not only throughout the country but also twice to Nepal, twice to India, Thailand several times and once to Burma. Along with a side trip to Hong Kong and a brief, but illegal, crossing of the Bhutanese border. Not only had I great memories from those travels, but I had made, as with Brussels, life-long friends. One of them, who had been literally in the next office for my whole posting, I would work with again some twenty-two years later on one of the most remote islands on the planet – Pitcairn.

Anyone from those bygone halcyon Dhaka days reading this might spot the missing person in the room. Yep, I had met a delightful young lady who, in about twelve months, would be my bride. That did not last long.

Two Temporary Duties –
Jeddah (Saudi Arabia)
and Baghdad (Iraq)

Jeddah (Saudi Arabia): June 1986 – November 1986

So it came to pass that, as I awaited a job back in London, there was an offer of a Temporary Duty in Beirut (yes, I know it says Jeddah in the chapter heading, but stay with me for a few sentences). They needed someone in the visa section of our Embassy in the Lebanon pretty pronto and I was on leave. I happily said yes. However, the situation in the Lebanon at that time meant that the two adjectives that did not immediately spring to mind were peace and tranquillity – chaos, killing and kidnapping were nearer the mark – but I did not join the FCO to sit back either in Whitehall drinking warm bitter in pubs filled with bitter Civil servants or on sun-drenched beaches sipping chilled Sauvignon blanc (unless, of course, I was in the Seychelles, but I am jumping ahead of myself). I joined for adventure and war – but not too much war. HM Diplomatic Service was there to prevent wars, something that we have singularly failed to do lately.

With my Lebanese visa in my diplomatic passport, I awaited flight details for Beirut. Somehow, they omitted to tell me that no sensible airlines were flying into Beirut in the middle of 1986 and I would be taking a helicopter from Cyprus to part of the Promised Land. I waited and waited but in the end, they said it was not safe and therefore asked for me to go to Jeddah, in the Kingdom of Saudi Arabia, for five months. I could and I did.

I was met airside (before immigration and customs clearances) in Jeddah airport by our very tall vice-consul. His opening greeting was, "Do you have any magazines?" Obviously, I had not got the memo about some sort of coded greeting that would spirit me quickly away to our Consulate (the Embassy was in Riyadh). I replied in the negative. He then explained that whilst the Saudi authorities could not open my suitcase, we liked to keep them happy (think oil, gas, defence sales, civil sales and their expenditure in the hotels and casinos of London) and thus we liked to oblige when asked to open baggage. The Saudi customs officers took offence at any magazines that hinted at bare female flesh above the wrist or ankle. I had no such goodies and we proceeded through unhindered.

The job in the Consulate in Jeddah was again visas (after two years in the front line in Dhaka, the powers in personnel obviously felt I needed more of the same). But Jeddah was different. It was mainly a fast production line to get the Saudis their visas issued as soon as possible so that they could go to the UK and spend their wealth. Wealth derived from trees falling down in their particular part of the world millions of years ago. Imagine what the world would be like if Moses, upon parting the Red Sea and crossing the sodden land revealed by his partition, had decided to turn right, headed down the coast, set up in Jeddah and then created the Kingdom of Moses in that oil-rich desert. I cannot speculate, but the Middle East might be a lot different today. I digress.

Back to the visa production line. The visa section in Jeddah was the direct opposite of the one in Dhaka. Here, we were basically an issuing office, whereas in Dhaka, most applications were treated with some level of suspicion, sad but true. In the Consulate, and indeed in the Embassy in Riyadh, we were regarded as key staff who were there to help oil the wheels of UK/Saudi relations. That is, if Prince so-and-so and his entourage of helpers, servants, hangers-on, family and friends (which could range from two or three to the sixties, seventies or higher) wanted to go to London at short notice – lots of these people had their own planes and were not subject to the vagaries of international airports and commercial airlines – we would facilitate that and everyone would be happy. There were glitches – some of my more hardline colleagues treated too many people as potentially illegal immigrants and senior officers would have to step in to smooth ruffled feathers. They then would ask me to do the necessary and expedite the matter. I had soon realised that a national requiring a visa for the UK, who worked in the Kingdom of Saudi Arabia, with a tax free salary, pleasant accommodation provided, flights home and various other perks, would rarely want to sacrifice all that for a clandestine life as an illegal immigrant living in a garage in Walthamstow.

And so, life for me was fairly comfortable, until one day I was not feeling too good.

There is very little water in the desert Kingdom (the very name gives that away). However, I managed to get water on the lung, and I am not sure to this day how. The medical term is pleural effusion. Luckily, mine was uncomplicated and so, whilst recuperating, I came up with the brilliant money-making idea that, as water is one of the most precious and necessary commodities in Saudi Arabia (the other contenders in the top five of much needed, valuable commodities being oil and booze, but more of the booze later), I could sell my lung created water – speciality water. However, after checking the Treasury guidance, I was disappointed to see that making money on the side by virtue of one's job or place of work was forbidden. Or at least one had to seek permission from a senior officer to do so. I am not sure how the Consul General would have received my money-making idea and so, with some misgivings, I let that one pass. And, apparently, a pleural effusion can make one temporarily insane to the point that ludicrous ideas like selling lung water seem perfectly reasonable.

As I say, life in the Jeddah compound was pleasant enough, but let us not forget that there are no bars or pubs, theatres or cinemas in the Kingdom of Saudi Arabia. There are segregated restaurants – men only or families. Nor are there many cultural or other activities (including fraternising with the opposite sex – unless one is married to that person or they are an immediate relative. But who would want to fraternise with one's sister?). And so life was focused on self-entertainment on the compound and that consisted of the swimming pool, the club, the hall for films and that was about it. But there was a good group of people and we all made the best of it.

My pleural effusion prevented me from learning how to scuba dive (a male-only event, starting far away from Jeddah, far away from the prying eyes that could not bear the thought of human flesh being revealed in the land of Mecca and Medina). But I had also heard that there was a particularly nasty fish called stone fish. As the name says, it looks like a stone, behaves like a stone, and thinks like a stone (work that one out!). But tread on it or touch it at your peril – it will not be a stone, it will be one of the most dangerous fish in the world. It can literally kill humans (no wonder Moses had to part the red sea: the Jews with their open-toed sandals, would have been at the mercy of this evil predator. The chasing Egyptians would have been the least of their worries). And once its thorns are in the flesh, if you do not die, you will be in agony for many hours. So perhaps the pleural effusion was a sign from Allah (peace be upon him) and here I am today to tell the story of Moses and the stone fish.

As the months passed by, the busy visa section slowly wound down; there was not enough work to fill the day. But soon I was to be saved from boredom in Boring Land. An amazing opportunity came my way. It was akin to *The Great Escape* (without the tunnels, the casualties, World War II or Sir Richard Attenborough – actually it was nothing like *The Great Escape* at all). Our Embassy in Sana'a in the Yemen had arranged the delivery to Jeddah port of a brand new fancy four-wheel Mitsubishi long wheel-based Pajero that needed to be driven from Jeddah to Sana'a. And I and the Second Secretary Commercial were just the people to do it. The drive would be from Jeddah to Hodeidah, then from Hodeidah up the Sarawat Mountains, onto the Yemeni plain and into Sana'a, which was well over a thousand kilometres. An adventure if ever there was one.

Note: Nowadays, do not try this at home. The whole of Yemen is in the middle of a civil war. Al-Qaeda is there, the Saudis and Iranians are fighting a proxy war between North and South; there are mines and missiles and a massive humanitarian disaster that the UN seems to have conveniently forgotten – as have we, but then we have forgotten everything except Brexit. But in 1986, life was more peaceful.

Our plan was simple. Load up the car with supplies for the Embassy in Sana'a (wherein worked a dear friend from my Brussels days). In addition to that, we had been asked to bring various types of cheeses to some British veterinarians working in Hodeidah. The journey, with an overnight stay in Hodeidah, should have taken about five days and then a long weekend in Sana'a, a nice break from the heat and abstinence of Jeddah.

With my Dear Leader (an Arabic speaker, thank Allah), we left the shelter of the Consulate compound at 0400. To get out of Jeddah we had to head, in the first instance, towards Mecca (the birthplace of Mohammed – peace be upon him – the founder of Islam) and the 'Christian Highway', so called because this highway did not go to Mecca. It took non-Muslim people away from Mecca. In fact, the penalty for Christians (or any other non-Muslims for that matter) entering the holy area of Mecca was castration, so for obvious reasons, or at least two very obvious reasons (or four, if I generously included my co-driver), we did not want to take the wrong road. However, take the wrong road we did.

For the first time in millennia, a thick fog settled over our unlit motorway. I could hardly see and plodded on, following my own sense of direction. I was quite comfortable until a scream from the passenger seat alerted me that we were heading for the first checkpoint, which was just inside the Muslim zone or, in our case, the testicle-free zone. A quick U-turn, balls checked, and we headed out, due south towards the land that would not remove testicles for a simple driving error.

The key to getting to the border and thereafter to Hodeidah was simple. Keep the Red Sea on the right. There was also another fundamental objective we needed to achieve. Get to the border before about 1300 hours. Why? A long lunch perhaps? Nope. 1300 hours was the time the Yemeni people (everyone from the President down through the border control officials to the humblest nomadic herdsmen and women) started to chew the Khat. The Khat is a plant that grows abundantly in the mountains of the Yemen and the leaves of which, if chewed over a long period, will create a high… and not much else matters after that. We really did not want to be greeted on the Yemeni side of the border by stoned customs officials. It is an interesting juxtaposition that in Europe, we have customs officials whose main job is to stop society from getting stoned on illegal plants and chemicals. But at the Yemeni border things seemed to be quite the opposite. However, we will get to the Yemeni side later, much later. We had arrived at the Saudi side of the border.

We pulled up at the Saudi customs controls. Not much traffic – a very good sign. We handed over our documents and passports and sat quietly. Knowing a little about the Arab culture, we expected to be there about an hour. However, after a fifteen-minute wait, we were beckoned forward, delight in our hearts, only to be herded into a locked wire compound. I could bore you with what happened over the next few hours. But here is the short version. Every orifice of the car was searched, cheese smelt, fruit pinched and squashed, the deckchairs and TV tested (by the border guards setting it up on the sand and, for some thirty minutes, sitting comfortably on the deckchairs watching a marine documentary involving lustful female surfers). Thereafter, there were some rather lustful looks towards our good selves – castration was now looking good – not for us, for them.

We were moved from one hut to another, saw several serious looking officials and eventually, five hours later, with the Saudi number plates removed from our Pajero, we were allowed to pass. A close look at our new revised travel document showed that we had permission to drive without number plates (we would see how long that would last). There were also twenty-three signatures on the document, although it was only signed by three different people. From that point on, I swore not to moan about any UK bureaucracy ever again.

Now we headed to the Yemeni side. They had been watching and chewing (Khat) on their side. They were stoned and only interested in the Saudi document. After a cursory inspection of our vehicle and a warning that without number plates, we would have to stop at every checkpoint, they wished us a pleasant journey. Hodeidah was three checkpoints away. About seven hours later than expected, we got to our hotel. But we were not particularly worried about the seven-hour delay, we had our balls still attached and had experienced no man-to-man interference from the sex-starved border guards.

The Yemen, unlike Saudi Arabia, has alcohol. The hotel had a bar and a restaurant and there we decided to freshen up, eat and get ready to meet the cheese-eating vets in the morning, and thereafter, head up the mountains to Sana'a. The change in elevation (we were at sea-level) would be some 7,500 feet, along treacherous winding narrow roads with cliff walls on one side and dangerous drops on the other. So we settled into a rather strange hotel with a bar and even stranger clientele. There seemed to be a holiday atmosphere and we were informed that the following day was National Revolution Day – a public holiday. That was comforting – less traffic on our road to Sana'a.

We munched on lamb (it might have been camel for all I knew) and rice. To tell the truth, I had chips – after two years in Bangladesh with rice for breakfast, lunch and dinner, I no longer wanted ever again to have one grain of rice pass my lips – and that is still true to this day (just in case you are thinking of inviting me round for dinner). As we ate, we could not help but notice that our fellow Yemeni guests, or perhaps just visitors off the street, had not only been consuming Khat since lunchtime, but now also seemed to have a penchant for drinking vast amounts of neat whiskey direct from the bottle. *Not a good combination*, I thought. But more worrying to a pacifist (aka coward) like me was that to a man (and they were all men – no women in the bar area) they all had large, vicious-looking daggers – curved and double-bladed – tucked into their belts. If a fight had broken out, we'd have stood no chance. In addition to this crowd, there were a few scowling gentlemen clearly advertising that they were supporters of the Palestinian Liberation Organisation (PLO). During 1986 (and various other years), the PLO was not to be trifled with. This bar was rapidly turning into Chalmun's bar in the pirate city on the planet Tatooine in *Star Wars*.

My co-driver, somewhat of an expert in Middle East matters, explained to me that the daggers were purely symbolic and almost like a part of their clothing, rather than a weapon for inflicting serious injury on two British Diplomats. Nowadays, the daggers were only unsheathed for cultural events. It is still sad to note that the Yemenis crave that the hilt of their daggers be made from rhino horn. But that is another story. Of course, now that I was fully aware of the history of the dagger (in Yemeni Arabic, a Janbiya), I was much more comfortable. Not.

With the amount of Khat these people had chewed and whiskey they had drunk, I was not sure that they could differentiate between a cultural event and mass slaughter. After the mass slaughter, they would retire to bed and, upon waking in the morning, would not care. Instead, they would head for the hills, await the lunchtime delivery of Khat and that would be the start of a brand new exciting day for them. Not for me – I would be dead.

But, as I am writing here in 2018, I was obviously neither filleted by my Yemeni friends, nor assassinated by some members of the PLO who had somehow lost their way to wherever Palestine was in 1986.

In the morning, we unpacked the cheese from the car and prepared to meet the cheese-eating vets of Hodeidah. For some reason, we were under the watchful eye of a man with a serious uniform and some serious gold epaulettes and, in turn, behind him were some other serious men without epaulettes but with rifles, guns and the ubiquitous dagger. After a while, he approached us and, to cut a long Arabic conversation short and put it into English, we were told that, as it was National Revolution Day, no foreigners, especially diplomats with a car without number plates, were allowed to leave the city. We could have debated the issue, but I do not think we would have won.

But to be fair, the military said that they had extended our stay in the hotel and would guide us out of the city the following morning and into the foothills of the Sarawat Mountains. How kind.

The morning was bright, the sun was shining and the sky was blue. And we had a day off. Our vets arrived – they all had rather long Ben Gunn-type beards (I wondered if this was linked to their craving for cheese) – at the hotel to collect their dairy products. We made them aware of our predicament (if a day off is a predicament) and they ensured that we had a pleasant day in Hodeidah, including snorkelling in the Red Sea. I spent most of my time looking out for stones that were not stones. As for the vets, they were wonderful people. If memory serves me correctly, they were in the Yemen on an aid project helping with camel diseases. Most of the diseases had probably emigrated to their beards.

Tomorrow came and, true to his word, the senior military man was at our hotel at 0600 and guided us at breakneck speed to the outskirts of the city, where he and his mini-convoy stopped, rechecked our papers, wished us luck and then, ominously, prayed for us. At this, I wondered if my Christian God would accept this man's entreaties to Allah – in the event of my death, I came to the conclusion that the two celestial colossi of the Earth's religions would come to some happy agreement as to where I would spend the hereafter. And so I was happy.

For the moment, there stood the Sarawat Mountains, as did our 140-mile, five-hour trip, to the Embassy in Sana'a. The road, we knew, was steep, mountainous, curvy and poorly maintained, with sheer drops in certain places. From all accounts, the stepped hillsides were littered with lorries and cars that had failed to negotiate the highway. So with bacon for breakfast, a treat in itself, as pork meat is banned in Saudi Arabia, and trepidation in our heart, we headed up and up and up.

The road was as bad as we thought but just about manageable. Having said that the road was just about manageable, the Yemeni truck drivers had to be seen to be believed. Their life expectancy could not have been more than thirty years. Whilst our average speed in the mountains was, in reality, twenty miles per hour, the Yemeni truck drivers hurtled up and down and round and round at breakneck speeds. I now understand the origin of that expression.

As foreseen, crashed lorries and cars (and the occasional tank from the 1962 - 1967 Civil war) littered the valley floors closest to the hairpin bends. There were times when the direct route to these valley floors, hundreds of feet below us, was within inches of our wheels. During those times, neither of us dared to look out over the splendid vistas that could be seen within inches of our offside front wheel. If we had, we might have died, or better – just stopped and walked the rest of the way to Sana'a. Even if it meant carrying our cargo on our backs.

We lived and came out of a gorge about 7,500 feet higher up than four hours earlier. Spreading out in front of us like a green and brown intricate tapestry of the Garden of Eden (who knows, it might have been here) was a vast resplendent plain. It was flat with a good road all the way into Sana'a. Blessing Allah, Jesus, Buddha, the Dal Lai Lama, and the Queen, for our good fortune in overcoming the Sarawat. We made haste for the Embassy.

We were aware of the joys that our cargo would bring to our colleagues – Sana'a was quite a difficult posting (I think the Embassy is currently closed for security reasons). In Saudi Arabia, we could not purchase alcohol or pork products, but everything else was available in massive superstores. In the Yemen, most everyday household items were difficult to obtain. Our arrival would be a mini-Christmas for our deprived colleagues. We would be greeted as heroes for undertaking this death-defying expedition.

Two things were to mar our wishful thinking (only partially actually). When we arrived at the Embassy, there were no throngs of deprived diplomats, no garlands, no popping of champagne corks, no nothing. The Embassy was closed (as part of the National Revolution Day holidays). The other mar for me was altitude sickness, but we will get to that.

After the Embassy guard made some frantic telephone calls, the British diplomatic cavalry arrived and, without much fanfare (indeed, it is difficult to get much fanfare in an Embassy garage), we unloaded and distributed the Christmas goodies. Then, we officially handed over our trusty steed – the Mitsubishi Pajero – intact, believe it or not!

We were then invited to lunch by my colleague from the Brussels days. Later in the evening, we were to be guests of honour at a British Council (then the FCO's cultural wing) mini-folk concert. Both my co-driver and I were pleased to be rid of our responsibilities for the next two days; we checked into the only reasonable hotel, grabbed a celebratory beer and headed out to lunch. The lunch was a splendid affair, but to be honest, this whole day and evening is difficult to recall. At the lunch, the wine and beer were both flowing. I imbibed to my heart and liver's content vast amounts of the aforementioned beer and wine. Now, whilst I knew that we had travelled up high and one could feel the effects of the thin air on the body, what I did not appreciate was the much-strengthened effect that alcohol had on one at altitude. It did not happen straight away. But it happened.

After lunch, we headed for the hotel. Wisely, my co-driver decided to rest before the equivalent of Glastonbury in Sana'a later that evening. Not for me such time wasting. Very lightheadedly, I headed for the bar and imbibed more beer and became a good friend with anybody who would listen – that was no one. I spent a couple of hours talking to myself.

After a quick shower, eye drops (my eyes were incredibly red and it looked like I had been chewing the Khat – which I had not) and a snack (should have eaten more), we headed for the concert. Another couple of pre-concert drinks and we were set for the show. At least, I thought I was set for the show. My memory here is very much based on haziness, altitude and beer, but mostly from anecdotes told the following day. The bands were a mixture of British Council staff and local Yemenis – all of whom blurred together in one big beardy folk music fest. To this day, I am not sure whether the event was culturally progressive or regressive for Yemeni culture, which (despite numerous wars and inter-tribal conflicts) goes back much further than Glastonbury circa 1970. As the show headed to its big finish, my colleague and I were invited onto the stage for a brief talking heads discussion on our expedition through the Sarawat (we had learnt that very few Westerners do this drive, because of the risk of death, serious injury, kidnapping and general mayhem from various tribes who might have taken a shine to our shiny new Mitsubishi). Nobody told us that before we left the warm womb of the compound in Jeddah.

At this point (or rather pint), I decided silence was a virtue because, basically, I was incapable of speaking any known language. I nodded and made lots of complimentary grunts as my co-driver expertly described our journey. However, the interviewer was not going to let me escape without something for the audience. And when asked if I would like to enhance the big finish, I said, "Of course, I can play the guitar." Now, I am not sure what came over me; actually, I am very sure – it was beer, wine and altitude. People who know me and have bothered to read this far will easily spot the flaw in the preceding sentence. I have never ever been able to play any musical instrument, ever – not then, not before, not now – and I cannot see any viable prospect of acquiring such a skill in the foreseeable future, or even before death, which at sixty is the foreseeable future. But apparently, I played the stringed instrument (not solo). To the aficionados of the Spanish guitar, it was obvious I was a complete fraud, but looking back, most of the cast and audience had sunk a fair few during this cultural extravaganza, enough for them to forgive, or not notice, or not really care. A star was not born, but neither was Her Majesty's Consulate in Jeddah disgraced – at least, I think not.

I awoke the following morning with the Mother of All Hangovers combined with altitude sickness. But I was not going to miss the sights and scenes of the old city of Sana'a. An amazing place of densely packed earth and burnt brick houses rising up to three floors. I am not sure how old they were (the Old City has probably been destroyed by the modern-day fighting – I do not know and do not want to know) but it was very impressive. We walked through the numerous 'souks' (markets) and bought souvenirs – yep two Yemeni daggers without, I hasten to add, the rhino horn hilt. They are in my attic as I type.

The next day was a trip out onto the plateau surrounding Sana'a for a picnic before heading to the airport and back to Jeddah. All in all, a trip to treasure for a lifetime – if only I could remember the Sana'a part.

We came back as diplomatic couriers and, for some reason, there was a mini-reception in the Consulate club awaiting our safe return. I thought that was very nice and touching, but everyone seemed to be more interested in the contents of the diplomatic bags than any stories of derring-do from the freshly self-proclaimed Conquerors of the Yemen. I soon realised why; whilst there was the usual diplomatic mail, there appeared also to be packets of food in the diplomatic bags (totally against the Vienna Convention on the Carriage and Inviolability of Diplomatic Mail). On close inspection, it appeared that I had been carrying back bacon, pork pies and pork chops. Naughty – it will not happen again.

I spent my last few weeks (of a five-month stay) in Jeddah finishing up the summer visa rush, visiting Riyadh (not knowing then that I would, with a new family, spend three years in the Saudi capital), manning the bar and generally lazing about. I had made good friends, who are no longer in touch, but in memory, and that is the main thing. On my last day in Jeddah, I telephoned the New Inn in Deal and said I would be in for my pint the following day.

I was and the FCO were keen to find me. They wanted me to help out in Baghdad.

Baghdad (Iraq):
December 1986 – January 1987

If memory serves me correctly, I arrived in Baghdad on 22 December 1986 to cover Christmas leave, but there were also rumours that Madman (Saddam) Hussein and the Ayatollah (not much, if at all, saner) were about to breach their unwritten undertakings of not bombing each other's capital cities. No point in killing the two main causes of this horrific war was there?

Anyway, it would not have mattered if these unwritten undertakings had been cast in stone – both leaders were not renowned for their adherence (written or unwritten) to any undertakings and agreements whatsoever. Indeed, the Ayatollah's main hobby seemed to be enacting an Old Testament punishment by ensuring that the Republican Guard cast stones at any unsuspecting non-veil wearing female until they died. In 2018, I am not sure much has changed! And of course, Madman Hussein was not much better. Saddam Hussein had other more horrific means of dealing with anyone he did not like – with or without a veil. Not him with the veil, I hasten to add, the females of the Iraqi nation.

The West was in a quandary. Which of the devils to support? I will not dwell on that – suffice to say that, because of the still-recent memory of the US hostages in Tehran and America's hatred of the Ayatollah and all things Iranian (no change there in 2018), I can tell you we were supporting Madman Hussein. But the French seemed to have had the best idea. They supported both sides! Anyway, I digress.

The British Airways flight to Baghdad was uneventful, except there were only three of us in Business Class and not many more in Economy. People had noticed there was a war on. My two fellow business class passengers were not to be trifled with (and they neither ate nor drank throughout the flight. Did they know something I did not know?). They were on some sort of mission and I was not going to risk life and limb by asking them. We landed early in the morning.

The journey from the airport to the Embassy was fascinating – it was like going back to what I imagine Britain would have been like in 1940 (except then we had the late great Winston Churchill and now Iraq had a nutter). Khaki-clad gun-toting troops were everywhere;

there were tanks, jeeps, and roadblocks and, on top of the high-rises (most of which, I assume, are now low-rises), were anti-aircraft guns.

On arrival at the Embassy, I was given the usual security briefing. Actually, I lie – it was far from the usual security briefing (which, in normal circumstances, consisted of a mixture of not drinking too much, only sleeping with NATO females, reporting contacts with communist nationals and other nationals, who shall remain nameless, behaving oneself and not bringing HM Diplomatic Service into disrepute). This briefing was, after the sights from the airport to downtown Baghdad, a bit more serious. It went something like this:

Deputy Head of Mission (then called the Head of Chancery (H of C):

H of C: "Welcome, Kevin. Glad you are here to help with the evacuation of the Embassy wives and their families."

Me: "Interesting, I thought I was here to cover the Entry Clearance Operation whilst the ECO was on Christmas leave."

HoC: "Ah yes, that is partly true."

[Note: this is an FCO euphemism meaning that something completely unexpected is coming around the corner and whatever is coming around the aforementioned corner is coming straight at you].

He continued, "But we have got wind (code for, this is the best guess the whole of the FCO could make from the plethora of information to hand) that the Ayatollah is going to bomb Baghdad, breaching an unwritten undertaking, and that President Hussein will retaliate against Tehran. We need to be ready to downsize the Embassy in a hurry. They could engage in a war of the cities."

Me: "I was not told that."

H of C: "No. We were afraid you might not come."

Me: "You were afraid! How do you think I feel?"

Suffice to say, I got on with the job. And to be fair, it did include visa work and that was not without its excitements. At one point, I had been told to refuse a visa to a very dodgy and nasty Iraqi whose entry into the UK would have been far from conducive to the public good. This gentleman did not take kindly to not getting his visa. His revenge was to send some Stasi-trained Iraqi government thugs into my flat to break the light bulbs in my bathroom and leave the shards of glass on the tiled floor. They hoped that, at some stage, I would go into the bathroom barefooted and the rest would be, shall we say, not nice. On the day of the state-sponsored house invasion, I unusually (and perhaps here, my Christian God was looking after me) had had a couple of beers with a colleague and needed the loo as soon as I got into the flat – straight in with my nice black brogues securely fastened to my feet. And lo, the bloody lights did not work! What a pain – but I soon noticed (the definitive sound of crunching glass gave the game way) that the light bulbs, in some sort of mass bulb suicide pact, had hurled themselves from their secure fittings to an early disintegration on my bathroom floor. It did not take long to put two and two together. To show typical British annoyance at this attack on my feet, the following day we delayed opening the visa section for thirty minutes – that showed them!

As is my wont, when overseas, when I am not visiting the local hostelries and trying out different beers and wines (except of course in serious Muslim countries, such as Saudi Arabia) and conversing with the locals, I like to get out and about. I was, therefore, more than pleased to accept an invitation from a colleague and his lady friend to get out of Baghdad. We would follow the Tigris as far as we could, and then get a possible sight of the Hanging Gardens of Babylon (if memory serves me correctly, the original site has never been found, but that small detail was not going to deter us). Apparently, we would see the 'Lion of Babylon', or at least one of the statues of the Lion of Babylon. The one I found – I have a photograph somewhere – has probably now been blown to smithereens.

We had cleared the journey with the security people at the Embassy and the Iraqi authorities. Nowadays, there would be a twenty-page risk assessment to memorise and sign in ten different places. Even after that, we would all be obliged to sign numerous pieces of paper telling everyone from the Pope, to the Queen, to the respective Foreign Ministers and many others that, if anything untoward occurred, it was our fault and that neither we (living or dead) or our next of kin or third cousin removed could hold anyone in authority responsible. But 1986 was a simpler time and so, after the convivial briefing and the mandatory cup of tea, off we went... nearly to war!

We set off early in the morning, heading south. My companions were amiable and a pleasant conversation ensued. We drove along, passing buses of ordinary Iraqis going about their business, pedestrians plodding to their workplaces, farm labourers heading to their fields – all pretty idyllic. That was soon going to change.

We were frequently passed by drivers who had decided to literally take Allah at his Word – that is, if the aforementioned drivers were killed in head-on collisions driving around a blind bend at eighty miles per hour, it was the will of Allah that they should die. And thus the souls of the deceased would, because their death was the will of Allah, be taken directly (hopefully not by car) to the Islamic heaven. All well and good if you believe in Islam (nothing wrong with that, I hasten to add, just in case a fanatical or radicalised reader decides to issue a fatwa against me). But if you are non-Muslim, such as a Christian, Zoroastrian, Yazdani or Jew, one is not going to be too pleased that a fellow of a different faith has caused you to shuffle off your mortal coil because he believes he has a divine right to drive like a lunatic to hell (or in his case, heaven), sodding the consequences because his God will look after him. I would have been totally miffed if this had happened to us on our little journey, but worse might have happened.

Along with the civilian traffic, the trappings of a country at war were easily visible. There were convoys of open-topped lorries carrying young soldiers to the deadly marshes in the South (I would subsequently deal with one of these poor young men in, believe it or not, Geneva). In addition, there were armoured personnel carriers, jeeps for the officers and the occasional tank rumbling along. As we turned a corner, a forlorn young soldier was hitch-hiking, his rifle and overloaded backpack looking like two unbearable burdens.

My driver who, by his own admission, did not speak very good Arabic, stopped to ask if we could give him a lift to the next village. I did not understand the exchange but I was told that the soldier was a conscript who had been in basic training in Baghdad and was now going on leave before heading to the Front. That is complicated enough in English and I am not sure that my driver fully understood what was going on. We were soon to be proved right.

For the next few hours, I was seated next to the soldier who needed no encouragement to direct us to his 'village'. He was also waving with much enthusiasm at his fellow soldiers each time we passed a slow-moving convoy. For a new conscript, he seemed to know lots of people heading to their destiny. And so further and further south we headed. As civilian traffic slowly disappeared off the road and more and more military checkpoints were crossed (our military passenger was as good as any military pass), it dawned on all of us that Private Hussein – not his real name or rank – was taking us for the proverbial ride all the way to his unit, which seemed to be at the front line of the front line, deep in the marshland surrounding Basra.

In a very diplomatic manner, principally because the man had a rifle and a uniform and, therefore, some basic knowledge of shooting, we managed to persuade him to get out. We then promptly did a U-turn and headed back. Believe it or not, we then found the Euphrates and some sort of mock-up of the Hanging Gardens of Babylon. Although the 'Hanging Gardens of Babylon' seemed to me to be a very recent addition to the landscape hereabouts. The brickwork was twentieth century and every other brick had either Saddam Hussein's name thereon or the name of a member of his family. And then we came upon a Lion of Babylon – fortunately, with no Hussein graffiti. So the day out was not entirely lost; we did not lose our lives or ourselves in the remake of parts of the 1914-1918 Western Front that was now taking place in the marshland in Southern Iraq. Iraq itself was soon to completely lose its way, Saddam was to lose his head (remember the statue being pulled down), and his life. But I will leave Iraqi historians to follow all that up.

Meanwhile, back at the Embassy, apart from running the visa section, I was tasked with setting up evacuation kits. No training for this – common sense and ask when needed. Common sense is not to be trifled with. Ignore it at your peril, as one of my Iraqi helpers nearly did and that nearly did for him. As part of the evacuation process, we had to restock the empty jerry cans with diesel and petrol. The Embassy in Baghdad in 1986 was massive and a search of the compound brought out numerous jerry cans – one of which was half full. We reckoned that that particular can had been around for a while and that, with the heat of the summers and the cold of the winters, whatever was inside was probably quite volatile. And so we chose our favourite Iraqi member of staff (who was also known to spy on us on behalf of the Iraqi government – no point in sacking him; better the devil you know!) to undo the cap and see what happened. We expected some proof of Boyle's law. To do this, we sent him out, suitably briefed and with protective clothing, onto the Embassy football pitch – I said it was a big Embassy.

When he reached the centre spot, he carefully undid the cap and, as we suspected, there was a hiss of gas followed by a fountain stream of petrol. Alas, our poor member of staff was covered in the combustible liquid, but the job was done and he was proud. As were we, we cheered and clapped from the touchline. Alas, our collective pride and joy turned to mass panic as our beloved spy, as if to celebrate his achievement, decided to light up a cigarette as he sauntered towards us. With much shouting, most of it over our shoulders as we ran for the bomb shelter, our Iraqi colleague eventually got the message and did not partake of, possibly his last, nicotine hit. And we managed to avoid what would have been the first ever example of self-immolation of a member of the FCO Local Staff in the history of the Foreign Office.

Just a small note on the size of the Embassy. The Iraqi authorities did not like the fact that the British government had such a large amount of real estate in the centre of their capital city. This land was probably (I have not checked) a relic of when Iraq was red on the map and was part of the British 'Mandate' (I assume we used 'Mandate' back in those days because we had overused the word 'Empire'). In order to rectify this perceived imperial intrusion, every now and again the Iraqis would arrange for a large vehicle to crash into certain parts of the Embassy wall or perimeter fencing. There would then follow profuse apologies, the Iraqi authorities would later claim that the errant driver had been punished, but the reality was that he had no doubt been paid handsomely for his trouble as soon as he got back to the Iraqi Ministry of Transport. Next, the Ministry of Foreign Affairs would (very kindly, don't you know) send around their team of builders to immediately repair and reconstruct the damage.

With careful planning, exact measurements and maps of their own making, they would, in making good the damage, pinch part of our UK sovereign land. This land, despite protests, was never returned. The Embassy was an onion slowly being peeled. But that is all academic now; like most things in Iraq, there is very little left that remotely resembles Iraq in 1986.

I had always wanted to do something special on my twenty-ninth birthday (I was born on 29 December), but here I was in Baghdad. Still, to save the day, there was to be an early New Year's Eve party on 29th December (why not on New Year's Eve? I never found out – something to do with an offensive... well, an offensive what? As I say, I never found out). The party was to be full of music merriment and games. I decided not to reveal that it was my birthday – I would celebrate when I got back to Blighty.

There were not many of us in the Embassy, but we did have the British Council (BC). After the obligatory toasts to HM the Queen and President Hussein, the first order of the evening was a Trivial Pursuit quiz – the Embassy versus the British Council. *Jolly good fun*, I thought. I was mistaken! There was deep, deep competition between the Embassy and the BC and none of the pseudo-intellectuals on either side were going to give any quarter. Answers had to be exact – "I will only accept the answer as written on the card" was the loudest slogan of the evening. A key moment in the game brought out the true colours of each side – hatred, I think, is a good word!

The Embassy delicately asked, "Who said – 'I am going outside and maybe some time'?"

Up jumped a BC staffer to exclaim for all to hear (except, as we shall see, the BC team) "Captain Oakes."

"Wrong," declared the Embassy captain. "Oates is the correct answer".

There then ensued an argument about who had heard what, this was swiftly followed by threats and fisticuffs. As we were already in the middle of a war, I thought this was rather intemperate behaviour on behalf of representatives of Her Majesty's Government and decided to call it a night. I headed back to my flat pondering the beauty of being born on 29th Dec, being twenty-nine and wondering about the absurdity of this trivial war within the real war just outside our shrinking walls.

I left Baghdad and, some two or three weeks later, I was told that I had caught the last British Airways flight out of Bagdad for many a year.

Part Four

Home Posting London/ Geneva/London

January 1987 – May 1990

Chapter 12

London: Marriage, Maths and Machinations

Back in London, now in a cold January 1987, with a flat purchased and a wedding to arrange (mine, but that did not last long, so we will not dwell on that), I still had to find a job to see me through my next three years in England.

One of the nice idiosyncrasies of the FCO, excluding most of its idiosyncratic staff, is its cyclical nature. At that time, in the late Eighties, although not set in stone, Her Majesty's finest diplomats would ordinarily be out of London for two postings (see above, Brussels and Bangladesh for me) and, as with me, perhaps have an odd temporary duty thrown in for good measure. This meant that after about six to eight years, old friends would reappear in the corridors of power in London. These old friends had made new friends, and so old friends too would make new friends of the new friends of the old friends. So there was, on returning to London, a ready-made friendly social base to keep body and soul together. We all had in common a life overseas. We were all now in our late twenties or early thirties (IQ as well as age). Some had settled down and married, some still had partners in far-flung parts of the globe (mine was in Geneva), some were still seeking life-long partners, others were seeking solace from their life-long partners, and still others were quite happy as they were. The majority of this band of brothers and sisters tended to socialise in the bars of Westminster for the next three years before we headed off to, once again, serve one's country in whichever part of the globe that demanded our particular skills.

After a little leave (holiday), sorting out flats and baggage from abroad, I received news that I was to join the Personnel Services Department, as Head of the Overseas Allowances team. Not my cup of tea, but turning down jobs was not really the done thing then. So with no staff management training whatsoever, just a basic knowledge of currencies and exchange rates, alongside a basic knowledge of economics, I was managing four young members of HM Diplomatic Service, none of whom had served abroad. Millions of pounds sterling in overseas allowances was in our capable hands. To add to that chaotic mix, my boss preferred Guinness to graft. And to top it all, there was a mirror of our section in Her Majesty's Treasury to ensure that Her Majesty's Diplomatic Service did not pay Her Majesty's diplomats too much money. On the social side, every other weekend, I would leave work on a Friday at 1600 hours to fly to Geneva for a weekend with my fiancée, get back to Gatwick late on a Sunday evening, and then the whole fortnightly cycle would start again.

So began the rhythm of my life in 1987-1988, but I had a plan. More of that later. I gradually learnt the names of almost every currency on the planet. And on a good day, could even quote the pound sterling exchange rate for most of them. Eventually, I was sent away on a one-week residential course to learn about managing staff. I then attended a three-week intensive Economic course (with the late great Ian Goatman as our lecturer), followed by a week in a converted monastery, where we had to roleplay directors of companies. My company went bankrupt. However, I still got the equivalent of an A-level in economics in four weeks – not bad. And during all that, I developed close relations with our minders in HM Treasury. Very close relations with one, in fact.

Weekends not in Geneva were gradually taken up with meet-ups in London with friends both old and new. These invariably started about Friday lunchtime in a local Westminster hostelry, where plots were hatched on the whereabouts of the fun and games for the upcoming weekend. Aside from that socialising, there was a wedding to attend (mine) in Felixstowe and a honeymoon to be arranged. Life was getting pretty hectic and the bank balance pretty manic. But I had a plan.

Winter became spring and we headed into summer. My engagement had been announced in *The Times* and I had met the future mother-in-law – she did not like me. But there was no escaping the wedding now. A stag do (day and night) in Calais followed. Even in the depths of beer and wine, ever the professional, I was the only one who could calculate the exchange rate properly – I made a profit on my stag do. Then there was a splendid white wedding in Felixstowe, with lots of friends attending. There were friends from my youth in Deal, friends from the FCO, friends of the family, family and other hangers-on. Of course, the bride had friends and family too.

Vows and rings were exchanged, followed by a splendid wedding feast, with a well-behaved best man and speeches that were nowhere near the truth of my past life. With a hasty escape from the obligatory disco/dance party, I and my new bride drove off into the sunset for a night in a magnificent mansion. Then, the following morning, we flew to Geneva for a three-week honeymoon, touring Switzerland and France. All a waste of time and money with hindsight.

After the honeymoon, my bride duly returned to duty in Geneva and I returned to work in Whitehall. And started to implement my plan. I had noticed during the summer months that the visa section of the Consulate-General (attached to our Mission to the United Nations in Geneva) needed reinforcing with an Entry Clearance Officer. The position was normally filled by a member of the Immigration Service. I had actually trained the current incumbent whilst in Bangladesh. Personnel Services worked closely with our overseas Postings people in Personnel Operations Department (POD), so I made a bid for that job for May-October 1988. It was only ten months away. With my wife already in post, they really could not reject my application (much to the annoyance of the Immigration Service, but my experience in Bangladesh trumped their pleas for an 'expert' to get the job). Autumn came and went, as did winter and then spring, and I moved out of Overseas Allowances (privately vowing never to go back), rented out the flat and headed off to live in Geneva with wife number one (there is a hint there – as there is at the end of the previous paragraph, in case you missed it).

Chapter 13

Geneva: Legless Football

I settled into domestic bliss in Geneva, and bliss it was. My wife was working in the UK Mission to the United Nations and I was working in the Consulate, so there were double salaries, married allowances, a flat just a stone's throw away from Lake Geneva and the flat in London rented out. And every Friday, filets de perches avec frites and superb dry Alsace white wine on the shores of Lake Geneva – and that was just to start the weekend.

I was also there to work, a shame really. In the mid-eighties, we had closed our Embassies in Iraq, Iran and the Lebanon. Something to do with wars, kidnapping and terrorism, if I recall correctly.

For visas to the UK, many of these nationalities travelled to Switzerland to obtain whatever type of entry clearance they required. Or, in the minority of cases, to be refused visas. As with all Entry Clearance operations, there was, however, a little, shall we say, deviousness going on.

Medical treatment in Switzerland was very expensive for residents and non-residents alike, so some of our customers would pretend they were going on a tourist visit to the UK, but then check into an NHS hospital and get treatment, sometimes substantial treatment, for free. It was illegal but free – no change in 2018. Part of my work was to establish the real reason for travel. Others were genuinely seeking medical treatment and could afford it, but they did not want to go back to a war zone (who could blame them?). Neither could they afford to live in Switzerland (even if they were given a residence permit, which was highly unlikely). Thus, they were likely to try and settle in the UK, which they were not allowed to do. But you will have had enough of that from the chapter on Bangladesh, I am sure. Still, bear with me for a couple of paragraphs.

On one occasion, an Iraqi mother and three children, with their ages ranging from twelve to about twenty-four, came into the narrow interview booth. There was a bullet-resistant window, a microphone either side and a door on their side that locked behind them to save interference from numerous other applicants. I controlled the lock.

From the paperwork, I ascertained that the visit was a mixture of medical and tourism, but I was not convinced they would leave the UK once in.

After a few questions, I asked about the medical treatment and the mother said her eldest son, who was about twenty-four years old, had a sore leg. He was standing in front me and looked perfectly healthy (never judge a book by its cover – although I quite like the cover of this book, an idea courtesy of the great Tom Burke, MBE). I asked the nature of the problem. He pulled up his trouser leg and showed me a fine specimen of a below the knee leg, unshaven, but not unusual to my untrained eye. I, therefore, expressed some scepticism about the need for medical treatment and began pondering the real reason for their visit. The next thing I knew, the eldest son had fallen over; his mother had pulled off his prosthetic leg and was banging it against the bullet-resistant glass. She was shouting in a mixture of Arabic and English, "Now will you believe us?" I left the booth to gather my thoughts and not to be seen laughing hysterically. There was more banging. I had forgotten to let them out of their side of the interview booth. I re-entered my side and did the necessary. The mother led the way out into the waiting room, leg in hand, her two children crying and the eldest son demanding (I assume, I did not speak Arabic) his leg back.

After sanity had resumed, I called the family back into the booth. It transpired that the son had been fighting in the Iran/Iraq war and had stepped on a mine. Whilst surgeons had done a good job, it was far from perfect (so the mother said). They had managed to get exit visas from Iraq, had plenty of money and, quite rightly, the mother wanted her son fixed up as best she could. Thinking back to my time in Iraq, and giving a lift to that young soldier heading for the front, I suspected that this family were not going back to Iraq and probably never would. I issued the visas. I hope they are well.

One bonus from this little escapade was that all the other visa applicants in the waiting room who had heard and witnessed these events had decided the UK was not for them and disappeared. I had the afternoon free to sip white wine and ponder the woes of the world while watching luxury yachts sail off to dine in luxury in Monteux, or some other shoreside millionaire's retreat.

Apart from that little scene, the days and weeks in idyllic Switzerland passed gently by. On one occasion, a colleague from the Mission registry asked if I wanted to play in a one-off football game against the local British School teachers. Of course. One summer evening, we turned up for the game. It was a close match, but I recognised one of their teachers, at least I thought I did; he had one of those unmistakeable faces and an unusual name, Mr Pasternak. I could not approach him during the game, which we won and I scored the third goal, but while we were shaking hands at the end, I asked him if he was a Mr Pasternak who had taught me (and others) PE at my grammar school way back in the early seventies. And indeed it was. And, although he could not remember my face, he remembered the name and that he used to live quite close to my parents' house in Deal – small world. We met again a few times and swapped stories, but I have not seen him since 1988. Probably lives next door.

We made friends with lots of people in the United Nations, and indeed a couple from CERN – the European Organisation for Nuclear Research. Very nice people but my brain could only take so much of the large Hadron Collider (up until that point, I thought that it was a strong cocktail), particle physics, particle accelerators and the elusive Higgs Boson (I think they have found it now – it was hiding in Ramsgate). I should have listened. In the not too distant future, I was going to have a brother-in-law who was (and still is) a Doctor of Physics. In Denver, I would be hanging out with two people who regularly discussed 'string theory'. I can explain string theory. Actually, I cannot. Here is an extract from Wikipedia:

"In physics, string theory is a theoretical framework in which the point-like particles of particle physics are replaced by one-dimensional objects called strings. It describes how these strings propagate through space and interact with each other."

Good, I am glad you understand that. Back through a black hole, now that we are all string theorists, to Geneva. Switzerland is quaintly portrayed as a land of peace, mountains, cheese, valleys, cuckoo clocks, skiing, fondue, money (but do not mention money laundering) and finishing schools.

But what is not widely advertised is the bureaucracy of having to live in such a precious place. In blocks of flats in the cities, there are laws about flushing the loo at certain times of night. There are decibel laws about your music and your conversation at dinner, including, of course, during dinner parties with friends. I am not talking about blasting out the 'hood with Bruce Springsteen or loud drink-fuelled political arguments concerning whether Einstein really did develop his special theory of relativity whilst in Berne. If you were discussing this at one of my dinner parties, you really would have been fuelled with drink.

At dinner parties, after 10.00pm, the music and conversation had to be at decibels of such a low intensity that conversation resembled the gentle rustling of leaves on a quiet autumnal morning. At one dinner party, the local municipal police arrived to tell us to quieten down our leaf rustling or face a hefty fine. On another occasion, they arrived with two Alsatians (not two people from the Alsace region of Eastern France, but two dogs commonly mistaken for German Shepherds – no, not sheepherders from Germany, but dogs, big dogs). Apparently, one of our guests had committed a hideous crime: they had flushed the loo after midnight. Peace and stability returned when I assured my police colleagues and their canine companions that such a national disaster would not recur until the following morning.

Over the centuries, European countries have engaged in battles (Agincourt being my favourite), wars (no favourite here), revolutions (the Russian one just about beats the French one) and breaking treaties (Chamberlain and Hitler in Munich springs to mind). Whilst all this was going on, Switzerland remained pretty much neutral and unscathed. Swiss neutrality can be traced back to 1515 (a quarter past three, to you and me). Thinking about it, they have had over five hundred years to profit from the misfortunes of their neighbours. They could even do it in four official languages – French, German, Italian and Romansch – whilst most now speak English.

But just in case a punch-up beckons, which might involve them, the Swiss have, over the years, built up a network of shelters (some would say nuclear shelters) so that, in the event of an invasion, they can get into these bunkers and hunker down until the invaders have got bored with fondue, skiing, dry white wine, lakes, valleys, clocks and chocolate. Even if it takes years, the Swiss will be impregnable in their shelters. Then, with the enemy gone to somewhere less idyllic but more exciting, the Swiss will carry on as usual.

For this salvation of Switzerland to work, everyone must know where their shelter is (a good start) and that the shelter, be it individual or collective, is fully stocked for a lengthy stay. With the usual Swiss efficiency, the shelters were regularly inspected and fines dished out for those who had not kept the prescribed list of goodies for a long and happy life underground. I was regularly rebuked for having no idea where my shelter was, and, thereafter, for not keeping stock in date (I thought the point about such stock was that it should not expire – such as honey, everyone could live on stale bread and honey for years, at least that is what I thought. The Swiss authorities have a different and dimmer view).

Just before I finish with Switzerland, there's a last note on finishing schools. I wonder if either the International School of Berne or the Liebefelz Steinholzi school of Berne have a certain Kim Jong-Un as one of their alumni. For fear of North Korean nuclear annihilation, they probably have.

I left Geneva after six good months, made lots of friends and generally had a very pleasant experience. As I packed to return to London – not knowing what job I would be assigned for the next eighteen months – I had a pleasant dinner with my wife, whose name escapes me, and she declared that she did not want to be married anymore. It must have been something I said. And that was that particular part of life's great adventure over.

Chapter 14

London (again): London Ladies

And so back to the FCO in London. With the marital demise, I bought my estranged wife out of the London flat, and my mortgage went through the roof. I started socialising much more frequently than hitherto and, alas, found myself back in Personnel Services dealing with a mountainous backlog of allowance-related work. The upside of the downside of dealing with allowances again was that my opposite number in Her Majesty's Treasury was a rather attractive young lady whom I got to know very well. The work was non-stop but, between me and my new friend in the Treasury, we managed to get through it. We also managed to get through numerous bottles of wine and the occasional Magnum of champagne.

For me, life in London in the late eighties revolved around work, the pub, weekends following the FCO cricket and football teams, the pub, not opening letters from my bank (see mortgage above), not opening letters from my credit card companies (see pub above), ordering the occasional Magnum of champagne (see letters from credit card companies above) and generally having a rather good time.

On the sports front, the cricket team toured The Hague. The captain knew that I was probably nowhere near as good as other players, but being my best mate, I was selected to go on the tour (a decision both he and the vice-captain would very much regret by the first innings of the first game). Our vice-captain (a dear friend, taken far too early by cancer) happened to have the same name as one of our most senior diplomats. So, mistakenly, the senior diplomats in our Embassy in The Hague believed that this cricket team would be the Who's Who of the FCO. To ingratiate themselves with the great and good of the FO, they had made VIP arrangements that were not usually expected of anything below a visit by a senior Minister. Official cars met us at The Hague airport, very nice accommodation was arranged throughout the city, and there was to be an official reception on our second night (we were there for three matches and a long weekend).

Of course, the reality was that the team was the Who is not Who of the FCO. This became obvious when we got off the plane and headed for the nearest bars. The other giveaway was that our vice-captain was not a knight of the realm and told everybody to stop calling him Sir X (protecting the innocent here) and to get on with the real business at hand, which was to buy him copious amounts of Carlsberg lager (a double offence as Carlsberg is Danish beer). I tried to persuade him to at least order Heineken, but he was having none of it. Once our Embassy in The Hague had worked out their error, things changed, and changed fast. There were no cars, no reception, but luckily, we had accommodation. We had planned that we would call on the Consul if we were made homeless and demand that, as British nationals, we were entitled to help from our Embassy. Now, if ever there was one, that was a career limiting idea. Fortunately, the idea was shelved and other shelves were emptied of their liquor stocks.

The cricket was secondary to our intention of having a good time in Holland; secondary in that we came second in all three of the matches. Our first match was a bit of a disaster. I alone dropped three simple catches. The Dutch are renowned for their football, but they are not bad at cricket either. I put it down to the fact that the country is very flat, so they are good at sports requiring expanses of green (but not snooker). I will not give you a ball-by-ball commentary of the first game (or any other) but suffice to say that the first game, in particular, finished very early.

I blamed the team leadership who had, the night before, decided on a team-building exercise. This meant that anyone who went home before 0500 in the morning would be put on box-cleaning duties – for non-cricketers, please ask a cricketer about this, but not in front of the children. Basically, the FCO IX had had four hours sleep each, and prior to those four hours there were the numerous rounds of drinks, drinking games, a transvestite disco (entered by accident, but left by design) and nightcaps – to be strictly accurate, dawn caps, on the very nice Scheveningen beach. A lot of fun, but not conducive to good cricket.

I could go on about the next three nights and two days but, basically, with the exception of the transvestite disco, they were the same: losing at cricket, enjoying Dutch hospitality, avoiding Embassy types (who were keen that UK/Dutch diplomatic relations remained just that – diplomatic) and, in general, having a rather good time. Talking of good times, it should also be noted that our second slip, every evening, kept disappearing, claiming he had left his house keys in a bar too close for comfort to the aforementioned transvestite disco. He seemed to have brought numerous copies of his house keys on a cricket trip. Our one other overseas cricket trip that year was to Dublin in October. There were two flaws in this. The Irish do not play cricket, but even if they did, the season would certainly be over by October. This sporting adventure was designed to give a well-earned break to various partners, be they wives, husbands or boyfriends or girlfriends. Strangely, it turned into a stag do without a stag. Not strangely, it turned into The Hague without the cricket or the transvestite disco. A new and more naïve member of our motley crew actually brought his cricket whites and pads. As a penalty, he had to go out wearing the whites and pads. And good on him; he did.

On this non-cricket Dublin trip, life seemed to revolve around the over-sixties disco underneath our hotel. After a day exploring Dublin, pretending (and failing badly) not to be English, and more importantly denying any knowledge of being Civil Servants (let alone British diplomats on a party weekend), the tired group retired to the sixties disco to dance the night away with Dublin's more long-lived residents. Some of whom could probably remember the Easter Uprising and being extras in *Ryan's Daughter*. Our funky attempts at breakdancing did not really fit in with the waltzes and foxtrots, so we were glad to be asked to leave.

Life was not all sporting weekends away and work. The management consultants that were starting to infect many government departments had infiltrated the FCO. One of their latest mantras was that training and learning never stops. Relentlessly, managers encouraged us to go away on training courses, forgetting about our front-line work. Whilst the whole of the FCO was on training courses, Thatcher, Reagan and Gorbachev declared an end to the Cold War. Perhaps we should go on training courses more often – we could solve the Middle East. But I digress again.

Taking this training to heart (and getting out of the office for a week) I, with two best friends and nine fast-stream new entrants, found ourselves blindfolded at the midnight hour, on top of a Welsh mountain, either quacking like a duck, mooing like a cow or barking like a dog. We were on a management, communications and leadership residential course in the mountains of Snowdonia. Not just us, as we were with three highly-paid management consultants, skilled in mountaineering, map-reading, kayaking and torturing civil servants into their way of thinking. Not one of them would have lasted five minutes in a hardship post.

For the next five days, these management consultants took us out into the depths of Snowdonia where we, as a team, had to kayak, abseil, climb waterfalls (one was frozen), map read, explore caves, measure the depths of lakes and generally behave like trainee officers for the SAS. Which, of course, we were not. We got lost in the mountains, we got lost in the caves, we got lost on a lake. (Even though we could see both banks, we got the depth of the lake wrong – it was three feet, not four – who knew, who cared?). In addition, all the time while we were pretending to be Rambo, our trainers were trying to impart the management, communication and leadership skills that would take us up to the stratospheric heights of the top echelons of the FCO. I am convinced that only one of the fast-streamer trainees on this course is still in the FCO. I suspect that the other eight were so enthralled by the lake-measuring exercise that they decided high-flying diplomacy was not for them and became hydrologists. Of the three not-so-fast streamers, one is doing rather nicely, whilst I and one of my best mates (the Stick Insect, as he is sometimes called) survived many more years with Her Majesty's Diplomatic Service and then happily retired. We did not set the foreign policy world alight, but then again, if we had, we would probably only have burnt down some much-admired edifice that was dedicated to the magnificence of the FCO.

I went to Algiers to stay with a friend for a rest from all the exertions and learning in Snowdonia and living in London. And, small world again, I met the Australian Consul who had been a big buddy in Dhaka. We had a splendid reunion in a Kasbah bar, wherein he proceeded to drink the bar dry of all their Algerian wine, as he thought, in his befuddled state, that the description on the wine bottles was 'Made in Australia' rather than 'Produit d'Algerie'. He eventually ended up in a very senior position in a very senior French country – I hope that his command of written French has improved. His drinking never would.

I travelled out to the great Atlas Mountains, had a picnic in a dry riverbed (it would not have worked in a wet riverbed), joined the Embassy darts team for a night and thrashed the American embassy. I admired the Notre Dame d'Afrique (two Notre Dames behind me now – there are many more, but two is enough for me at the moment), and visited the Monument of the Martyrs, commemorating the Algerian War of Independence. Alas, there are too many such commemorations to wars around the world; it's time to start building things commemorating happier events, a grand edifice celebrating the publishing of this book might be one.

Returning to my accommodation in downtown Algiers, I put on the TV. I was surprised to see what I thought were images on French television of my hometown of Deal. It was Deal. The IRA had bombed the Royal Marine School of Music, killing eleven young marines. The evil people who committed this atrocity have never been caught. There is a memorial bandstand at Walmer Green. If you are ever in the area, please pay your respects

I had now been in London for nearly two and a half years. Another overseas posting was imminent, and the cycle of farewell lunches, dinners and drinks parties had slowly started. Not just for me, but for everyone who had arrived back in London in early 1987.

The economists will tell you that times were tight in the UK in the late eighties. Actually, that is a lie. Economists would never make such a straightforward statement. So for now, take my word for it. Inflation was running at eight per cent and mortgage interest rates about twelve per cent. But, of course, the biggest drain on the economy was pubs being open all day. Obviously, not a drain on the breweries or the publicans, but a drain on the Whitehall Civil Servants who, because of inflation and interest rates worries, sought refuge in the bottom of a glass. There were many of us. I had had to move out of my flat and rent it out, and moved in with a couple in East Croydon. The couple were fantastic. East Croydon was not. And at this time of rising debts, what is not a wise thing to do? Let me tell you. It is not wise to have two girlfriends at the same time.

Alternating dates and visits, and keeping them apart, was both mentally and monetarily very stressful. I know, I should have chosen one or the other, but as with most men, I thought I could get away with it. Also, I had an escape plan. I had heard, not long after my return from Algiers, that my next job was as the Vice-Consul in Dakar, Senegal, in Francophone West Africa. They wanted me out there in about five months, but before that, I would be training and learning French. Not being tied to a desk and telephone in the FCO building, I thought I could continue my subterfuge uncaught. And then fly away unscathed. Stupid me.

As the rounds of farewells gathered momentum, these two particular ladies (who to this day have my greatest respect – but probably not vice versa) were being invited. They knew each other – actually we had all been friends in the same social circles and so it was no surprise that at events, not just for me, they would be at the same social gatherings. My life was becoming more and more fraught. I knew that sooner rather than later the game would be up. My deceit would be exposed and there would be an unmarked plot in the garden museum just across Lambeth Bridge, wherein my cold lifeless body would be secreted in the dead of night by a person or persons unknown – probably two persons and probably both female. My posting to Dakar would then have been cancelled and you would not be reading this book but, obviously, that was not to be.

They did find out. They were both talking to each other at a rather convivial garden party to the North of London. Each was telling the other how much they were looking forward to visiting me in Dakar, and how nice and wonderful I was (it's my book, I shall put in what I want). And, of course, it did not take long for the penny to drop. Actually, it was a bit more nuclear than that. In the middle of a beautiful spring day, as word of my deception spread, the convivial garden party became a very frosty reception – verging on a nuclear winter. Questions (interrogations is a better word) were asked. At one point, I was locked in a cupboard. I am not sure whether this was for my own safety or a plan had been hatched to leave me in there to die a slow death. Suffice to say that the plane to Dakar now could not come fast enough, but before that, I had some training to do and Paris to visit. The training (away from the FCO and Whitehall) and the brief sojourn in Paris learning French enabled me to escape the worst of the wrath of these ladies. I have found that hiding is sometimes the best solution to awkward moments such as these. But best of all, some months later, both ladies came to the airport to see me off (not in a nice way, if I recall – just to make me suffer).

One lady did come and visit me in Dakar, but that did not end well – not the visit, that was good, but the relationship. We went our separate ways.

En Route to Senegal

As mentioned earlier, prior to my departure for Dakar, I had some training to do. A bit of operational stuff – budgets, estates and consular work – but the best was the French language training. I had also found out that soon I was going to be only one of three members of the double D club. Not the bra size, but those of us who had served both in Dhaka (Bangladesh) and Dakar (Senegal) – both pronounced in an almost identical fashion. Later in my career that was to become a mere bagatelle – I am probably one of the very few people on the planet to have been to North Korea, Siberia and Pitcairn. That is probably not an envious accolade with which to burden oneself, but there it is – and later, we shall come to those inglorious places, but for now, back to learning French.

I had A-level French from school and this had – blowing my own trumpet here – vastly improved since my posting to Brussels. And so, as I joined my French class in the wonderful FCO language centre (part of a large Training department), I had no fear of resuming my learning of this great language. My classmates were a mixture: some new fast streamers, who needed to be given some basic French for their first jobs in the FCO, and others (older, probably much wiser, and vastly experienced in the FCO) on their way to French-speaking posts: Dakar (me), Paris, Berne and Kinshasa, if I remember correctly.

At first, the lessons were of a classroom nature. All the French teachers in the language centre taught all of us different aspects of the French language, culture and customs; as well as the nuances of certain words and phrases not taught at school or University. We were educated in slang and colloquialisms. Well, at least some of us were. Some of the graduates straight from University thought that they were still at primary school and behaved similarly until it came to the point that our teachers had had enough and the classes were reconstructed. We all then worked differently. Those of us going abroad were expected to pass exams and thus behaved somewhat more maturely. while the graduates who were not going abroad and so did not have the same pressure, were left to waste taxpayers' money. Looking back, I think only one of the graduates is still in the Diplomatic Service and he is a fluent Italian speaker. Still, after ten weeks, we all regrouped for our final mission – two weeks of intensive

French in Paris. We would be staying separately with French families, be further trained (no English allowed) in a glorious building next to le Jardin de Luxembourg, and were expected to eat, drink, breath and sleep French (my attempts to sleep French failed miserably).

The FCO excels at this type of training. This was mini-immersion; some people now go through months, if not years of training, followed by immersion far away from the Embassy prior to being let loose to work with their foreign counterparts. For two weeks, we worked in French, occasionally in the classroom, but more often than not out on the streets of Paris and in some of their greatest institutions.

There was lunch in the Sorbonne, an afternoon in La Defense, a visit to the Quai D'Orsay (the French equivalent of our Foreign Office), a privileged visit to the Ecole d'Administration National – an elite establishment (perhaps the most elite in France) for training senior civil servants and diplomats in the dark arts of government. In the evenings, dinners in exclusive French restaurants and, to give it all a sense of balance, dinners in the less salubrious parts of Paris – where accents were difficult and slang plentiful. But the food and wine still good. There were visits to the theatre – the world famous Opera, the Louvre and, of course, Versailles.

Versailles deserves a special mention. We had to make our own way there from our accommodation, using certain prescribed routes (to test our ability to buy discount tickets and use public transport). Our man going to Kinshasa got lost. It was probably a good omen for someone who was going to a country that did not even know its own name – it was originally the Congo Free State, then the Belgian Congo, then the Democratic Republic of the Congo (DRC), next Zaire – as it was in the 1990s – and then back to the DRC.

The graduates arrived together with a taxi suspiciously disappearing around a corner. On its side were the telltale words 'Driver speak engilshe'; he might be able to speak it, but his spelling and grammar needed some help. Huddled together now for our last cultural adventure before returning to England, we were joined by our guide and Versailles was all ours. It literally was. Not for us the tourist walkways trodden by millions of others. We were to see into the depths of the Chateau of Versailles.

We spent hours in rooms behind rooms behind rooms, in secret passageways, viewing anything from magnificent statues and portraits to peering into the cubby holes that were the rooms for the servants to the servants who, in turn, served more superior servants. Of course, we also saw the Royal Apartments, the Royal Chapel,

Marie Antoinette's Private Chambers, but the piece de resistance (already my French is flowing back), the best bit, was stepping out of a concealed door and directly into the public side of the Hall of Mirrors. Imagine the surprise of the numerous tourists admiring the Hall of Mirrors as one of those glorious mirrors opened and out traipsed the future of Her Majesty's Diplomatic Corps – the tourists did not know that, of course. Perhaps it was wise that they did not, but it was still a fine ending to our training in Paris.

I would and should, of course, thank my hosts, the French family who had a lovely flat in the Third Arrondissement, but I only met them at the beginning of my stay to get the keys and rudimentary directions. After that, they had been instructed that I may or may not be there for breakfast (depending on that day's activities) and that they should not speak English to me. I think this last point was lost in translation somewhere. When very occasionally our paths crossed in their own home, they would avoid me. But to be fair, I was hardly ever there. And today, I would probably not recognise the street that housed me for two wonderful weeks of learning and culture.

Lastly, I should say that some years later, some unthinking senior and probably monoglot managers and ministers decided to close down the Language Centre. Big mistake, but I am pleased to report that sense has prevailed (it does not take a genius to know that our diplomats should be able to converse, write and read foreign languages) and it has now reopened.

Part Five

Dakar (Senegal)

May 1990 – May 1993

Chapter 15

An Inauspicious Arrival

Well, that was some home tour (a posting in London). Engaged, married, bought a flat, temporary duty and living with my wife in Geneva, separated (not sure what happened there, but do not dwell on it), a side visit to Algiers and lunch in the Atlas Mountains; and after the proverbial female famine, the proverbial feast – a bit awkward when more than one delightful lady turned up at Gatwick to say farewell. But, for now, I was off to a new adventure in French West Africa.

I stopped over in Geneva (Swiss Air was the only decent, value for money airline flying in and out of Dakar then) to see some friends. Two days later, I was picked up at Dakar airport by an Embassy driver and taken to stay with my predecessor. This gentleman understood handovers. Neither of us wanted the other to be there. He wanted to leave having done his bit, and I wanted to start without having the 'professional' looking over my shoulder, so we kept it short.

There are two key early memories concerning my arrival. I loved the drive from the airport to downtown Dakar – a rugged coastline interspersed with white sands, an amazing beachside fish market (where else would you put a fish market?) and then onto the Dakar peninsula and the Embassy compound. The compound contained the Ambassador's residence, wherein I would spend many a happy hour sharing a cold beer with the Ambassador (the late great Roger Beetham, LVO CMG, a well-deserved CMG and the best boss I ever had). We would often stand in the kitchen and discuss budgets; how to fix the ailing residence; French/UK/Senegal relations; who should go to Guinea, Mali, Guinea Bissau and the Cape Verde Islands; the monkey with the erection (more of that later); and beer and wine – he was a sommelier and taught me a few things about wine. But I am getting ahead of myself.

At that time, in early 1990, the Embassy was nice, neat and compact. Six staff from London, about thirteen (excluding the Residence gardeners and Residence staff) Senegalese staff, one aid worker (water projects) and two from the British Council (I hoped that they had not heard about my concert in Sana'a). Under the leadership of the Ambassador and his equally wonderful wife, Christine, this was more of one big happy family than one of Her Majesty's far-flung representations in Africa.

Our Embassy in Dakar was multi-accredited. That is to say, we covered more than one country. In countries where we had little influence, did not care about or had forgotten about, we did not make the effort to build and staff Embassies or High Commissions, so our little Embassy in Senegal was also accredited to Guinea (capital Conakry), Guinea Bissau (capital Bissau), Mali (capital Bamako) and the Cape Verde Islands (capital Praia). Why should we not have proper Embassies in these countries, you may ask? Simply put, we knew when we were, in diplomatic influence, out-ranked. We did not cover Guinea and Mali because the French were the key players. We did not cover Guinea Bissau and the Cape Verde Islands because the Portuguese were the key players. We did keep our Honorary Consuls, however, who were our eyes and ears on the spot.

My job as the Vice-Consul and Administration Officer basically consisted of running and getting the finance to pay for the place and all our activities. As Vice-Consul, I was basically dealing with a trickle of visa applications (most people in this area, thankfully, wanted to go to France or Portugal) and the trickle of British passport holding lunatics who had crossed the Sahara the hard way and now had no money to get home.

As with almost every overseas Posting, once your successor has gone, you do the rounds, meeting your opposite numbers in the 'friendly' Embassies. There was no point in those days going to the Russians (and certainly not nowadays in 2018 – one might be offered Poisson-a-la-nerve agent), Chinese, Cubans etc. During such introductory visits, one would hopefully meet some professional kindred spirits in the NATO and EU missions (although probably not now in these days of Brexit), as well as some social kindred spirits who would, when the weekend came, spirit one away to the local nightlife, clubs, bars, sports events and restaurants. Museums, theatres and other cultural centres, had I wanted to visit them, were thin on the ground in Dakar. And so, very reluctantly, I found it was the bars and nightlife that helped me to keep body and soul together. Although my first introduction to a very popular bar/restaurant was inauspicious, to say the least.

On my second weekend, I put on my glad rags to venture out with my new-found friends. We were meeting at a bar downtown in which all the various nationalities hung out. Numerous members of the local young diplomatic corps would be there. The influential French would be there. Relics from the French Foreign legion would be there. Influential Senegalese ladies and gentlemen would be there. I was the new boy and would be under scrutiny. So, with a spring in my step, I headed out to meet my future friends and colleagues in Senegal. But first, a quick bit of history and local knowledge.

When the French were colonising various parts of the world, they tried to turn the capital cities of their newly acquired lands into mini versions of Paris. There were bakeries providing baguettes three times a day, decent restaurants, French wines and, generally, a French feel to the places. Upon independence, some of the standards slipped, but there was no mistaking the totality of the French influence. Including, unfortunately, the old-fashioned hole in the ground toilets – squat toilets. And there we have it, a potted very short lesson in the history of French colonisation.

Back to my big night out; still with a spring in my step, I entered the bar wearing my smart light-brown lightweight brogues, khaki lightweight chinos and smart Lacoste T-shirt. The new cool guy had arrived. I was having a thoroughly pleasant evening, chatting to one and all in English and French. The model of sophistication. Even attracting a few amorous looks from the ladies. Unfortunately, and very unusually for me (probably the change to West African food), I needed to go to the loo rather urgently. I found it quite quickly and, to my horror, it was a squat loo. The only time outside of my own home I needed to sit down and here was my worldwide nemesis. I cannot squat, or at least if I try, it is not for long and I fall over. But I had to do what I had to do. So, thinking clearly and logically, I removed my trousers so that they did not touch the rather grubby floor and made an attempt at squatting. It was not to be. However, thinking outside the box, I noticed that the flush pipe was attached to the wall and went all the way down to the floor into the toilet. I could use this as balance.

I reversed myself, squatted and gripped the downpipe. I manoeuvred myself into a comfortable situation – well, as comfortable as one could be in such a precarious position. I hoped to all the Gods in the universe that I had remembered to lock the door and, whilst I thought about that, I noticed that water was leaking from the top of the pipe. My weight was detaching the pipe from the wall. And then, in slow motion (and that, thankfully, was the only motion at that moment), the pipe came away (I had visions of the shower incident in Bangladesh), and I fell into the squat toilet as water cascaded over me and my smart new clothes.

I immediately sorted myself out, stuck the offending pipe in a corner and went back into the bar. I ignored entreaties from new-found friends and colleagues for conversation and dashed headlong into the early evening to get a taxi home. I suspect the flow of water from the loo and the trail of drips following me might have given some a clue as to what had just occurred. But I was not hanging about to tell the story. I never went back to that bar and, after many months, only told trusted friends what had happened. And did they laugh? Yes. Did they spend much time telling everyone in this small corner of the French empire the story of the British Vice-Consul and the squat toilet? Yes. I suspect, in thousands of years, it will be some sort of prophetic legend.

Chapter 16

Consular Affairs and the Erect Monkey

After the loo-quake, I got on with learning the job. A major part of this was the partial rebuilding and complete refurbishment of the magnificent Ambassadorial residence. We had teams of Senegalese workers, we had teams of builders out from the UK, and we had estate experts from the UK and various parts of Africa. Tea drinking by these people must be a worldwide phenomenon. Rather than just getting on with the jobs in hand, they tended to sit in my office drinking tea until either the Ambassador and his wife decided to see how their new home was progressing (or not, as the case was most of the time) or there was some sort of building crisis. There were many of those, but the first prize goes to the case of the mad monkey.

It was a slow day, the sun was shining, the temperature pleasant, the weaver birds were happily building their nests (a lot faster and more effectively than we were building the residence) and nothing much else was happening. This idyll was broken by shrieks coming from the half-built kitchen. A posse from the Embassy tea drinking club, with all haste, strolled to see what the problem was. It transpired that the Ambassador's wife had seen a monkey (a rare sight in Senegal) in the kitchen. Monkeys bite and can be quite vicious and destructive – the last thing we needed in our new residence. Search parties were formed and a grid created to cover every inch of the residence and the grounds. It did not take us long to find our missing primate.

He had taken up gardening. He was in the garden pulling up the plants and throwing them at anyone who approached him (and it was a him). Although not large, no one in their right mind would want to approach, negotiate with or indeed attempt to get near an unknown West African monkey. One bite might lead to a rather horrific and painful death (I once knew a girl like that).

For reasons known only to our Maker, the usual crowd congregated and stood at a respectful distance, wondering what to do. The monkey knew what to do. He stood on his hind legs, and with one hand waved a recently removed plant at us and with the other pointed to his erect member. At this point, the Ambassador whispered, "I do not care what you have to do, including if necessary, with extreme prejudice. Just get rid of it." I think he had recently been watching Martin Sheen in *Apocalypse Now*. After issuing these clear instructions, he then took his dear wife away – I think she needed a lie-down.

It did not take long for a professional monkey catcher to be found. He arrived with his sidekick, a thick stick, a bag and a bunch of bananas – no mod cons here. He approached the monkey, sat down and placed the bananas about a foot away from himself. The monkey catcher held the bag open. His sidekick with the stick sat nearby, and everyone was asked to move back and remain very silent.

After a little while, our monkey friend decided to have lunch and warily approached the bananas. The monkey chose a banana and cautiously started to eat, his member still erect. Then, with the skills borne out of generations of monkey hunting, the monkey catcher hit the monkey on the head. He (the monkey) turned to see from where the offending tap had originated. The monkey catcher's sidekick then tapped him (the monkey) on his still erect member to further confuse him. Then the main man grabbed him, the monkey – not his sidekick – by the scruff of the neck and expertly deposited our plant-stealing, pornographic primate into the bag. And another day in paradise passed.

Just off the coast of Dakar lies the island of Goree. Now a World Heritage site, but back in history, it was an infamous slave island. The whole island was geared for the transportation of slaves. The House of Slaves is still there and has been visited by the likes of Nelson Mandela, George W. Bush, Bill Clinton, Barack Obama and Michel Rocard (the former French Prime Minister). And me. Inside the House of Slaves is the 'Door of no return'. For those slaves taken to Goree, this was the last piece of Africa that these poor souls passed through before being herded onto ships for the Caribbean and America. Interestingly, later in my travels, I was to discover there was a 'Bridge of no return', which crosses the Demilitarised Zone, the border between North and South Korea. But that comes later.

Back to Goree. All official and family visitors were taken there as part of their official visits or holidays. Not all of the island was the dark history of the slave trade. On the mini-beach, by the mini-port of Goree, were al-fresco restaurants (shacks actually) that served up the Senegalese traditional dishes of Thieboudienne and Poulet (Chicken) Yassa. Thieboudienne is really rice and fish; it is probably much more than that, but I am not a cook. Nice, if you like rice, I don't and so rarely ate it. Poulet Yassa is chicken with lots of different flavourings and served with white rice. Nice if you like rice, I don't and so always ordered it with chips. So I was really eating chicken and chips. If they had had smaller baskets, I would have had chicken and chips in a basket – I knew how to live way back then.

Leaving Goree, just off the Dakar peninsula, is the most Westerly point on mainland Africa. This most Westerly point is La Pointe des Almadies on the Cap Vert Peninsula. I believe, from a photo I have seen, it has been redeveloped now. But back in the early nineties, it consisted of a handful of very nice French and Lebanese restaurants, where rice was not mandatory with every morsel of food. The waiting staff got to know me and my friends so well that frites and salads were the accompaniments to our meals. So much so, in fact, that a trend started and, towards the end of my tour in Dakar, not much rice was seen at these particular restaurants. Believe it or not, in all my travels, here on the westernmost point of Africa, one can find the best Irish coffees in the world. I kid you not. So much so that one quiet Sunday afternoon and evening, I sipped five of them. I did not go to sleep until the following Wednesday.

Both the fresh fish and seafood in Senegal were to die for (but only if caught in a sewer and eaten raw, but I did not do this). Regularly, I would head for the fishing village and go out into the wild Atlantic Ocean with some friends and nothing more than bait, a rod and a few cans of beer (and, I forgot a boat – in these neighbourhoods called a pirogue – a small wooden canoe-shaped boat with a small outboard motor). We would trail our lures looking for various types of fish. I caught mainly bonito (related to the tuna; first cousin removed, I think), and on the beach, it was cleaned and filleted and taken to be cooked – magnificent with chips or salad. Not rice. The fish cleaning ladies of the fishing village were more than delighted to filet our fish – as payment, they accepted the heads, gills, fins and skin of the fish, and could not understand why we foreigners did not want to eat these delicious morsels when mixed into a fish soup. Probably because, in relative terms, we were rich and did not need to, that was my only thought.

Over the months and years, we all got to know our colleagues in our fellow friendly embassies – especially the Anglophone Canadians and Americans. We were also close to the Danes and Dutch. This camaraderie was reinforced when through our savings we had a slight surplus in our budget, and with that money, I built a British

Embassy club on a small plot of vacant land attached to our Embassy. Whilst only open once a week, this brought like-minded diplomats, consular and support staff together. Work (exchange information and ideas), rest (a nice, air-conditioned, sanitary pristine, Anglophone environment) and play (beer, wine and simple pub grub) were the order of the evening. It was here, in the club, that I was invited onto my first helicopter flight.

My American opposite number told me that he was flying out to an American oil rig some eleven miles offshore. He said that he had been informed there were five British nationals on the rig and asked if I, as the Vice-Consul, would like to pay a pastoral visit.

The American Ambassador spoke to my Ambassador, who agreed whole-heartedly) that my presence was much needed. The day of the visit came and out at the airport was the oil company's helicopter, my opposite number from the US Embassy, the pilot (of course) and the local representative of the oil company. The local representative, Bill, was a good beer-drinking friend of Polish extraction and a larger than life character. After the safety briefings – a key part of which was that I could not sue or blame any American on the planet in the unlikely event of my demise, either on the helicopter or on the oil rig – Bill, my Polish friend, explained that he had not been in this type of helicopter since his days in 'Nam. I was not sure how to take that. I was soon to find out.

Just before take-off, Bill asked the pilot (who apparently had also been in 'Nam and who also was called Bill) to let us have an 'Operation Rolling Thunder' take-off. Well, not slowly and sedately straight up for us. Oh no. Seven feet above the airport bush, eighty miles an hour for one hundred yards and a sudden banked steep climb to our altitude (whatever that was) was the start of our day. As this was going on, two young Vice-Consuls stared at each other in total fear of losing their lives. Meanwhile, our two Vietnam vets were hollering and shouting and reminiscing and declaring that Lt. Colonel Bill Kilgore from *Apocalypse Now* should be the next President of the USA, if not the world. All we now needed was the *Ride of the Valkyries* blasting out over the quiet, far from Vietnam, peninsula below us and our two Vietnam vets would have been in their own little Heaven.

To be honest, after that, the rest of the day was somewhat tame. Very tame. We landed very sensibly. But, judging by the take-off, had we been under some sort of enemy fire, we would have easily survived and our antagonists would have rued the day they took on Bill and Bill from 'Nam.

I had a nice chat with the Brits on the rig, had a nice lunch and then got back on board. The helicopter, as in Vietnam, had to have its own personal name and so, after some thought, we christened it (later on in the Embassy bar) 'The Ass Kicker'. But our flight was not yet finished. It was not as bad as the take-off, but the pilot kindly flew us low over the island of Goree and the whole Dakar peninsula, including Les Almadies – which provided great unforgettable views. And I was getting paid to do all this.

You are probably now travel sick, but there was one last mode of transportation I was privileged to experience in Senegal or, more accurately, off the coast of Senegal – a fully functioning sailing vessel. Not too big, not too small. It was in Dakar prior to crossing the Atlantic to Recife in Northern Brazil. The usual Consular Corps suspects were invited on board for a day of sailing. It was great fun helping with the steering, moving sails and avoiding sunstroke, and avoiding falling overboard. However, there was a weird practice in which most, if not all, indulged. And, an early warning here, do not try to do this at home or anywhere else.

A very long thick piece of rope was securely fastened to a mast and thrown overboard. People then – get this – jumped overboard (even though the ship was at sail and at about six knots per hour) and grabbed onto the rope for a seaborne, sail-assisted rope ride. All well and good. Until one had to get back on board. To do this, one had to pull oneself (against the waves and the sea hitting one at over six knots per hour) back to the ship and clamber aboard. The alternative was to let go and be caught up in the vicious currents of the West African Atlantic and end up as a corpse on the skeleton coast of Namibia thousands of miles away. Of course, I did not know about the difficulties of surviving the rope ride. With gay abandon (in the old sense of gay), I launched myself overboard, grabbed the rope and only then realised that I was already some forty yards away from my large lifeboat. At first, it was nice being pulled along through the aquamarine Atlantic Ocean, but one had to get back on board, sooner or later. So, I started the long grim haul to safety, arm over weary arm, grimace over weary grimace (on the plus side, I was grimacing so much that the seawater could not miss my teeth and the force, power and weight of the salt water gave me the best teeth whitening cosmetic dentistry I will ever have). Eventually, exhausted, I made it back on board. Sailing on sailing ships is good, but avoid the rope ride at all costs.

Chapter 17

The Shipping News

Under the leadership of Ambassador Roger Beetham and his wife, the Embassy had built up a reputation as being very welcoming for visits by ships from our Royal Navy. These ships were either on their way to the Gulf or the Falklands, or on their way back from the Gulf or the Falklands. We could expect two or three a year. As was expected of the Rolls Royce FCO, we used these visits to enhance diplomatic relations with Senegal, reinforce our military cooperation with the French Navy and to look after, to the highest standards possible, the officers and crews of the ships. The officers liked the highest standards – cocktail parties, tennis matches and tours of Goree and la Pointe des Almadies. The crew liked nothing more than the downtown culture of certain parts of Dakar where diplomats fear to tread. Dakar was (and I hope still is) not a violent place. The worst that could happen was one's pockets being picked or rip-off prices in a dark and sleazy bar. I only know about the latter because someone told me, but as Vice-Consul (or should that be Consul of Vice), I was occasionally despatched with the Shore Patrol to find some errant seamen to ensure they returned to their bunks and were on board for whatever travels were in front of them – some straight to the doctor, I should imagine.

The highlight of all these ship's visits was not once, but twice receiving visits from Her Majesty's Yacht Britannia (disposed of later, very unwisely, by Tony Blair). There was never Royalty on-board, which made the visits more relaxed, at least for protocol purposes. The yachtsmen and women were totally professional. They knew the diplomatic value of the yacht (unlike Tony Blair – I was to meet the PM later on in another posting, but for career purposes, I did not raise the subject then). The visits were organised so that representational work was done early on and, thereafter, the crew could relax before heading off into the deep blue yonder. This relaxation included the usual Ambassadorial challenge to the captain (or in this case, the Commander) of the ship or the yacht to partake of an Embassy versus ship tennis tournament. The social aspect of these tennis tournaments had spread far and wide across Her Majesty's Navy. There was free beer, wine and a good lunch for one and all, and the challenge was always accepted. And we always won, with one major exception.

It must be said that we had a slight advantage, in that we had a well-utilised tennis court in the Embassy grounds. On my various tours of ships and two tours of HM Yacht Britannia, I did not spot a tennis court anywhere on board. I am sure I would have noticed if any ship or yacht had had one.

And so, on a convivial Sunday morning, the Embassy team proceeded to beat the yacht team. All well and good. There was always a quiet bet of a good bottle of single malt between the top bosses. On this particular occasion, for reasons unknown to all but the two men, a 'double or quits' game was organised for after lunch.

Now hear this! Now hear this! The Commander gently rounded up his team and quietly suggested that they take it easy on lunchtime vino in order that he could save himself parting with two fine single malts housed somewhere in the bowels of HMY Britannia. Of course, it should be known that when one as illustrious as a Commander of the Royal Yacht 'suggests' something, it is, in fact, to be done on pain of keelhauling. When our Ambassador suggested to his team that we might consider moderating our consumption of the lunchtime vino so that he could imbibe, later on, some fine Scotch whisky, we thought he was joking. No orders for us. And a very merry lunch was partaken of by the home team.

Then the afternoon entertainment began. It did not last long. Our star player, on his first serve, completely missed the ball, his racket flew forwards and hit his doubles partner. He then stepped on the ball that his serve had missed and came crashing down to earth. I am afraid that most of the rest of the tournament followed suit. Points were won and lost – actually very few points were won by the Embassy on account of the very many pints that had been consumed. The yachtsmen won. The Commander gloated; the Ambassador threatened reprisals – I'm not sure what, as they were never implemented, but once again, British Embassy Dakar and Royal Navy relations were the subject of the talk of the fleet.

Whilst the Royal Yacht did not have Royalty on board, and Royal visits to French West Africa were a rarity (must have had something to do with the French Revolution) we were, some months later, privileged to have a visit by HRH Prince Philip. He was on his way to Brazil for a meeting of the World Wildlife Fund. Dakar was a convenient refuelling route and so arrangements were made for some diplomatic calls and a reception during his short one-day and one-night stopover at the Residence. This was to turn out to be a strange day.

On the morning of the arrival of HRH, everyone was busy ensuring a Rolls-Royce service for the meetings and the reception. Rule number one for the reception was that no one was to be late – guests and staff, especially staff. On that same morning, I was called to Dakar port to deal with some Ghanaian stowaways. There was an agreement that should Commonwealth stowaways be found on a ship in Senegalese waters, they could, on the authority of the British Embassy, be offloaded and returned to their country of origin. All pretty straightforward normally.

Usually, the removal of the stowaways entailed using our resident Ghanaian chief (Head of the Commercial Section in the Embassy), who would accompany me and two Senegalese immigration police on board the vessel. The Chief would, soon after boarding, be able to tell me that the stowaways were Ghanaian. Paperwork would be exchanged, the stowaways removed and later deported back to Ghana and our job was done. On this day of all days, it was different, very different.

On arrival at the port, we were directed to the pilot boat (nothing unusual here, sometimes the vessels holding the offending fugitives were moored a little way out in the harbour). As we set off, we were getting closer and closer to the harbour exit. I asked the pilot where the ship was. He pointed to a large container ship a long way in the distance. There was nothing to do now but to head out into the rough sea. And it was rough. That did not bother me then, but it would soon bother me very much. After some thirty minutes, we were nearly upon a very large, five or six storey high container ship. Ominously, there was a rope ladder hanging down the side awaiting our arrival. I turned to my Ghanaian expert for guidance, only to notice that the poor man had been seasick, not only over himself, but also our nice shiny FCO briefcase. His look said very clearly that he was far from happy and no way was he going to climb up the side of this huge container ship. The (British) captain of the container ship had radioed the pilot boat to say he was looking forward to seeing us and had laid on some afternoon tea and snacks. That was nice, except the first problem was scaling the side of a very high ship using a very small, loose rope ladder. And to add to my woes, I was starting to get worried about the time and being out of contact with the Embassy. I was sure they would be looking for me to help with some last minute royalty-related chore.

The pilot boat pulled up alongside the rope ladder and, bobbing like the proverbial cork, we needed to step from the shifting deck of the pilot boat onto the ladder steps and grip the ropes. If you missed, you would quite simply fall between the container ship and the pilot boat, which would then probably hit you on the head and Her Majesty's Vice-Consul would be no more. But I did it and then, with the seasick covered FCO briefcase tied to my back (by the way, for the fashion conscious, I was wearing a nice shirt, nice tie and fancy black brogues), made it up the side of the ship and safely onto the deck. Not a chore for the faint-hearted, I should say.

I had the usual courtesy chat with the captain, met with the first mate who showed me the Ghanaian passports of our unwelcome guests, signed the paperwork and then, with the Senegalese immigration police, started the reverse of what we had already done. It was only then that the captain, inviting me onto the bridge, pointed out that my Ghanaian colleague had had enough bouncing around on the wild Atlantic, mutinied and ordered the pilot boat back to port. From the bridge, I could see it disappearing into the distance. I was stuck there for a while, knowing that, back on dry land there was a Royal visit happening. After a few frantic phone calls (using a very expensive satellite telephone), I managed to speak to the Ambassador who, for some reason, was not his usual calm and collected self – mainly because his 'can-do' man was marooned some eight miles off the coast. Even he could not persuade the captain to up anchor and move his forty thousand ton container ship closer to shore. So, I waited patiently for the return of the pilot boat – some two hours later.

Back on dry land, I was covered in oil and dirt from the outside and inside of the ship, I needed to get home and changed for the reception. I was late – not good form. However, I thought that my story, to a fellow seafarer, would take the edge off my tardiness. Alas, the story was never told (at least not to a member of the Royal family – unless they are reading this now). I had a brief five minutes with HRH discussing the rebuilding of the residence. It was not for one as lowly as I to try to change the subject (something I should have remembered later in life when I was at a meeting in Buckingham Palace). So it came to pass that HRH Prince Philip had a short, successful visit to Senegal, whilst four Ghanaian stowaways also had a short, but less successful visit to Senegal.

As a postscript to the visit, on HRH's return a week later from Brazil, his flight had a brief refuelling stop at Dakar airport. Only an hour stopover. I was designated for airport duty to ensure that, if HRH or the crew needed anything, I would be on hand to help. To cut a long story short, the plane arrived an hour earlier than expected and, somewhat dishevelled, I arrived at the airport, got out onto the tarmac to meet the plane and greet HRH just as he was disembarking for a short stroll. He asked me to accompany him. We made small talk and, just before he rejoined the aircraft, I asked why the aircraft was an hour early, to which he replied, "Wouldn't you be in a rush if your house was on fire?" This was November 1992, when Windsor castle had caught fire. I did not have an answer, and he rejoined the aircraft and headed home. I returned to a BBQ that I had earlier left in a hurry and pondered my future.

Talking of the future, history, of course, was made when Saddam Hussein invaded and annexed Kuwait in August 1990. The world was determined to kick him out. The UK and the USA were, for the want of a better expression, team leaders, and the little old British Embassy Dakar was to play its part. Single-handedly, I was despatched to liberate Kuwait. No, not really.

An Oberon class submarine that was on its way to the Gulf, moored in Dakar port for some fuel and spare parts. We looked after the submariners, who were very much determined to enjoy the full delights of Dakar prior to returning to their undersea odyssey. We even managed to host a mini-reception on board. Only the captain has any privacy on a submarine this small; everyone 'hot bunks'. That is, if you are working, another member of the crew will be sleeping in your bunk. The Ward Room was a cupboard and the NCO's mess was a space made by folding up a couple of bunks. After the reception, there were private drinks for the Embassy staff, a few more beers in downtown Dakar and then finally a head count to ensure that no one had been left in some dubious portside bar, before we waved our new-found submariner friends off to save the Western world, or at least to save the oil suppliers to the Western world.

Now amongst all this tennis, shipping, roping, fishing, helicoptering, submarining, fine French dining, and fine French wineing (made-up word), there was work to be done. Apart from the estates' budget residence rebuilds, there were my Consular chores and visits to The Gambia, Guinea and Mali.

Chapter 18

The BBC in West Africa – Banjul, Bamako and Conakry

On the consular side, this mainly consisted of helping British nationals (aged anything between twenty and sixty), who had crossed the Sahara the hard (and cheap) way by lorry, car, motorbike, camel or on foot; basically, any way but the easy option of flying over the top of it, landing in Dakar with money and a credit card (not maxed out). Nope, the hard way for a foolhardy few meant arriving in Dakar, tired, sunburnt, dehydrated, destitute, and pleading with the British government for funds to go home. My job was to try to ensure that public funds were not used on these people. I had to try to extract details of parents or relatives or friends or old teachers, or previous university professors, or long-lost lovers (some of whom sought reconciliation, while others sought retribution for past misdemeanours) in the hope that someone would come up with funds to enable the Destitute of Dakar (I should have had T-shirts printed) to get back to Blighty. Inevitably, there is someone somewhere who loves somebody. Usually, someone provided the airfare home and everyone was happy.

A desperate minority (through embarrassment more than anything else) fought this system of asking others for financial assistance. They steadfastly claimed that, as taxpayers, Her Majesty's Government should get them home (Business Class preferred, don't you know), and should do so with all possible haste. However, when this assistance was not forthcoming and the consular case (as they were called back in the day) were left to their own devices for a few days, the lack of accommodation, lack of decent sanitary facilities and a diet of cheese and ham baguettes, paid for from my own pocket, meant that our desperate minority saw sense and the details of reluctant benefactors were provided.

In turn, funds were provided and then no more 'Destitute of Dakar' T-shirts but 'Happy to be Back' tattoos instead. In one particular case, a school friend from some forty years in the past provided the airfare for a particularly difficult (and, it has to be said, lonely case). The consular case in question did not make any contact with his benefactor when he was safely back in England. How sad and ungrateful.

Aside from these great consular affairs of state, there were the annual internal meetings deciding who should go, and when, to our outlying countries of Mali, Guinea, Guinea-Bissau and the Cape Verde Islands. In a coconut shell, I ended up with the responsibility of visiting Guinea and Mali. And on occasion, there would be the odd holiday visit to The Gambia.

Senegal encloses the former British colony of The Gambia and, on occasion, several of us would get together and drive (or rather be driven) down to Banjul, the capital. Once out of the city of Dakar, the level of sophistication changes. The French did not care much for anything outside the capital cities of their colonial conquests. The hinterland of Senegal was just bleak, poor villages with poor villagers and not much more. To get to Banjul, one has to pass through or by the town of Kaolack. Kaolack is best known (if it is known for anything – most people will not have heard of it) for three things: peanuts, a centre for Islamic studies and plastic bags (the last is my own addition). Above Kaolack, there must be (as yet undiscovered) a rare lifetime lasting vortex that quietly collects all the (mainly light blue) plastic bags in the vast West Africa region and, when no one is looking, dumps them all down on the outskirts of Kaolack. That is my one and only memory of Kaolack. A vast wasteland of used light blue plastic bags.

As I say, The Gambia is a former British colony and so, back in the nineties, there were no sophisticated restaurants, decent red wines or freshly baked baguettes. The beach bars thrived on serving English breakfasts (full), lunches of sausage egg and chips (Mighty White bread optional) and Indian meals in the evening (rice mandatory). These beach bars seemed to cater for sex-starved middle-aged European ladies and rather obese, old single men who seemed to like that part of the world – perhaps it was their interest in the historic colonial culture of The Gambia?

We band of brothers and sisters from the British Embassy in Dakar would, every now and then, while away a weekend with our friends from the British High Commission in Banjul. We did not spend our time drinking at dodgy beach bars, eating English bacon and eggs whilst simultaneously admiring the negotiating tactics of the sex-starved and obese European holidaymakers.

We were more adventurous (at least, I think so; negotiating with the natives for sex must have been a bit like Russian roulette – only

AIDS kills one more slowly). There were trips up the river Gambia; I recall a restaurant at the top of a tree where waiters would monitor alcohol consumption and guide the over-consumers down to the safety of terra firma, thus avoiding full grown adults falling out of trees (hence the expression, 'He is out of his tree'). Pleasant hours were spent floating around the mangrove swamps. I am not sure we were supposed to be in these mangrove swamps for hours; after a while, every waterway and mangrove looked the same and, to this day, I believe it was more by luck than judgement that we returned to our accommodation on the same day, if not the same week.

Guinea was the pits, man. It was so bad that I could not bear going there (I only went twice and that was twice too many). In economy class, only an hour's flight from Dakar but a million hours away from civilisation, my fellow passengers were overloaded, overweight and underfed. Underfed in the sense that when the little plastic tray of food and drink arrived, and the cabin crew had moved on, they put the whole tray into one of the many baskets they had between their legs, on their laps or on their heads. But that was not the end of it; once the cabin crew came back to pick up debris, all these people claimed that they had not received a meal and wanted another one. Suffice to say that, over the years, the cabin crew had gotten used to this ruse and so ignored everyone. I gave my food away to whoever was sitting next to me and became a minor celebrity for thirty odd minutes.

Guinea is an interesting colonial basket case. France got very annoyed with Guinea when they demanded independence in 1958. So annoyed that France is probably somewhere in *The Guinness Book of Records* for the fastest withdrawal in the history of withdrawals (I know what you are thinking – move on). When they left, they took everything that might be of use to the newly independent government – street maps, city plans, sewer plans, regional maps, nuclear codes (not really), the recipe for fresh baguettes three times a day and all the brie cheese in the country. This, of course, was not a good start for the newly independent country, but it was compounded by Guinea's new leadership flirting with Soviet Socialism and Chinese Communism (or was it the other way round?). Guinea, in return for supporting the policies of the Soviets in Africa, demanded aid – any kind of aid. On one occasion, the Soviets duly complied. They sent snowploughs.

Add to the dabbling in Communism and the other favourite African pastime of the sixties and seventies – the creation of a one-party state led by a dictator – and then add to that mix various coups and attempted coups and so, by the time I visited the country in the early 1990s, I am afraid to say that Guinea was a complete mess and the capital Conakry was right in the middle of that mess.

I tended not to stay very long in Conakry. The only hotel worth staying in was not worth staying in. It was ridden with mosquitoes that, through years of practice and evolution, could bite through mosquito nets; the lobby and corridors were ridden with prostitutes that could, through years of practice and evolution, bite through multi-locked doors – apparently, their only intention was to learn English. As I had no teacher training, I refrained from holding classes. The food in the restaurant (I use that term very loosely) was inedible. All in all, not really a family holiday resort destination.

With the usual British stiff upper lip (caused by a mosquito bite), I went about my business; business was mainly saying hello to the few Brits living in the city and dealing with visa and passport matters. But the real business was avoiding potholes, prostitutes, overflowing drains and sewers, circumnavigating huge piles of festering rubbish and, generally, not catching cholera, Lassa fever, green monkey disease and all sorts of other horrible conditions known only to be found in this corner of the globe. After all that, I went back to the airport and to my beloved Dakar. That is all I have to say about Guinea – apart from recognising the wonderfully efficient lady Honorary Consul we had in Conakry.

I am not sure why I liked Mali and its capital Bamako (Bammers, as some Eton-educated visitor (idiot) once called it). I think because, unlike Guinea, they did not take the nuclear option when France offered independence. They hung around and thought about it and, thus, the French left that particular colony in better shape than Guinea down the road. Saying that, Mali was poor then. It was poor in the nineties when I visited and, at present, I do not see it as a key member of any big serious economic grouping. Like a lot of countries freed from the yoke of colonialism, Mali dabbled in socialism, communism and one-party stateism (that's a made-up word). I am not sure why they did that; I think it was to spite their former colonial masters. It never worked, but I am drifting into areas about which I know very little, if anything.

To me, Bamako was cleaner, fresher and friendlier than Guinea. It had a much more easy-going atmosphere – apart from the usual coups that is, but coups in this part of the world had become the norm.

The city sits astride the great Niger River. There are two major bridges in the city, the Bridge of Martyrs and, as a donation from the then-King of Saudi Arabia, the King Fahd Bridge. Little did I know, but in a little over four years, I would be in Riyadh, the capital of Saudi Arabia. I should have thanked His Royal Highness for the bridge, as I crossed it often, but it's too late now; he has passed away. I digress again. Both bridges gave and give magnificent views of the busy business happening on the great river Niger below. A fantastic kaleidoscope of African life by the river – boats, nets, fishing, washing, eating, and generally having a nice time despite the heat and poverty.

My visits were basically pastoral, in the sense that the British residents needed to feel wanted and cherished and loved by their Embassy in Dakar. The visits were organised by our Honorary Consuls which consisted of tours of the city and river. And lunches and dinners. Unfortunately, the national dish of Mali is Maafe – a groundnut stew. Not for me, I am afraid. There was also lots of rice or millet or couscous (the Arabic influence from the North) – again, not for me. Some foreign foods I can go for, others I would rather poke red-hot needles under my fingernails. In Mali, I stuck with the river fish and French fries – good old fish and chips.

Not much to report from these visits to Mali, but there is an interesting little footnote for history. Whilst mooching about in the basement of the residence in Dakar, I came across a sign concerning one Major Alexander Gordon Laing. A little bit of research and I ascertained that Major Laing was the first European to reach Timbuktu by the North/South route. The sign in the basement detailed his short stay in Timbuktu and was originally attached to his house there. But I'm getting ahead of myself.

En route to Timbuktu, in Tripoli, Major Laing married the British Consul's daughter. The world is small, and it gets smaller. Major Laing's journey was funded by one Joseph Banks, then President of the African Society, and later on it was (Sir) Joseph Banks who supported one Captain Bligh; and one of Captain Bligh's sailings resulted in a certain mutiny. That mutiny led to the rediscovery of Pitcairn Island – an island that was to become a key chapter (literally) in my life. Destiny or fate or coincidence, who knows?

But for now, back to the sign in the basement (sounds like a Sir Arthur Conan Doyle Sherlock Holmes mystery). For whatever reason, this sign, obviously, was no longer attached to Major Laing's house in Timbuktu. A few conversations with the Ambassador and a plot was hatched. If memory serves me correctly, he paid an official visit to Timbuktu and duly returned the sign to the Timbuktu authorities.

In writing this piece, I have looked on the internet at the sign on the photo of Major Laing's house in Timbuktu and I am ninety-nine per cent certain it is the one I found in Dakar British Embassy Residence basement many moons ago. If you visit, say hello from me.

Time flew in this Francophone corner of West Africa, and so after three happy years, it was time to leave. Throughout my tour, I had a very close friend and I am much indebted for that companionship.

Just prior to leaving Dakar, I had just been informed that, subject to acceptance by the current Ambassador in Lithuania, I was off to Vilnius, as the Deputy Head of Mission.

Temporary Duty: The Seychelles

Well, one does not get many better jobs than this. As described elsewhere, the FCO quite often needs officers who are between postings, between jobs, on leave, in rehab, or on bail (only joking!) to cover absences or special events overseas where the current staff allocation cannot cope. I was awaiting confirmation of my posting to Vilnius and, whilst having a quiet pint in my local pub in Deal, the great New Inn, the Landlord informed me that my Mum had telephoned to say that the FCO wanted to speak to me quite urgently (this was a Friday – unusual for anything urgent to be needed on a Friday, especially after the all-day opening of pubs). The Landlord kindly offered me the use of his private telephone in his upstairs private home. I accepted with some trepidation – the last time this had happened (same pub, same Landlord) I ended up in Baghdad during the Iran/Iraq war over Christmas 1986… a time when I was expected to be with my future first wife and future mother-in-law. However, as that marriage did not last long, with hindsight, the experience of a war zone was preferable to that Christmas with my future first mother-in-law… no more to say on that!

Anyway, as I say, with some trepidation, but not spilling the pint that was still in my hand, I telephoned the number that I had gotten from my Mum. I actually did not catch the name of the person or the department from whoever had picked up the phone at the FCO end (no one does that any more for fear of having to take responsibility for their words, but that is another matter). All I heard was that I was being asked if I could be at Gatwick on Sunday evening – but they could not tell me why on the open line. I was informed that I did not need a visa and could I, kindly and as soon as possible, get out of the pub (my Mum had explained to the Personnel people that they could usually find me in the New Inn on any given day whilst on leave or hiding from a temporary job in the FCO in London!). The FCO wanted to see me pronto for a briefing.

At this point, I said rather hesitantly that I would be delighted to help out, but that I had not heard my destination. Somewhat irked, the Desk Officer for the Seychelles said I was needed in Victoria (capital of the Seychelles) rather rapidly and that I could expect to be away for about ten weeks. He continued (still irked, but now well and truly so) that if I had a problem with that, he assured me that there were plenty of others who might just, without hesitation, deviation or repetition of the country, throw their passports into the ring.

I needed no further convincing. Later, I found out that his irritation was not due to my lack of hearing or the fact that I was in the pub and he was not. It was simply that he had applied for this temporary duty and had not got it. I was the better person for the job; not sure how that happened, but I am not going to complain now.

So I appeared on a late Friday afternoon in King Charles Street to be told that HRH the Duchess of Kent was going to make an official visit to the Seychelles in early December 1993. I was needed to help with the on-island arrangements. I was told that I would be needed for the legwork, checking venues, routes and the other islands that HRH the Duchess would be visiting during her four-day official visit. I would be put up in a hotel for the ten weeks with the option of moving into a self-catering apartment if I so wished. Well, say no more, ten weeks in the Seychelles! The possibility that all or part of it would be in a beachfront hotel, visiting places other people would pay a fortune to visit, and seeing some of the most spectacular turquoise blue waters and white sands on the planet meant that, for obvious reasons, I was completely sold on the idea.

At the FCO, I was briefed that the visit was in recognition of a recent return to multi-party democracy in the Seychelles. At that time, the visit and the details of the visit were 'Confidential'. That was it. All I had to do was pack, get to Gatwick Airport on Sunday evening, where a ticket to the Seychelles would be awaiting my arrival, and I would be in Paradise Island the following morning! My then girlfriend was none too pleased, but, hey, sacrifices for Queen and country had to be made now and again and so I ignored her pleas to stay with her and not go.

I had now been in the FCO for some fifteen years, with three substantive postings (Belgium, Bangladesh and Senegal) behind me and three temporary duties (Jeddah, Baghdad and Geneva) to add to my travelogue. Whilst I was not as well travelled as other colleagues at that time, I would, by 2016, have a significant list of substantive postings, temporary duties and official visits under my belt. Such travels in today's modern FCO are probably a thing of the past (as am I), but again I digress.

One point about travelling that I learnt through bitter experience was that air travel is much more enjoyable when not talking to someone you do not know and with whom one, invariably, has nothing in common but a ticket on the same aircraft. I had at this early stage of my career developed my defences against unwanted conversation from the next seat. My first (there will be others if the reader can bear to keep going) was to say that I was an international undertaker going to collect a body for a client. That one worked on numerous occasions, and did so for this twelve-hour overnight flight to the Seychelles.

On arrival in Victoria, I disembarked, tired but enthusiastic. I, with many others, made my way across the blue sky covered tarmac towards the immigration/arrivals hall. As I made my way forward, a serious-looking gentleman with a serious amount of gold embroidery on his equally serious uniform stopped me and said something like, "Welcome to the Seychelles, Mr Lynch! We are very much looking forward to your visit and the visit of our special guest. I will guide you through immigration and customs and outside the High Commission has provided a car and a driver to take you to your hotel. The High Commissioner has left you a note in the car with some practical advice – he would like you to rest and be prepared for the High Commission tomorrow morning."

After exchanging further pleasantries, I, in front of everyone else on that flight, cleared immigration and collected my suitcase for my ten-week holiday (sorry, I meant to say for my ten-week intensive work-driven temporary duty, organising a serious high-level visit, which would forever and a day cement UK/Seychellois relations). Just before departing for my hotel, I gently enquired of my greeter how he had recognised me and was he aware that the imminent VIP visit was 'confidential'. On the first, he gently turned me around to look at my fellow travellers: they all had quite clearly, before landing, changed into shorts, T-shirts, sunglasses, flip-flops and hats. My grey pinstriped suit, white shirt and tie clearly gave the game away that I was not in the Seychelles for a two-week holiday. On the second question, he merely said that nothing was a secret on Mahe – everyone knew there was an imminent visit by a member of the British Royal family!

So to a day's rest in a very nice hotel on the North West coast of Mahe about a fifteen-minute lovely drive from the capital, Victoria. However, rest is not in the thinking of those of us in Her Majesty's Diplomatic Service, oh no! For work reasons (and having, for once, managed four hours sleep on the flight over), I decided that I should check out the beach, the hotel restaurants and bars. I also managed to reconnoitre the clear blue water – a good spot for snorkelling – a wood-fired pizza restaurant and clambered over some of the amazing granite boulders littering the beaches of the Seychelles. All in a day's work for the imminent VIP visit – even though, as yet, I was unaware of the actual details of the visit. But a good initiative, I thought!

The following morning, I duly reported for duty at the High Commission. The High Commissioner (HC) and his small team were all splendid and very welcoming. Apart from the HC from the UK, there was the Deputy High Commissioner (DHC) and a Registrar. All good people and, of course, there were Local Staff: the backbone of the FCO the world over (I do mean that – not just because, later in life, I was to marry a member of the locally engaged staff in a future Posting – I bet the suspense is killing you!).

Suffice to say, we covered my own administration arrangements – the main one being that I (not the taxpayer, but me personally) could save money if I wanted to move into a self-catering apartment, cook for myself, do my own cleaning and washing. Apparently, it was quite lucrative and other officers who had been sent out to cover leave absences jumped at the chance of saving a few pounds to spend back in England. Not me. No contest. When, in my life, would I get to stay in a five-star hotel in the Seychelles, where my food was served in one of three restaurants, my room was cleaned and made up every day and, for an extra small fee, my washing was done twice a week? And within a few feet of my room some of the best beaches, snorkelling and scuba diving in the world. As I say – no contest. Of course, this very generous system no longer exists, but it did then.

And so to the visit of HRH. The Duchess of Kent would visit the main island of Mahe (various meetings and receptions) and two other 'big' islands – La Digue and Praslin. One visit was to be to the small island of Aride to see one of the (then and probably now) rarest birds on the earth – the non-flying Seychelles Magpie-Robin.

Two weeks after my arrival, there would be a reconnoitre visit (recce) by HRH's detective and then, in early December, it would be the real McCoy. During the actual visit, HRH would be accompanied by three household staff and the detective. My main job, apart from the pre-visit preparations, was to be one step ahead of the official party to ensure all was shipshape for the arrival of the guest of honour. 'Why?' you might ask. Well, the Seychellois, wonderful people that they are, are quite laid-back – even when Royalty is about. But, never fear, the FCO was here and I would have it all under control. Famous last words!

I settled into the hotel very well. All the staff knew what I was doing in the Seychelles. The recce visit went well. The detective, perhaps in a moment of weakness or in a moment after several glasses of Seybrew lager – the beer of choice in the Seychelles – thought that I should learn how to scuba dive. He logically deduced that, in the unlikely event that we dropped something into the clear blue Indian Ocean that only a UK-based member of staff could and should retrieve (I think he was talking about his gun), I should be the one to do it. I could not have agreed more. Quite rightly, Her Majesty's Treasury baulked at the idea that my scuba course should be paid from the public purse. But, above and beyond the call of duty, I paid for the course myself and eventually left the Seychelles with my Open Water PADI certificate – not just that, but the lifelong memories of some of the most amazing and colourful underwater sights of my life – coral gardens, octopuses, turtles, sharks and other fish of all shapes, colours and sizes. And I did not have to dive for a misplaced Diplomatic Protection Group issued sidearm.

Visits such as these are meticulously planned, right down to the very last detail long before the VIP steps off the plane. And as we waited for the appointed day for the arrival of our VIP, I helped out in the Consular and Passport section. On one bright blue, frangipanied morning (they all seemed like that – it was autumn in England and so I was not going to complain) a middle-aged couple from my hotel came to High Commission; they had lost their passports – they might have been stolen but that would have been unusual in the Seychelles. Our job was to issue new passports. We did the usual checks and bureaucratic procedures and I had the passports ready in forty-eight hours. Rather than call them into the High Commission, I once again went beyond the call of duty and delivered them personally to the hotel reception. It was on the way to my room. No effort spared there.

That evening, as I was enjoying dinner, on my happy lonesome as usual, the couple who had lost their passports delicately approached me and, as a sign of their gratitude, invited me after dinner to join them and their daughter and soon to be son-in-law for a drink at the bar. I duly obliged. It turned out that, instead of having a big wedding back in England, there had been some sort of collective decision for the marriage to take place here on the Seychelles. Later, I was to find out that this was somewhat to the annoyance of one part of the four-fold wedding entourage – no point in telling who that person was; I would not like to start an inter-family marital tiff some twenty-five years later. So it came to pass that, after a few convivial drinks in a bar on an island in the middle of the Indian Ocean, I became (not necessarily in this order) a witness to the wedding, the best man, the ring bearer and finally the informal Wedding Organiser-in-Chief. The wedding was in forty-eight hours and the VIP visit in seventy-two – lots to do!

Actually, most of the wedding was prearranged by the travel agent acting on behalf of the wedding party. I was just an unintended add-on, or (as is to be seen) an unintended accident waiting to happen.

The groom-to-be insisted on a stag night. As we did not know anyone, the stag party consisted of two – me and him. We did not have transport and that limited us to the two hotel bars and one beach bar about a hundred yards along the beach. That would have been doable, except that the bride-to-be wanted a hen party (her, her Dad and her Mum – what fun!). The only rule was that the two parties could not meet (it was, after all, the night before the wedding). And so, quite possibly, two of the smallest stag parties in the history of marriage set out, at 1900 hours on the island of Mahe in the Seychelles, for a glorious three bar game of hide and not seek. Prior to this world-shattering revelry, I had detailed separate starting points and 'no-go' times in certain bars, and a no peeking rule. Again this was because of the old tried and tested adage that the bride should not be seen by the groom on the night before the nuptials, but this concept seemed to perplex the would be in-laws. I think they thought I was going to rustle up some hookers and a Seychelles strip-o-gram. I might have done this had I (a) known where to find them and (b) not been organising a Royal VIP visit.

And so a surreal game of stag hide and not seek played out over three bars for three (I must say, for me, long) hours. In the end, it was all pretty much of a non-event. We eventually met up, had coffees and liqueurs in the restaurant and went to bed for the big day – I had to go to work and then be back at 1600 hours for the wedding.

The next day came around too quickly (astronomically impossible, but we shall ignore that). I was late (last-minute hitches with the VIP visit). I had the rings, and when I arrived at the venue, the witness and signature table was, in my humble opinion, not where it should have been. I moved it. The groom demanded a pre-ceremony drink to calm his nerves – taken in full sight of the bride. Not a good start. And so the ceremony commenced until I was asked to produce the rings. Oops! They were in my hotel room. A quick dash and the problem was solved (at least to my satisfaction, but I am not sure everyone else enjoyed standing around with nothing much to do for ten or fifteen minutes – which probably seemed like a lifetime). That part of the ceremony went off without any further hitches.

And so a quick stroll, video going, to the newly located witness and signature table. As the proud couple posed, pen in hands, for the obligatory signature photograph, a small rogue wave trundled very nicely under the chair and knocked over the table. In the groom's haste to save the signature book, he knocked his bride into about a foot of clear blue Indian Ocean. He grabbed her, I grabbed the book. As the bedraggled bride was comforted, dried and placated by her new husband, the travel agent who was appointed as the Seychellois Master of Ceremonies was holding an immediate inquest as to which idiot had moved the table: the father-in-law was heading to the bar whilst his wife grabbed the nearest waiter, who happened to have a tray of drinks (not for us). After consuming the aforementioned hijacked drinks and some soothing words from the hotel management, all round became calm again. The Master of Ceremonies was still trying to track down the table-moving culprit.

The wedding party was flying out the next day and I would be tied up with the visit. Early in the evening, we exchanged addresses and agreed to meet up in England. I never heard from them again.

The next day was the Royal visit. I would like to say that this all passed off with the usual FCO brilliant efficiency – no hitches, no blemishes and a visit that cemented UK/Seychelles relations well into the 21st Century – it probably did and continues to do so. And I have no doubt that it is so described in Foreign Office reporting. But, on the other hand…

The island of Mahe is small, the roads are narrow and speed limits deliberately set at between twenty-five and forty mph. Often, it should have been much slower than this. Prior to the arrival of HRH the Duchess of Kent, we (as in me) stressed that, when travelling in the Seychelles, there would be absolutely no need for flashing blue lights, roadblocking, overtaking everything that moved, mowing down innocent humans and animals in high-speed cavalcades similar to those of unelected Heads of State desperate not to meet 'their people'. So on the appointed day, we met the Royal team and departed the airport with everyone accounted for, and the visit starting in earnest. I was in the lead car of a convoy of five vehicles as we sedately left the airport. Imagine my surprise then as my car was overtaken by a cavalcade of flashing blue lights, outriders and cars, all breaking the speed limits, mowing down humans and animals and generally ignoring everything about sedate and safe travelling. Still, we made it to the hotel.

The first order of the day was a private lunch with HRH, the High Commissioner, the Lady-in-Waiting and me. We had already greeted the Household team and welcomed back the detective. We briefed HRH on the visit programme, diplomatically ignoring the chaos already caused by the Seychellois drivers.

On that first afternoon and evening there were meetings, an evening reception where, brilliantly, HRH kicked off her shoes and joined in with the impromptu dancing that tends to happen in this happy part of the world. Talking of happiness, time and timetables are not issues in the Seychelles. And why should they be? An idyllic island in the middle of the turquoise blue Indian Ocean, palm trees, beaches to die for, fish to die for you, rice, coconuts, the very suggestive coco-de-mer and giant tortoises. The list goes on. The real world is another place far far away. And so, two hours after the scheduled end of the evening programme, we managed to get HRH back to her hotel and we all prepared for the next three days of meetings, island-hoping, lunches, photo opportunities and the search for the elusive Seychelles Magpie-Robin.

Even though the Duchess of Kent was somewhat removed from immediate accession to the throne, in the event of something happening to the nuclear Royal family, Royal protocol dictated that Royal blood was always on hand in the event of a ghastly accident happening to HRH. This was kept in a medical cool box. And wherever we went, it went – carried by either me or a member of the Royal Household. This was not a problem until we were into our second visit to one of the inner islands, which was to be reached from another island.

To get to that island, we had been in a very nice plane and now had to get to a very nice boat moored in a very nice inlet and thence onward to the island of our destination. During the recce, nature had conspired to bring us to that inlet during low tide. That basically meant a short walk in ankle deep water, where we would board the boat, be pushed off and head to another island. No problem – everyone had been advised that they might have to remove footwear or wear flip-flops or something similar. On arrival at our first island, the tide was in, which meant that the water was, instead of two to three inches deep, about two or three feet deep. There did not appear to be any little boats to get us (or more importantly HRH) out to our launch. HRH again, as with the previous night's dancing, was un-phased and headed out, not worrying about getting herself or her resplendent dress wet – despite a member of the team going above and beyond the call of duty and offering a piggyback, which was politely declined.

We, the support team, on the other hand, had to manage the paperwork, the very nice islanders who wanted photographs, the local security detail and the cool box containing the – untainted by the great unwashed – Royal blood. Our detective was having to think about where he could now move his gun, from where it was going to get wet to where he could easily reach it if it was needed (of course, the risk of any threat here was a million to one).

So whilst we were organising all this and ensuring that HRH was in good order (as mentioned above, HRH had gamely headed into the water and was nearly aboard our transportation to find the elusive Seychelles Magpie-Robin), we were arranging who was going to carry the shoes and keep the various visit papers from getting wet while, at the same time, politely wading towards our boat and trying to keep sightseers away. All in all, we did a good job, with one quite important omission. We failed to notice that the 'blood box' had decided to quietly float out to sea in the direction of – if my geography was correct – Jakarta, some thousands of miles away. And so, with a quiet wave of the hand, one of our party deftly moved into crawl mode and ploughed through the non-existent waves and collected the priceless plasma. Here was another piece of priceless British ingenuity; the rescuer of the Royal blood adroitly headed for the launch, pushing the cool box in front, and soon the precious cargo was aboard, we were aboard, the gun was aboard, but none of us was bored. Quite the opposite.

On Aride, the island where we had all been assured the elusive Seychelles Magpie-Robin could be found, we regrouped. I was pondering how our hosts could be so sure that, after all our efforts to get to Aride, we would not all be massively disappointed and not see the elusive bird. But we were all reassured by impeccable logic: some ten pairs of the birds had been moved here for their preservation. They had been moved to this particular island because, many moons ago, rat-bringing humans had arrived on the various Seychellois islands and their rat friends had fled from the dirty confines of their ships to the bounty of these pristine islands. Once there, they started to breed rapidly and colonise the erstwhile human, rat-free habitats of the birds. Pre-rat times, the birds had no natural predators on the ground and so had no need to fly – isn't nature wonderful – except for when we intruded. Rats eat bird eggs and probably would have eaten flightless birds as well. Aride was and still is a rat-free safe haven. Do not take your pet rat there – ever.

The island is small and there are few, if any, places to hide. Our quarry was bound to be found. I suspect that, if our quarry knew that they would be the subject of much cooing, photos and intelligent observations, such as "aren't we humans awful?", there would have been the fastest evolutionary change in history. The hitherto flightless Seychelles Magpie-Robin would have immediately (not waiting for evolution to kick in) relearnt to use its dormant wings and headed for some other uninhabited, far off predator-free island (Pitcairn springs to mind – but there are rats and humans there – not necessarily in that order).

But back to the hunt, sorry, the matter in hand. Our hosts (the Seychellois conservation people) lead our party very quietly and very precisely through the undergrowth and after thirty minutes, we were privileged to come across a pair of the birds. I am afraid the cynic in me believes that they had been rounded up from elsewhere that morning and planted directly in our path just minutes before we came across them. But, my cynicism aside, it was a rare and wonderful privilege to see these rare feathered friends.

And so the visit went on for the next two days without many more hitches. The timetable was always being altered and everything was now on Seychelles time. That is not late: on the Seychelles, being late is our (FCO) concept. On the Seychelles, time is measured in daylight hours, fishing hours, eating hours, relaxing hours (lots of those) and not by looking at clocks and watches. Not a bad way of living, except if you have a plane to catch. But then why would a Seychellois want to catch a plane? And to be honest, after the first day, the whole group was pretty relaxed about time, unlike some other visits I have been involved with. Say no more.

On the eve of departure, after ensuring that the VIPS (HRH, Her Majesty's Representative the High Commissioner and the Lady-in-Waiting) had safely retired, the remainder of the Royal team (including myself) retired to the bar and then, for good measure, we all went for a midnight swim at a nearby private beach. The turquoise warm water was lit up by a full moon, the beach enclosed by million-year-old massive granite boulders, and there was chilled white wine and Seychelles beers cooling on the whiter than white sand. Not a bad way to end ten weeks of work.

The visit itself was a success (although you will never hear of an overseas visit run by the FCO not being a success). And I do mean that. It was a privilege for me working with great people and getting ten weeks in the Seychelles – well, you do not get that in many jobs! And, of course, I should note that I am a Roman Catholic and that, soon after the visit, the Duchess of Kent converted to Catholicism (and thus lost her position in the succession ladder). Was it something I said?

Finally, on this small chapter of FCO life, our High Commissioner kindly informed me that my next posting had now been confirmed by the powers that be – two Ambassadors, the outgoing one and the incoming one. After language training in London, I was heading for Vilnius, Lithuania. Good news and it got better. On the return flight to London from the Seychelles, I was upgraded to First Class.

Part Six

London/Lithuania

September 1994 – April 1997

Chapter 19

London: Learning Lithuanian

The job in Lithuania was as Deputy Head of Mission (DHM). Our Embassy in Vilnius was a two-British-diplomat post, me and the Ambassador (who was my Head of Chancery in Dhaka, Bangladesh). In those days, all Ambassadors had the right to accept or refuse their deputies. Michael (a great man, no longer with us) seemed to take his time accepting me. I am not surprised after Bangladesh! But accept me, he did. However, as we were only going to be together for three months, he ran my CV past his successor. Accepted by two Ambassadors, what were they thinking of? And three years later, both would come to my home (now with wife and child – my wife and child, I hasten to add) to bid me and Leone and Benny farewell. But I am jumping ahead of myself by some three years.

As DHM, I would basically run the Embassy, jack of all trades and master of none. I was to be Head of Commercial Section, Head of Press and Public Affairs, Head of Administration, Entry Clearance Officer and Entry Clearance Manager (not visas again!!), Acting Ambassador when he was on leave, and Acting the Fool when I could.

After various London-based briefings, covering all aspects of Embassy work, I started full-time Lithuanian language training in February 1994. Shifting from almost daily use of French in Senegal (as well as some use in the Seychelles) was difficult; attempting to speak Lithuanian with a French accent and French words is not to be recommended. My (first) teacher was a kind young lady who worked me hard – homework, tests, more homework and more tests.

To get my pronunciation correct, I had a small mirror which I had to hold up on every possible occasion, so that it reflected my open mouth and I could see how to position my tongue to the back of my front teeth and say 'R' like a drunk Glaswegian at three o'clock in the morning. On the commuter trains, this attempt at enunciating correctly some words from Europe's most archaic Indo-European language attracted lots of looks; ranging from utter disgust through to looks that said that this poor young man needs help, needs serious professional help. To date (2018), every Lithuanian I know will tell you that I am incapable of rolling my 'r' the way they do. Well, to be honest, I do not carrrrrrrre anymore.

I was due to get to Lithuania by September (1994) and the expectation was that I would have at least reached A-level standard by then. To prove that it had not been a complete waste of my time and taxpayers money, I would be expected to sit (and pass) the FCO Lithuanian Intermediate exam – translations from English to Lithuanian and vice versa, writing in Lithuanian, summarising a piece from the Lithuanian press, and an oral exam. And I would get paid a nice 'Language Allowance' if I passed the exam. Knowing this, I did try my best – unusual for me, but money talks and if I needed to talk in Lithuanian for money, then who was I to argue?

I did find it difficult. My teacher did not give up and show her exasperation, but nor did she reveal too much about herself when we had a free-ranging conversation. This was 1994, prior to Lithuania being in the EU, and so with my visa hat on, I deduced that my teacher (about twenty-five years old) and on the FCO payroll, was probably living and working in the UK illegally. Oh well, not my problem, but some three months later, I turned up for my lesson and no teacher. I never saw her again.

I then had two more teachers who seemed to be more mature and had, if memory serves me correctly, the correct immigration status to teach me. Slowly but surely, for the next five months, I ploughed through the complicated grammar, vocabulary, syntax, declensions, pronunciations that make up the Lithuanian language. I never would have thought that the two years of Latin that I did at my grammar school would come in useful – believe me, they did.

And so, after the usual round of farewell parties in the pubs of Whitehall, where after several pints of lager, I became fluent in Lithuanian and so conversed with my friends until last orders. My friends will claim that I became incoherent, but that is because of their limited mastery of Europe's most archaic Indo-European language. But at some point, after these splendid farewells, I headed to the airport. I was heading for an amazing little country, nestled between the Baltic Sea, Poland, Latvia, Belarus and the Russian Oblast of Kaliningrad. A little country, with big people, one of whom in particular was to change my life forever; for the good (not that it was particularly bad thus far).

Chapter 20

Lithuania: Power Plants, Prisons and Pharisites

And so it came to pass that, on a bleak grey September morn, I landed at Vilnius airport to start another chapter in my life. As usual, I was met by my predecessor (a friend before my posting to Vilnius and still a good friend to this day), and we had the usual formal handover; lots of handshakes and farewell events for my predecessor. These were combined with welcomes for me, but in reality, as with any handover, these were farewell parties for the officer departing. Unless, of course, one's predecessor has been a complete dickhead. Then the parties, lunches and dinners really are to get rid of your predecessor and welcome you, the new guy or girl, in the hope you will be an improvement. Fortunately, I have never had this problem. I have succeeded very fine people. The reverse might not be true.

A little bit more background on Lithuania before I go into the fun and games of being Deputy Head of Mission in this newly independent country (actually, newly independent again – it gets complicated). It is a country sitting on the shores of the Baltic Sea and is surrounded by countries that had, for whatever reasons, taken exception to its very existence. They had, over the years and centuries, invaded and occupied it. Even the Germans had had a go – they even crossed Poland to get there. But then again, in the 1940s, the Germans were up to no good in a lot of places. If the inhabitants of Gotland had been so minded, I am sure they too would have tried their hand at a quick invasion whilst no one was looking.

As the Soviet Union collapsed, a plethora of countries re-emerged on the world stage. The 'West', if the 'West' still existed, wanted, as usual, to exert its influence on these new countries and so, in the very early 1990s, the UK reopened its Embassy in Vilnius. We wanted to help (also known as getting it under our sphere of influence) and whilst we were hoping that little Lithuania would turn more to the West rather than back to its former master in the East, there were some big diplomatic issues to try to resolve.

The Russians still needed access to their Oblast (an exclave county) Kaliningrad and, even after independence, fully-armed Russian soldiers were travelling across Lithuania in sealed trains (and goodness knows what was inside those sealed carriages, but a good bet was that it was not boxes of Cadbury's Dairy Milk chocolates). That was not good for little Lithuania.

One big diplomatic issue was the big nuclear power station to the North of Vilnius. Nothing wrong with that, one might think, we in the West have nuclear power stations, except that Russia provided the nuclear fuel rods (Lithuania's energy was then 90% dependent on this nuclear power). This gave the former occupying power massive leverage on its West-leaning neighbour and – a minor point I know – the reactor at the Ignalina Nuclear Power Plant (INPP) was an old, unmaintained, leaky, Chernobyl-type reactor. That is, there was the imminent likelihood of a catastrophic disaster. But hey, what was that to us sturdy diplomats of the West? If it was good enough for Chernobyl, it was good enough for us.

The Lithuanians seemed desperate to move from the malign dictatorship of Moscow to the benign (I use that word loosely) dictatorship of Brussels, in the form of the EU and NATO. To get them officially to join the EU and NATO would take time and lots of diplomatic work from NATO and the EU, and lots of undiplomatic attempts by Russia to disrupt that process.

But enough of that big boy policy stuff for the moment. On my arrival at Vilnius, arrangements had been made for me to continue with my Lithuanian language training. There had also been arrangements made for me to visit the Ignalina Nuclear Power Plant but no one, at that time, was willing to impart to me that vital piece of information. I think they were waiting to see how expendable I was – the powers that be would have said amenable, but I think expendable is closer to the truth. More of Ignalina later.

In late 1994, at the start of my posting, I would disappear every afternoon to continue with my Lithuanian language training. At times this consisted of conversations over, quite possibly, the most awful food on the planet. My worst was Plov – which, culturally, was an odd dish in itself. It was Russian. And if the Russians ate it, I could understand their massive consumption of vodka. You needed to be drunk to eat it, or at least you had to be if you were facing the one I had in front of me. It was rice (you may have gathered by now that I do not eat rice!) with a chicken that had seen better days (not much better days, I hasten to add, looking at its skin, meat – I use that term very loosely – and bones. I think the chicken would have actually welcomed its demise as a preference to whatever existence it was having in life). To add to the attraction, the mess was covered in some sort of heart-stopping clot-forming translucent fatty material unknown to the Western world. I managed two bites and then explained (lied) that there was an emergency at work, left, threw up and went for a lie-down.

Other Lithuanian language-learning activities consisted of visiting churches, museums, the University of Vilnius and shops. In 1994, the Vilnius old town, thanks to the Soviet-planned economy, was run down and dilapidated and needed lots of help to bring it back to its former glory. It is magnificent now – worth a visit, but not for stag or hen parties. These I expressly forbid.

Just a quick cultural note on Vilnius University; it is well worth a visit. During one visit, I picked up a brochure which noted that a teacher at the University was one Johann Georg Adam Forster (1754-1794). Nothing special about that... except that young Forster travelled on HMS Resolution during Captain Cook's second voyage of exploration in the Pacific. The Master of HMS Resolution on Captain Cook's third voyage was one Captain Bligh. His argument in 1788 with Fletcher Christian would, some seventeen years later on from 1994, keep me in a job in Pitcairn and Auckland for over five years. A small world – a bit like the church in Brussels. Or was it all destiny leading me to Pitcairn? One has to wonder.

But back to 1994 (maybe that should read 1984). I dragged my teacher into all sorts of courtyards in a desperate search to find a bar so that I could rid my palate of the taste of Plov, or other dishes such as Cepelinai (Zeppelins) or deep-fried bread (with the emphasis on fried). To be fair, the ingredients are much better nowadays and the national dishes are worth a try. The bars I found were old and dirty and the beer awful. Still, the beers and bars are much better nowadays and worth a try. On one occasion, we found a quite presentable restaurant and bar. It was open and the barman and waiting staff appeared to have been waiting all their natural lives for customers. On entering the restaurant, we were told that we needed a reservation. There was no one there. I said, in my best Lithuanian, that we would just like a nice beer at the bar. The reply was less than friendly, saying that the bar was too busy. Again there was no one there and, back in 1994, coach loads of tourists were not descending on the city. I was standing my ground until a Norman Bates-type character appeared and spoke in Russian to my teacher. At that point, she took my arm and we meekly went back out onto the now dark streets of downtown Vilnius. I never found out why we were not allowed in and, believe me, I had been barred from better places than this one.

I passed my Lithuanian language exam. And the time had come to start some real work. I was about to become an expert in nuclear energy. Did you know that nuclear is an anagram of unclear?

It seemed to me that the whole of Her Majesty's government, the EU, the USA, the Atomic Energy Authority in Vienna, my Dad, and practically everyone else bar me, was interested in the Ignalina Nuclear Power Station. And so a visit by a nuclear power plant expert from Vienna was arranged. And I was just the man to accompany him. There were those back in the UK and Vienna who thought that, whilst the expert could do, via an interpreter, the technical stuff, I would give a layman's view of the plant and, with my new command of the Lithuanian language, pick up any snippets whilst our hosts conversed in Lithuanian. There was one big flaw in that idea. As we quickly discovered at the plant, everyone spoke in Russian. Russians 1 the West 0.

The plant, as I recall, was on its last legs. Bits of plaster were literally falling off everywhere; the radiation protective uniforms we had to wear had seen better days; people were smoking in the control room; the radiation detector stick (not sure that that is the correct terminology) occasionally bleeped and went red but no one took any notice. And finally, we were honoured to be able to stand on top of the reactor itself. Well, I have done some things for Queen and country, but that took the biscuit. Many thoughts entered my head. If Ignalina did do a Chernobyl, I would be blown to smithereens and lots of schools and hospitals named after me, but I was not ready for that, nor was I ready to be exposed to lethal doses of uranium or plutonium; in fact, I was wondering what I was doing there in the first place, and why I was being paid a pittance to be there. And to add to my woes, I was wondering if the bad guys on the Russian side were secretly irradiating my testes to ensure that a future line of adventurous British diplomats would not be created to eventually annoy the Russian Bear.

None of the above came true, unless I am ghostwriting this. But I am not. At least, I think not. I could have been blown into a parallel universe, who knows? But even so, it was not all bad. There was a team of Brits working on helping the Russian/Lithuanian Ignalina team prepare for decommissioning (a must for joining the EU). And indeed, I formed a bit of a short but pleasant relationship with a nice

British girl working for that team. Contrary to remarks from friends in Lithuania and England, she did not glow in the dark.

Ignalina is now safely decommissioned and everyone in the region is living happily ever after. Except that next door to the region is Mr Putin. He has nuclear weapons and an inclination to invade sovereign states – Crimea to name but one. The nuclear threat has not totally gone way – it is there but in a different guise. And in 2018, he has been up to no good in Salisbury, England.

That visit was a niche part of the work in Lithuania. The key foreign policy objectives of the former Eastern bloc countries, including the Baltic States and, of course, my own parish of Lithuania, were joining the EU and NATO. Joining NATO will come later. Joining the EU was the first priority (interesting that as I write, the UK is in the middle of leaving the EU). And, of course, it was in the EU's interests that these countries should join the EU in order to form an economic bulwark against Russia and the newly formed Commonwealth of Independent States (the former Soviet Union bar the Baltics). One would have hoped that the Russians would have had the good grace (good sense even) to avoid the use of the word 'Commonwealth' had they known that there were very few things that we in the UK had in common with our Commonwealth, and there was, nor is, nothing wealthy about the whole institution.

To join the EU was pretty simple. All the country in question had to do was to sign on the dotted line on a one-page, plain English and convoluted French document. This document merely said that the aforementioned country would like to join the EU and the EU representatives agreed, signatures were signed and that was that. The country was in and everyone was happy.

No, that was in my dreams and in the dreams of all those wanting to join the exclusive EU club. The reality was that there was (and probably still is) an EU volume of work called the *acquis communautaire*. This was, in 1994, thirty-one chapters containing about 80,000 pages of laws, guidance, rules, recipes, jokes (not many of those), multiple choice questions and paintings by numbers that the applicant country had to abide by, cook, tell and paint and then submit into the EU's massive bureaucratic machine. And then the applicant country had to sit and wait whilst the EU bureaucracy dismantled and quibbled everything that, in our case, the fledgling Lithuanian Ministry of Foreign Affairs had spent years meticulously preparing. And in 2005, after much heart and bureaucratic ache, Lithuania did indeed join the Holy Economic Grail that was the EU. And most of their population scarpered and are resident everywhere bar Lithuania – but mostly in the United Kingdom. And now, in 2018, the UK has a year to extract itself from the *acquis communautaire*; good luck with that.

But back to 1994-1997. In order to help Lithuania join the EU, the EU had set up a fund called the PHARE fund. PHARE is short for "Poland and Hungary Assistance with Restructuring the Economy". So much for everyone else then. But it did later involve the Baltics and others. PHARE, as my fluent French speaking colleague Monsieur Jarrett will tell you, is also French for lighthouse. Lighthouses, by the way, tend to mark dangerous coastlines and other dangerous maritime bits of the sea. Is there a subliminal link here between the EU (and later NATO) and the last bit of the Baltic coast accessible to Russia – that is the Kaliningrad Oblast? A question for the scholars, so we will not dwell on that.

Café des Phares is also a very nice bar on Place de Bastille in Paris. Bastille, by the way, was a fortress originally built to keep the English out of Paris. It is no longer there. Is there a subliminal link between that and the fact that soon the English will no longer be in the EU? Another question for the scholars, so we will not dwell on that one either. But the Café des Phares is well worth a visit.

And so, via funding from the PHARE programme, Lithuania was quickly overrun with EU experts working on restructuring the economy – from planned to unplanned (oops, that should be capitalist). The Lithuanian economy would have been much improved far earlier if the extortionate consultancy fees paid to the so-called experts in banking, finance, energy, city planning, judicial, agricultural, sandwich making and tea-making had gone straight into the Lithuanian Treasury. In my head, I had nicknamed these expensive PHARE consultants the Pharisites (with a silent "h" – no disrespect to those of a similar name that are mentioned in the bible). I wanted to call them the Hittites with a silent "S" but that did not work with the acronym PHARE.

To get our own bit of influence over Lithuania, the UK government created the bilateral 'Know How Fund'. Condescending or what? The Lithuanians, bar the elderly Sovietised generation (and that is a generalisation), were, and are to this day, highly educated, very intelligent, pragmatic, can-do, hard-working, dynamic people – they have a bad taste in national dishes but they can be forgiven for that. Whilst being glad of the EU/UK and other bilateral assistance, they have, over the centuries, got fed up with Johnny (Johannes, Ivan and Janusz) Foreigner telling them what to do and how to do it.

Our Embassy team were not short of a few marbles. All were fluent in English; their university degrees covered almost every possible subject in the Sciences and the Arts. One of the Residence domestic staff (as opposed to the undomesticated staff of the Residence) even had a degree in nuclear fusion or fission, or was it just plain fishing? They were young (still are) and determined to do the best for their country. They were determined that, whilst EU and bilateral funding was helpful and much needed, they would only make use of these funds as long as they needed and wanted them. They were not beggars and certainly did not want to be financially and politically beholden to outsiders. They had had enough of that.

All the team were, and still are, delightful. From the chess-playing Administration Officer to the Ambassador's Personal Assistant (who could almost outdrink me) to Stasys, the man who cleared a path through the snow from my cottage to the Embassy – it was only fifty yards, but when the snow was two or three feet deep, a Herculean task. And Stasys was about a hundred years old. Sadly, he is now no longer with us. The Defence Attaché's Assistant (who also acted as interpreter and translator) was rather nice. Still is. I married her, but more of that later.

My main partner in crime (also known as work) was the young and clever Press and Public Affairs Officer (PPAO) – Mida Babiliene. Mida, her husband and family are still great friends to this day. Alas, rather than getting out and about meeting the people during the very early days of my posting – learning more about the country and culture, briefing the media and other stuff – I seemed to be going backwards: I appeared to be back where I started – in prison.

Two British Nationals had been arrested for allegedly having numerous Russian icons in the back of their van as they avoided a customs post by driving in the woods across the Latvian and Lithuanian border. They had made national news and were about to make national news in the UK. Of course, they were entitled to Consular Assistance and, as Her Majesty's Consul, that would be me. To help me deal with the Lithuanian authorities, I had my trusty sidekick, Mida B. It was not going to be easy. And the Lithuanian jail in Vilnius was a relic from the Soviet era. Not nice, far from it and far from UK penal standards. But the cardinal rule for straightforward foreign prisoners is that their detention should be no worse than that of the local inmates. In the case of the Vilnius central prison, the black hole of Calcutta might have been preferable. But I thought it unwise to suggest to our prisoners, or the Lithuanian prison authorities, a prison transfer to Calcutta.

After months of fruitless pleas for bail, by independent lawyers, not the FCO, our fellow Brits were eventually allowed bail in the country. That was awkward as I was the only other English person they knew and they delighted in turning up at my favourite bar pretending to be visiting British businessmen (I suppose technically they were). As the conversations developed, my friends would be telling them to watch out as there were already two British businessmen in jail. And that the jails were far from nice. Invariably, this meant that my two 'friends' left pretty quickly. Eventually, the court ruled that our two friends could travel to England whilst on bail. I never heard if they returned to face trial. Probably not.

Chapter 21

Marriage, Mother-in-Law and Dressing Father-in-Law

A lot of Embassies and High Commissions nowadays have 'Away Days' to help team bonding, thus making them more productive. I seem to have taken this practice to its ultimate conclusion.

It was New Year's Eve 1995/1996 and most of the Lithuanian staff were heading to a remote farmhouse in the middle of the coldest place in Lithuania to celebrate the New Year. There would be music, beer, wine and vodka. There would be a sauna, deep snow and singing and dancing. I was invited and could hardly say no – I had no other plans. And so, on the afternoon of 31st December, at the tender age of thirty-eight and two days, I headed out to a place called Varena. And it was cold. Very, very cold – minus twenty centigrade. And there did not seem to be too many bedrooms and the loo was outside. I decided there and then to refrain from using the loo for twenty-four hours.

The party began and, before I knew it, people were coming out of the sauna in their swimming togs and running around in the deep snow outside. Utter madness and not for this stuck-up diplomat. I sat at the grossly overloaded table and tucked into the (edible) food, Georgian wines and the occasional vodka. Everyone was pleading with me to join in this icy death game. I held out until such a time as the Georgian wine and Lithuanian vodka altered the common sense part of my brain. Before I knew it, I was in the sauna with many others, getting very hot. Beer was poured on the molten rocks to give the place a rather pleasant smell and opposite me, on some sort of sacrificial altar, the Embassy translator was being birched. All pretty normal for Lithuanians on New Year's Eve. For us reserved British people, all pretty abnormal, bordering on insane.

The sauna was getting hotter and hotter. And by biological osmosis, so was I. I feared going outside – it cannot be right to go from about plus sixty-five degrees centigrade to minus thirty-five degrees centigrade in one small step. But yes, I did it. I did it on several occasions, actually, and even ended up standing outside with a nice wine in hand, talking to the birched Embassy translator. As we chatted, it was very nice of her to say that I was the worst boss she had ever worked for. I put this down to the birching, heat, cold and vodka, and ignored it. Eventually, we had a stroll in the three feet deep snow, I stroked her hair and it was frozen. As friends, we went back in, but I declined being birched – not for me, at least not on our first short outing. Especially after the remark about my staff management skills – I could see revenge coming a mile away.

New Year came and went and needing sleep, I found myself huddled up on a sofa next to Leone, the lady formerly known as the birched one. We were now on first-name terms.

Early the following morning, once the frozen diesel in my car had been melted with the aid of a hairdryer, we headed back to the normality of Vilnius and an inside loo. In early January, I started to date Leone and, after a whirlwind romance, we married on 18th May 1996. Benny was born on 22nd November 1996. And we are still happily married to this day.

But I get ahead of myself; prior to marriage, I had to meet the parents and prospective brother-in-law (one brother was in the USA and we would not meet until 2002). We duly travelled to Leone's hometown, Baisogala (which, roughly translated, means 'worst place'), where I asked her father for his daughter's hand in marriage. He said yes very quickly, very quickly indeed. We then had a very pleasant afternoon where I diplomatically tried to avoid the range of Lithuanian snacks carefully prepared for my arrival.

There was only one minor glitch in the coming nuptials. Lithuania is a Catholic country. I am a Catholic and so is Leone. And so was the Archbishop of Vilnius. Because of my previous (short) marriage, he would not allow us to marry in the Cathedral, or any other Catholic church for that matter. *Not very Christian*, I thought. Later, in our next posting, I worked for a direct descendant of a Catholic Saint – the martyred Saint (Sir) Thomas More. We related our story to him and he contacted the Pope's senior legal advisor (hard to believe I know, but true) who advised us that under canon law (internal Catholic laws) my first marriage did not really happen in the eyes of the Catholic Church and technically we could have married in the Catholic Cathedral. That was history then. But, as we married in the Lithuanian equivalent of a Registry Office (and very nice it was too and a great day too), we could do it now if we so wished. Perhaps one day.

Here, I must tell you about my mother-in-law (she is called Danute). To be politically incorrect, generalising and joking, it is somewhat true to say that most husbands would like to send their mothers-in-law to Siberia. Well, Danute was in Siberia, against her will – courtesy of one Joseph Stalin. Danute has had the last laugh and outlived him by sixty-five years.

Her story began way back in the late 1940s when the Soviets brutally occupied Lithuania. The Lithuanian 'Forest Brothers' were the partisans of occupied Lithuania. They were fighting a rearguard action against the might of the Soviet military machine in Lithuania. Danute was helping them by supplying food and medicines. Without her knowing, one doctor she had approached (whilst she was pretending to be ill, but really getting pharmaceuticals for the partisans) was KGB. He noticed something odd (probably the fact that she was very healthy and not ill) and reported Danute to his superiors and much more nasty people.

Danute was arrested, held and tortured in the infamous KGB building in the centre of Vilnius. Over a thousand people were executed there and thousands more tortured. I have seen the cell where Danute was held, the cell in which she was tortured and the door through which she left Vilnius for a twenty-five-year sentence in Siberia, a place inside the Arctic Circle. A place designed more for death than rehabilitation. It was Danute who showed me around the KGB hell that she had to endure for nearly three months in her early twenties. She is still alive and has forgiven her tormentors. She writes poetry. She has written a book in Lithuanian about her experiences. We could all learn from this great lady.

Leone and I were duly married on 18ᵗʰ May. We had a grand wedding day. Everybody from the Embassy was in attendance. Leone's friends travelled from far and wide. My Mum and Dad and younger brother came from England. The great and the good from Lithuanian society were also there. We had a fine Lithuanian feast that went on until the early hours of the morning; the following day, we headed for a glorious honeymoon in Cyprus – three different venues and a welcoming bottle of Champagne awaited us in each of them. A wedding day and honeymoon always to be remembered. Except, probably, for the Ambassador; if memory serves me correctly, he had over-imbibed and cannot remember much.

Sadly, a little while after our wedding, Leone's father (Benediktas) passed away in our Embassy-provided house. It was late, it was freezing outside and we did not know how to get hold of an undertaker. As a Consul, I had instructions on how to deal with dead British Nationals overseas, but these were not much use in newly re-established Lithuania. Apparently, culture demanded that the main thing to do was to make the deceased presentable. The death was not unexpected and a suit, shoes, shirt and tie had been prepared. Leone was obviously upset, so I and my brother-in-law dressed the corpse as best we could. I am not sure that there is anywhere in the world a training course for dressing the dead. We tried our best to make Benediktas as sartorially elegant as possible and, in so doing so, became quite hot and opened the window onto a cold Lithuanian night.

It was a stressful time for one and all. Leone came to visit her late father and pointed to the open window and said that he (her father) would get cold. Not being a doctor, but with O-level biology, I pointed out that as Benediktas was no longer with us, he would not feel the cold. Losing that particular skirmish, Leone then pointed out that his tie was not straight. Now, putting a tie on a dead man is not an everyday occurrence and it had taken me a great deal of time and exertion (obviously with no help from Benediktas) to tie the perfect double Windsor knot. I am afraid that I then pointed out in my A-level English that Benediktas would not notice. And that if he had noticed, then we should sack the doctor who had confirmed his demise, cancel the undertaker and any other funeral arrangements that might thus far have been made. Suffice to say, we all ended up in tears and Benediktas was later buried with a fine funeral and is probably the best-dressed man in the graveyard.

Time passed and soon my posting (and Leone's life) in Vilnius was sadly coming to an end. Leone's life was not coming to an end – just her time in Vilnius. I just wanted to make that clear. In actual fact, we had managed to create our firstborn – the wonderful Benny (Benediktas), named after his late grandfather; and my Dad, coincidentally, was nicknamed "Benny" after the famous 1930s boxer.

After nearly three years in Vilnius, the overseas adventures continued. This time with me, allegedly, as an adult father and husband, accompanied by Leone, my lovely Lithuanian wife, and six-month-old Benediktas (Benny). We were heading to Riyadh, the capital of the desert Kingdom of Saudi Arabia and the personal fiefdom of King Fahd, the Bridge Builder of the Bamako.

When I received news of the Riyadh posting, I somehow neglected to tell Leone that the Kingdom of Saudi Arabia was probably one of the most restrictive societies on the planet. Pretty important, bearing in mind that her family had struggled, strived and fought for Lithuania's independence from the restrictive yoke of the Soviet Union.

Women were not allowed to drive; they had to wear, when outside the home, the ubiquitous abaya (black cloak, to put it very simply);

they could not travel with a member of the opposite sex unless he was a member of the immediate family; there were no bars, theatres or cinemas. The restaurants (no alcohol, of course) were segregated. The male side was pristine, quite Western. On the family side, families were shut away behind thick drapes and the décor was consistently shabby. All in all, it was not really a society conducive to the females of the species. But why should I bother my new(ish) bride with these trivialities? Benny was OK. He was male and at six months could do anything; even drive, if he wanted.

But a last word on Lithuania and Lithuanians. Many unforgettable memories, but I think what is key to the whole character of the country and its people and turbulent history is the Lithuanian ethos that Lithuania was only ever occupied, never conquered.

Part Seven

Riyadh (Saudi Arabia)

July 1997 – December 2000

Chapter 22

Wine, Work and Panto in the Desert Kingdom

And so it was that we headed out to the desert Kingdom. We were in Business Class on British Airways. One knew when one was getting close to Saudi Arabia; even in Business Class, the drinks trolley and all the drinks were removed thirty minutes before entering Saudi airspace. The majority of the British businessmen (and they were almost a hundred per cent men) in Business Class had, anyway, tried to completely demolish the whole bar and any trolley drinks within reaching distance. No more pubs for them for a while.

On leaving the aircraft, we were met with a wall of very hot air. Welcome to the desert and Riyadh – a city that was (and probably still is) in a permanent competition with Kuwait City and Baghdad for being in *The Guinness Book of Records* as the hottest city on planet Earth. But probably, because of the word 'Guinness', Saudi Arabia does not submit temperature readings.

We went to our new home for the next three years. By way of background, Jeddah used to house the Saudi Foreign Ministry and all the foreign embassies, but back in 1975, the King, in his infinite wisdom, decided that rather than continuing to have his diplomats and the foreign diplomats living by the Red Sea, with a sea breeze, seashore, some of the best scuba diving in the world (apart from the infamous stone fish, of course) and Saudi airspace from the West limited to about twelve miles (and, therefore, more on plane drinking time) – yes, rather than having all that and more – His Royal Highness decided we should all live slap bang in the middle of the desert. And so, by the mid-eighties, over eighty embassies found themselves in the Riyadh Diplomatic Quarter – colloquially the DQ. The DQ was (and probably still is) the size of a small town ten minutes away from downtown Riyadh.

Moving our Embassy from Jeddah to Riyadh was going to cost money, a lot of money, and as usual, HM Treasury was reluctant to pay more than the bare minimum. The Embassy itself was rather grandiose. In its grounds, we had the Ambassadorial Residence, two swimming pools, squash court, tennis court, gym, function hall and last, but from far from least, our very own fully-stocked pub/club (but more of that later). HM Treasury ensured that staff accommodation was purpose-built to exact and exacting standards that matched the grade of the officer – no matter the size of his or her family. So the British estate consisted of streets for the most junior (maximum of two bedrooms) to the 'Counsellors cul-de-sac' – big houses, but not really that big. The house I was about to buy in Deal was bigger and I was far from the rank of Counsellor, very far. As a matter of fact, so far was I from being a Counsellor that I thought they had something to do with fixing broken marriages.

In essence, the British diplomatic housing estate reflected the various socio-economic classes of the United Kingdom. One could not hide from one's low or high status. George Orwell and Aldous Huxley would have loved this place. Karl Marx and Lenin, not so much.

The Embassy consisted of a big commercial section; the sole purpose of this was to sell, from Britain, everything that was needed to live in the vast desert Kingdom of Saudi Arabia... everything bar alcohol, pork products and Bibles – all banned in the Islamic Kingdom. In addition to the commercial section, there was a big defence section; the sole purpose of the defence section was to sell, from Britain, everything that was needed to bomb or beat the shit out of anyone trespassing into Saudi Arabia. Those potential trespassers were, in reality, most of its neighbours. Overseeing these two big sections was the political section, whose sole purpose in life was to ensure that we (every living or dead British citizen) did not offend any (living or dead) rich Saudi citizen, so that they bought anything and everything from our country. All pretty simple – after twenty years, I had worked out diplomacy.

I quickly settled into life in the commercial section. The work was varied and interesting. It enabled me to travel to Jeddah (I saw some old Consulate friends there), the Western Province (and, therefore, a quick nip over to Bahrain for wine with my meal), and to the North to a very conservative town called Buraidah (which is equidistant from the Red Sea to the Arabian Gulf). Here, I had Saudi minders to prevent me, I think, from proselytization. The idea behind these visits was to visit factories, firms and companies in order to persuade them to buy British. It worked; Saudi Arabia, for the UK, was a thriving market and probably still is. In addition to this in-country travel, each year we would make an official visit back to the UK (including

Northern Ireland), linking up British companies and their products to the Saudi companies that needed those products. A travelling salesman really. These UK travels enabled me to get to know my own country better. In Northern Ireland, I passed by my old primary school – which is a lot smaller now. I had single-malt Scotch whisky in Scotland, Aberdeen Angus filet in Aberdeen, Welsh rarebit in the Mumbles in South Wales, got lost in Redruth and discovered that the Bull Ring in Birmingham is not a bullring.

The bosses in Riyadh were all good news and the last two had both attended Eton. I harboured dark thoughts that they planned to turn me into their fag, but no, great guys both. One had reached the dizzy heights of Head of School at Eton (they do not have Head Boy, don't you know) and he had a good friend who was the Pope's lawyer and even, as relayed earlier, interceded on our behalf concerning our Lithuanian registry office wedding.

Whilst I was out working (a term others would say is loose), Leone and Benny quickly adapted to the life of having a maid and a driver. And, on the accommodation front, to be fair, our house was more than adequate for our small family. We were three but soon to be four. Adele was on her way. In the cool season, Leone and Benny were to be found walking (or in Benny's case, being pushed) in the dry riverbed that went through the DQ. Leone was learning how to play tennis. She was, in addition to being a mother, tennis player, and a great hostess, a superb supporter of yours truly in my quest to be salesperson of the year – which was never achieved. Leone eventually joined the visa section, which would stand her in good stead for future employment in Ghana and her adopted hometown of sunny Deal.

Apart from the embassy bar, pool, tennis and squash (I did not go to the gym), there was not a lot else to do. But one thing one should never do in HM Diplomatic Service is to volunteer for anything, anything at all. I did. A big mistake.

The club was on diplomatic premises and, with the knowledge of the Saudi Authorities, but probably not their blessing, we had alcohol. A lot of alcohol. Alcohol that was worth a lot of money on the Saudi black market. Other diplomatic missions, who shall remain nameless, partially funded their running costs from illegally selling alcohol. But not us Brits. Individually, we had our quotas, carefully monitored by management. The bar stock was also very carefully controlled. On the club committee was an 'Alcohol Officer'. His or her job was to keep an eye on stocks. Unfortunately, prior to our arrival, the Alcohol Officer had taken his job literally and not only kept a close eye on the stock but also kept his liver in work by consuming large amounts of the stock, so much so that the books were in a mess, the stock was in a mess and he was in a mess. He went back to London to dry out – funny, is it not, that we sent an alcoholic away from a place where alcohol is banned to a place that gave birth to Public Houses, where anything from shandy to meths is widely available? Yes, I know pubs do not, or at least should not, sell methylated spirits, but you have not been to a very dodgy pub just on the outskirts of Dumfries.

In the absence of the alcoholic Alcohol Officer, I volunteered to become the aforementioned Alcohol Officer. My wife Leone, how she did laugh. But within a few months, the bar was shipshape – a ship in a desert. Although later on I was nearly lynched as I had under-ordered and the club was down to its last bottle of alcohol – Bailey's Irish Cream, if I recall correctly. I drank that to dull the pain of the retribution I would receive from diplomatic colleagues who enjoyed the odd lager after a hard day's work. However, two things happened; firstly, the container arrived in the nick of time and secondly, since that cliffhanger, I have never been able to drink or even smell Bailey's Irish Cream.

With a paucity of other things to do, the social life and pastimes consisted of socialising around the pool (both table and swimming), dinner parties, sports, pantomimes, camping in the desert, going to Bahrain (allegedly, another country, but since it was linked to Saudi Arabia by a giant causeway, it was the world's biggest Public House). But I had developed a favourite pastime: avoiding the non-diplomatic British ex-patriates who only befriend you to get access to real booze. 'False friends', I called them.

There was a thriving illicit brewing industry amongst the ex-pats, but the product made one either blind or fall over very quickly or, indeed, both. One particular brew was called 'Sid', not after Sidney or Sydney, but apparently from the Arabic for 'my friend'. No friend of mine has made me blind or made me fall over very suddenly. Nor, indeed, would I risk five hundred lashes of the Saudi whip just for the odd tipple (or maybe I would). So false friends befriended diplomats in order to have healthy booze and to not become blind and legless on the Saudi homebrew.

The dinner party circuit was hectic and incestuous. Regularly, one would see the same faces at different dinner parties three or four times a month. As if the repetitiveness of seeing work colleagues at work, at the club, at the pool and at dinner parties and lunch parties was not bad enough, all the houses had the same style, and were only marginally different in size, and the furniture everywhere was pretty much identical (thank you, HM Treasury). At times, it really did feel like Groundhog Day.

Leone is an excellent cook and so I was one day despatched to the supermarket to get the necessary for a dinner party. I had my trusty list. We had a delightful menu lined up, finishing up with tiramisu. My wife is a professional, fully-trained, university-graduated interpreter and translator, so I found it rather odd that she should spell macaroni cheese as mascarpone cheese. Never mind – none of us is perfect. Everything, including the macaroni cheese, was duly purchased. Pleased with my efforts, I dropped the shopping at home and headed out for a game of squash. A little while later, the call came through to the club. It was my darling wife asking where the macaroni cheese was. I explained that it was there and, politely, educated her in the fine art of spelling macaroni. At this point, there was an ominous silence. She asked if there was anyone else, preferably sane, in the club. I handed over the phone to her work colleague who, after five seconds, collapsed in a hysterical heap. It did not take long for me to earn the nickname 'the macaroni kid'. I cannot now face either tiramisu or macaroni cheese. And I am banned for life from the kitchen. For those not in the know, tiramisu is not made with macaroni cheese.

Camping in the desert was a great a pastime for many. For me, it was an experience never to be repeated. OK, the dark sky at night, without any light around, was quite magnificent: thousands of stars, satellites, meteor showers and the odd Iraqi missile heading for goodness knows where. But camping itself is most uncomfortable. Firstly, one cannot camp on the sand. The tent poles will not grip, and so the 'desert' is, in actual fact, bits of rock, stone, sand and dirt. Their sole purpose in life is to prevent poles being implanted into the earth, and to make one fall over and very badly cut oneself when one is hundreds of miles away from any medical facilities whatsoever. Once the tent is pitched (and the pitching of many tents has been cited in many less than amicable divorce proceedings), everyone sits around the campfire and sings. Oh, what fun. Some brave souls will have risked the wrath of management by transporting beer to the campsite. At least, this took the edge off a never to be forgotten – and for me, never to be repeated – night of *Ging Gang Goolie*. And do not get me started on the toilet facilities.

I once heard a story that a senior British royal had pitched a tent (to be accurate, probably the senior butler had pitched the tent) in the 'Empty Quarter'; apparently, a really, really big bit of desert in Southern Saudi Arabia. As tents go, I expect it was a good, nice tent, basic but nice – one he could show off to his senior royal Saudi mate, who was on his way and had a reputation as a genuine Bedouin. Imagine our royal's surprise when the genuine Bedouin prince turned up in a forty-ton pantechnicon, inside which were all the modern-day accoutrements needed for camping in the desert: air-conditioning, a spa, double bed, private WC, satellite TV, sofa, mini-library and a mini-bar. That is my type of camping.

Sports days and sporting events were our other main sources of distraction. The annual tennis tournament was one such event – mainly men's doubles and mixed doubles, if I remember correctly. The Ambassador seemed, with a frequency too frequent to be believed, always to get one of the best players as his partner (and the Ambassador was not a bad player himself). We shall leave that thought there.

On one occasion, my wife, Leone, was partnered with probably the number one or number two player in the Embassy. This augured well for the Lynch family. Well, it augured well until her doubles partner went to the well and thoroughly refreshed himself prior to the first game, let alone their first match. However, much to the astonishment and amusement of the crowd, even whilst intoxicated, he could play a blinder (from where the expression 'blind drunk' emanates, methinks). Slowly, the dynamic duo progressed through the rounds, my wife on the tennis court and her partner buying the rounds in the bar. At one stage, he had reached the perfect place of tennis brilliance complimented by alcoholic confidence. However, as most of us know, this alcohol-induced perfect place only lasts until the next round – in this case, both the drinks round and the tennis round. It was bound to happen. On the way to the court, he fell into the swimming pool (shallow end, mercifully), extricated himself, got changed, had another beer, and appeared on court none the worse for wear it seemed to most of us. Although he had moved on from that perfect place of the previous round, in his head he had not. Suffice to say that the Lynch family (in the form of Mrs Lynch) did not, that day or any other day, take home the mixed doubles trophy. Her partner, on the other hand, did win the other mixed doubles trophy – the bar-made mixed doubles.

I cannot let the sports go without a quick reference to cricket, the Brigadier, his bowling and my two black eyes. Two or three times a year, en masse, the Embassy trooped out of the city to a hidden green field gem of a cricket ground. The Saudis do not play cricket and there was a law or by-law that expressly forbade more than eight foreigners hanging out together. Two teams of eleven equals twenty-two and once you add on the spectators, there would be about fifty foreigners breaking the law. But as I say, the cricket ground was nicely tucked away in the desert behind some well-watered palm trees. Of course, it was obvious what the place was, but our kindly hosts turned a blind eye to the idiosyncrasies of the British, Australian, Indian, Sri Lankan and Pakistani nationals – why not let these strange people stand around all day in the blazing sun, with no shade, trying to hit a small red ball into oblivion. And oblivion was nearly where I, rather than the ball, ended up.

Our Defence Attaché, the Brigadier – a great friend I might add – considered himself a demon bowler. But his field placing left much to be desired – not a good sign for a man who, in the event of war, would be in charge of a major tactical unit made up of two or three battalions, consisting of up to 5,000 men. If the Brigadier could not correctly place ten men on a cricket pitch, what hope did the West have in the event of a Russian invasion? Maybe that was why he was in Saudi Arabia? Anyway, on this particular day, I must have annoyed him.

There is a reason why the Sri Lankans are the best one-day cricketers in the world. They are good at it and hit the ball hard. Extremely hard. At the crease was a small wiry Sri Lankan gentleman who looked as if he could play. The Brigadier positioned me, his good friend, in a position which can only be described as an onside gully. In the real world, the real gully has to be constantly on his toes, as at some point in the match the ball will inevitably come towards gully very fast and at the body. In my world, if the Brigadier bowled down the leg side to a small wiry Sri Lankan gentleman who looked as if he could hit the ball hard – extremely hard – my reactions had better be measured in terms of light speed rather than miles per hour. The inevitable did not take long.

The ball hit me on the bridge of my Ray-Bans, knocking me to the ground. Dazed and dazzled, I picked myself up, grabbed the ball and threw it. I know not where I threw it, but I think the opposition got four runs courtesy of my throw.

Within hours, I had two very nice black eyes and within twenty-four hours I was sitting at the all staff Embassy meeting – to be chaired, as usual, by the Ambassador. Oddly, I was the only one wearing sunglasses. Stating the obvious, the meeting was not al fresco. When

Her Britannic Majesty's Ambassador (HMA) commented on my odd attire, I removed my sunglasses and informed him that "the Brigadier did it". Much laughter, mirth and merriment ensued as the Brigadier explained to HMA that he had not, in fact, engaged in fisticuffs with me, but that it was all my fault as I should have caught the ball rather than attempting to head it back to the wicketkeeper. HMA moved the meeting on to some problem with Iraq.

Technically, Christmas and Christianity are banned in Saudi Arabia. But ignoring that minor detail, the highlight of every Christmas in the Riyadh Embassy was the pantomime. To be honest, it was probably the highlight of the year for most people. The Embassy staff put on the panto, not just for us in the Embassy, but also for hundreds of ex-patriate Brits. Our function hall could hold up to four hundred people. There were seven back-to-back evening performances and one matinee for hundreds of children. Tickets sold out within hours. There were even rumours that they were being sold on the black market at four or five times their face value. Some people, and – it has to be said – sad people at that, bought tickets for themselves for every night and the matinee.

As you will have seen from my first posting in Brussels and my attempt at being Cher in the Sonny and Cher duo, I am not averse to the occasional cross-dressing. Someone in management might have noticed this and so my first role in *Mother Goose* was as a humble goose, not a cross-dressing part, not a speaking part and not much of a part at all. However, as with Hollywood, my small part was noticed. Almost comparable, in my eyes at least, to Jack Nicholson's big breakthrough in *Easy Rider*. And the next year, stardom beckoned. No auditions for me, the director begged for my talents. I accepted, perhaps with too much haste, but I was in, not quite top billing but in the top five credits. I got to dress up as the Pink Fairy in *Cinderella*. I am not sure there ever was a Pink Fairy in *Cinderella*, but whatever. This part was a continuity type role; my character had to appear in front of the curtain during the scene and set changes and keep the audience informed of the plots and sub-plots in the Riyadh production of *Cinderella*. Easy, you might think. But I had to do this in verse, alone on stage and dressed in a pink wig, pink blouse, pink shoes, pink hearts on my cheeks (facial) and a pink tutu. All of this in front of a lot of people who knew me as the suited, bespectacled, betrothed family man from the commercial section. And when I say, in verse, I use that term loosely; the example that sticks in my head is:-

"Oh dear, Oh dear, isn't it appallin'
Cinderella has nothing to go to the ball in."

Not exactly a Shakespearean soliloquy, but good enough for me to get a laugh out of the audience every night. Poor souls. As they say on Broadway and Theatreland in London, *Cinderella* could have run and run; and run all the way to Bahrain to get some much-needed libation. But the final curtain fell and soon we were in 1999 and, unbeknownst to me, my second greatest role was in front me – my first was being a brilliant father and husband.

Stepping out of panto-land, let's go back in time momentarily. On 19th January 1998, my daughter, Adele, came into the world. Giving birth in Riyadh was something of a spectator sport. Adele was born in a very good hospital in Riyadh in front of the United Nations. People with varying nationalities all wanted to be at the birth – not sure why. Probably because there is not a lot else to do in Saudi Arabia. But back to the United Nations.

The birth team consisted of Leone, a Lithuanian; the gynaecologist, an Iraqi; the nurse, a Filipina; the doctor, a Syrian. And Leone's friends in attendance were Singaporean, Maltese, Indian, Irish and Sri Lankan. I am pleased to say that all of these wonderful people were at the business end of the birth. I was holding Leone's fevered brow and the hand of a Welsh nurse. I found that Leone giving birth was quite stressful. I am pretty sure she would agree that I need not go through such stress again. And so I have decided that we shall stop at two – the great Benny and Adele. Incidentally, anyone born in Saudi Arabia is immediately a Muslim – some sort of Sharia law that says anyone born in the land of the two Holy Cities of Mecca and Medina must acquire, on pain of beheading, the Muslim faith. I think Adele is and always was non-practising.

Due to other acting commitments in Europe and America over the Christmas period, I was unavailable for the 1999 Riyadh panto season. However, I am sure you will all have read in the *Saudi Gazette*, *Tatler*, *The Broadway News*, *The LA Times*, *Playboy* and *Playgirl*, *The Times Sunday Supplement* and *The Beano* about my extraordinary portrayal of Dame Gertie in *Jack and Beanstalk* in 2000. Never in the history of pantomime has one performance been nominated for so many showbiz awards – the Oscar, the Bafta, the Emmy, the Grammy, the Tony, the Fred and the Dave. Never in the history of pantomime, has one ad-libbed so much, forgot one's lines so frequently, sang so badly and ingeniously changed the face of pantomime forever. From panto to farce-oh. Eight magnificent shows wherein I changed the script at my pleasure, changed my strip seven or eight times a performance and caused the audience to laugh, cry and die at the drop of my wig or the sound of my singing voice. Some were heard to say that they would never see the likes of Dame Gertie again – at least, I think that is what they said. Others tell me it was more like they would never like to see the likes of Dame Gertie again. A big difference.

Our last night in Riyadh was also, literally, my last night on stage. As I bade farewell to my loving fans (many of whom had endearingly waved white handkerchiefs during my award-winning rendition of *Something Good* from the Sound of Music), I knew I had reached the mountaintop of live performance. Silently and with heavy heart, tight bra and thigh-breaking high-heeled boots, I decided to quit the stage. No fanfare.

The following day we left Riyadh. Three fun years behind us. Although there was not much to do in Riyadh itself, the Embassy made its own fun; friends for life were made, Adele was made, there was the usual great spirit of camaraderie and, to this day, we are very much in touch with desert friends who have not deserted each other. Great people. One of whom starred with me in *Jack and the Beanstalk* and is now Head of the Diplomatic Service and will probably ban the publication of this book. Well, obviously not.

Two things happened as we were leaving, my next posting was confirmed – Accra in Ghana – and on boarding the plane, one of my admiring fans shouted, "It's Dame Gertie." The applause out-thundered the Rolls-Royce engines and lifted us up and onto our next escapade.

Part Eight

Accra (Ghana)

April 2001 – May 2004

Chapter 23

Back on the West African Coast: Snakes and Rats

At this point, I believe that our people in the Personnel Department had lost my file and were making up my career as they went along. I certainly was. Accra would be my fourth posting in a row (unheard of – they always liked to get you back to London every six or seven years) and mixed up in that was the horrendous ten weeks in a five-star hotel in the Seychelles.

As my dear friend from the Metropolitan Police described it – this Accra posting was the equivalent to a "three-year stag party!" We shall come on to that. In the meantime, after a short interlude in sunny Deal, we headed to West Africa. It was my second time but now, some eight years after leaving Dakar, here I was now travelling with Leone and two young children… oh, what fun for the other business class travellers!

The job was going to be interesting, I would be First Secretary Trade and Investment (and, by default, third in command of this large High Commission). I would have a team of five to help. As in Saudi Arabia, we were to persuade the Ghanaian business community and the Ghanaian government to buy British goods and services and invest in no other country but the United Kingdom. That all sounded good, but I could see one minor defect – Ghana in the early 21st century was in receipt of both UK and international aid. It was not a rich country and, indeed, was probably a poor country. Surely, it was in the interests of the Ghanaians to export as much as they possibly could to us and to get us to invest in Ghana. But who was I to argue? I suspected, probably much to the annoyance of the aid people, that the work of the Trade and Investment section was to generally find out where the UK and international aid money had gone and get the recipients of those funds to buy British goods. So we gave them money to buy British. I had an idea: why not cut out the middleman and not give the money at all. Instead, it could be given directly to British business. For obvious reasons (I would not have a job in

Ghana), I did not espouse such a thought publicly or even privately. Even, occasionally, I knew when to keep Mum

The High Commission also covered the ex-French colony of Togo. Perhaps there was a secret stash of wealth here that the Trade and Investment team could tap into. But no, Togo was very poor and, anyway, the French had that nano-market tied up.

The High Commission in Accra was pretty much the same model as the one in Dhaka, Bangladesh: it had a huge immigration section (a waiting area that held 400 people daily – all wanting to visit, settle, study, and seek medical treatment in the UK – some of whom were actually going to do that legally). And with the immigration section came, once again, the siege mentality. Alongside this siege mentality came the non-stop Friday afternoon anecdotes detailing the latest implausible reasons why one of our hard-working Entry Clearance Officers had decided not to issue a visa to one of our Ghanaian friends. Unbeknownst to one visa applicant, my Lithuanian wife Leone worked in the visa section.

That particular applicant, rather ingeniously, I thought, claimed to have studied for three years in Vilnius University. Quite possible, of course, but the high street bookies might have offered odds of over 1,000/1. And so the Entry Clearance Officer, following Sir Water Scott's inspiration in *Marmion* ("Oh, what a tangled web we weave... when first we practice to deceive."), let the applicant tell his story of his alleged three years studying in the Baltic state. The ECO eventually asked the question that would define the outcome of the interview. She asked, "Do you speak Lithuanian?" To which the applicant replied, "Yes, very well, thank you." From stage left, my wife duly appeared and had a rather one-sided conversation, in Lithuanian. One-sided because the applicant could neither speak nor understand one word of the language he was hearing. Rather strange, considering that he had spent three years surrounded by the language. The visa was duly refused.

One of the unintended consequences of this particular incident was that many Ghanaian applicants – be they genuine or fraudulent – now believed that the clever British government had trained their visa officers to master numerous languages in order to help with visa applicants who were claiming to have already lived or studied in foreign lands and returned to Ghana (always a positive in any visa application). We did not disabuse anyone of this notion.

In addition to the Immigration Section, there was us in Trade and Investment, the political section (as with Dhaka, there was tension between the immigration section and the politicos), the administration people trying to look after hundreds of locally-engaged Ghanaian staff and twenty or thirty staff from the UK. There was also a Defence Section with a Lt. Colonel and his Warrant Officer. To this day, I am not sure what their role was. It seemed to me that over the years, the British had trained enough – too many – Foreign and Commonwealth soldiers who had gone on to become unelected military dictators. And when that happened, we then spent an inordinate amount of time trying to get rid of them and, at the same time, wondering from whence they had acquired such good military skills and tactics.

Somewhere in downtown Accra, there was the Department of International Development (DFID). We did not see too much of these people. They were the people providing the aid money – we did not see too much of them because, probably, they did not want us to see the luxury in which, allegedly, they lived: large houses with swimming pools. It was not only me that saw the contradiction in HMG employees who were solely in the country to alleviate poverty, but who were at the same time living in accommodation far above their norm back in Blighty, and massively above the norm of the people they were trying to help. I was not advocating that they should live in abject poverty (maybe not a bad idea), but something more modest that might – presentationally, at least – have helped their cause.

In addition to all that British government representation, there was the Club. The usual throwback to the empire. Staffed by Ghanaians dressed in white. A kitchen, large bar, pool table, darts, BBQ and swimming pool. At that time, no members of the Ghanaian or other local staff were allowed to be members (that, rightly, changed during my time in Accra). It was called the 'Grasscutter's Return'. I am not sure who came up with this name. The name has nothing to do with some sort of moving memory of an old High Commissioner's faithful gardener; no, a grasscutter is the Ghanaian name for the Greater Cane Rat. Apparently, it is an edible rat, locally known as 'bushmeat'. A food well known for a series of effects on the body: at best, a temporary satiation of hunger, but more likely severe indigestion and then, much more likely, some very severe tropical diseases, such as Ebola, and then, it is very likely to be responsible for the not so good – actually, the very bad – condition known as death. I never ate a whole one, part of one or a morsel of one. And thus I am alive to tell the tale.

In addition to the joys of the Club and the numerous characters in the High Commission, I took on a beach house about forty minutes to the East of Accra. This was a bolthole where, once or twice a month, the Lynch family, with the late great Karen and Ken Simpson and the still with us Mic Higgins and Caroline Cross (and our combined total of six kids of varying ages), sojourned for a whole Sunday. Here, we hid from the poverty, smells, sweat and begging of the city of Accra. Here, we sat in glorious splendour – well, not that much splendour. When I say 'beach house', try not to think of Richard Branson and his estate on Necker Island. No, our beach house was a small concrete hut, a shower and a loo. A mini terrace with a largish sandy garden leading to an unswimmable rocky beach. But here we sat with our cheese and wine, our beer and sausage rolls, our boules and cribbage board, our sunhats and our kids getting sunburnt. We did this over a period of some twenty-four months until it dawned on me (I am slow at times) that we could do all the same things with the same food in our back gardens in Accra, saving on a designated driver. And so I gave up the beach house.

Later, it dawned on me: what was the point of living abroad? I had a big garden in Deal, I was (still am) half a mile away from the beach, and cheese, wine, beer, sausage rolls, boules and cribbage were in abundance in my hometown (I might have to check on boules). But then again, I thought about life overseas: travel, different countries, different cultures and people; more money, servants, officially-provided cars at times, drivers and more servants. There were the different kinds of food (but not grasscutter) and drinks (but no more vodka after Lithuania), and every three or four years something completely different, all courtesy of the great FCO. No, I was not ready to forsake all that for a few more years. Thank the Lord: Russia, USA, Pitcairn and New Zealand were still ahead of us.

Speaking of travels, as usual, the intrepid Lynch mob covered the country. But not before I had exposed not only my own family, but my Mum, Dad, sister and brother-in-law to the delights of impoverished Africa. Outside of Accra, the villages are basic but there is normally land, a well and crops. And near the coast there is, stating the obvious, the bountiful Atlantic Ocean. In East Accra (the older part of the city), life is not so clever. The population is densely packed and the drains are densely blocked. It was not unusual to see someone gently easing himself (normally a male) over an open sewer. And, by easing, I do not mean delicately climbing across the sewer. There is a myriad of smells, none of them, in my humble opinion, nice – quite revolting, actually. A place to be avoided during the rainy season or, for the squeamish, a place just to be avoided. I took the whole and extended family there. We did not tarry long.

Having survived East Accra, we headed further East, along the original Gold Coast. The Gold Coast has had an interesting multinational history; not only were the British involved but also the Portuguese, the Danes, the Swedes and the Prussians. They should have formed their own mini-European Union. Some of these Europeans built coastal forts ostensibly to trade European trinkets for gold (we were good like that), but later a darker trade evolved – slavery. As with the island of Goree in Senegal, these forts were the last part of Africa that some Africans would ever see. We stopped and paid our respects and drove on courtesy of our Ghanaian driver William, along the narrow potholed roads that were riddled with debris from numerous crashes.

The majority of the crashes were, in my humble opinion, caused by drivers being distracted by the local inhabitants stepping out into the road and waving various wares for sale. These consisted of anything from blue (they always seemed to be blue) plastic buckets to eviscerated grasscutters. The edible grasscutter (a contradiction in terms in my book) had been splayed, the four limbs covering the four Cardinal points of the compass, and then attached to some sort of tennis racket. And then the whole thing was waved in the face of unsuspecting drivers travelling at Mach 1 on a road originally built for cows and carts. Either shock or hunger then caused the driver to crash, eviscerate himself and any innocent bystanders or grasscutter sellers. If the dead grasscutter did not get you to the afterlife earlier than you expected, then the snake in a knot might be more to your taste.

In Ghana and other parts of West Africa can be found the ball python. It probably spent millions of years as the straight python and then humans came and captured it either for food or as a pet (pet snakes: another contradiction in terms). The consequence of the straight python being captured and/or killed after many millennia of minding one's own snake business was that he or she curled up in a ball and hoped for the best. Hence, its modern name: the curled-up-in-a-ball python, shortened to the ball python. Originally, as a defence, the ball python wanted to spit at its protagonists but the spitting cobra said it would sue – he had the patent for spitting snakes. I digress.

On the Gold Coast road, villagers would catch the ball python and tie it in a knot around a long stick and then, if a driver did not much fancy the eviscerated grasscutter, they would leap into the road and wave the ball python in the unsuspecting driver's face and the resulting crash would not be much different from the earlier grasscutter one.

Thankfully, William was a vegetarian and either avoided the snakes and rats of the region or, in a brave effort to save us all from the afterlife, he ran over everyone and everything until we got to the relative safety of Sekondi-Takoradi. Here, we all settled down to some authentic Ghanaian culture, including the purchase of the magnificent everlasting Kente cloth and the largest lobsters I have ever seen, or indeed eaten. We were not far from the Ivory Coast (Cote d'Ivoire for the French purists) border, but there was a serious civil war going on near there so we did not go.

On our way back to Accra, we stopped at a crocodile farm. A note here for parents of young children. Do not stop at a crocodile farm with young children. Ever. That is all I am going to say about that.

Chapter 24

The Great Cultural Escape

Our neighbours in Accra were Mic and Caroline; Caroline was our beloved Consul and Mic, her husband, was on unpaid leave from the Metropolitan Police. One day, it dawned on Inspector Higgins and I that we should get out amongst the local culture to experience the real Ghana, the real Africa. And so, on one Sunday when our wives, unwisely, sent us down to the local shop to pick up some eggs, we kept on walking. And we walked and walked until we deviated from the usual roadside tracks and headed into the bush – scrubland really.

We kept on walking until we came upon a 'Bush restaurant'. After much discussion, including me threatening to commit suicide, we agreed not to have grasscutter and settled instead for another well-known delicacy (well, perhaps only well known in the Ghanaian poverty-enhanced countryside): Ghanaian snails. Not any ordinary snail, I should say, but the giant tiger land snail, a giant air-breathing snail, no less – that begs the question, what else would it breathe? But I shall leave the gastropod experts to mull over that. More importantly, the snails came with chips. Alas, there was no decent dry white 1996 Bordeaux wine – actually, none at all – to further enhance our expedition to widen the knowledge of our taste buds. So we ordered beer. And beer was the only thing that enhanced the knowledge of our taste buds at that particular culinary experience. The snails and chips were delivered on plates that had probably been used during the Great Plague and had not seen hot water since. The forks (no knife) were either of a traditional rustic design from better days gone by or just rusty. Police forensic investigation by Inspector Higgins of the Yard concluded it was the latter. The snails themselves gave the appearance of wanting to better the grasscutter in how many ways they could destroy life in one's intestine or just simply to destroy life. The chips, to put it mildly, had seen better days, probably the days just before the Great Plague.

We did not want to offend our hosts and so quietly tipped our lunch into the bag provided for the eggs. And, in so doing, destroyed a perfectly good shopping bag. We lurched back, shopping bag in hand, to the nearest track and grabbed a bush taxi. The lexicographer in me was starting to note that everything was 'bush' related. Bushmeat, bush restaurants and bush taxis. We headed further into the bush and came upon some sort of bush festival, or what we thought was a bush festival. We paid our driver and asked him if he had had lunch. In response to his negative reply, we offered him the bush bag lunch (including bag). He was delighted and drove off to feed his entire village, leaving us with the impression that we might have over-ordered.

Our bush festival turned out to be a bush funeral. Funerals in Ghana appear to be happy occasions. Not for the corpse, of course. He or she might not have wanted to be where they currently were. More likely, they too wanted to join in the day's festivities, but I suppose that thought is not strictly unique to Ghanaian people. Or, alternatively, Ghanaian funerals might be quite sad, and this particular group of villagers were actually happy that the deceased was precisely that – deceased. Anyway, the village people made us welcome, sold us some cans of Guinness and offered us some rather splendid grasscutter adorned with giant air-breathing snails. *The local equivalent of turf and surf*, we thought. I politely explained (or rather lied), in every language that I knew, that this was a very kind offer but that we had already eaten. We consumed our cans of Guinness, danced with mourners and paid our respects to the deceased.

The deceased was resting in one of the most ornate, unique coffins I have ever seen or probably will ever see. The lid was a cross between ancient Egypt and new age drinking. There was the King Tut mask at the top end and then, halfway down one of the most important and famous sarcophagi in the world, the coffin morphed into the bottom half of a Star beer bottle. Whoever the deceased was, he or she must have been some sort of Living Beer God or Goddess (LBGG). As I say, we paid our respects and bade farewell to our new-found friends. We headed directly to the only five-star hotel for hundreds of miles and had a nice lunch with nice wine, bought some eggs and then returned to our wives, who for reasons known only to themselves, did not talk to us for a week or so. Inspector Higgins of the Yard and I called this day our Great Cultural Day of Escape. It has subsequently become just The Great Escape – nowhere near the great events of the real Great Escape or the great film of the same name. But just the mention of the film or its brilliant soundtrack, or German voices or accents, or sights of German Shepherds (the dogs, not Bavarian herders of sheep) or eggs will send our wives into apoplexy.

Meanwhile, back in the Club, preparations were being made for the obligatory High Commission pantomime. Rumours of my panto fame had reached all corners of the globe, probably not North Korea, but most corners of the globe. Anecdotes, true and false, about my cross-dressing skills were starting to spread throughout the Accra diplomatic community.

The panto director was the Deputy Head of the Immigration Section. Whenever I appeared in either the immigration section or in the club, he would size up my gait, and listen keenly to my enunciation or mentally measure me up for the costume. Or at least I think that was what he was doing. He had been tipped off that I had gone into panto retirement and would take some persuading to get back out on the boards. He went about it in the wrong way. He asked me to audition. I gently reminded him of my previous fame across the Middle East and, in a self-promoting, point making point (which proved to be my West African panto downfall), I emphasised that I, as the Robert De Niro of pantomimes, did not do auditions. I either got the part as the Dame or not. The panto director, a sensitive type, huffed and said that De Niro did not do pantomimes. And that was that.

Diplomatic life in Ghana went on as per normal. The Political Section politicked, the Trade and Investment section tried to trade and seek investment, the Administration Section administered, the Defence Section defended (what, I have no idea), the Immigration Section immigrated. Or, to be grammatically correct, the Immigration Section did not immigrate anywhere. It stayed in one place. And, to be fair, so did most of the Immigration Section's customers.

And, of course, we had the usual round of senior visitors when we all had to be on our best behaviour. Two were outstanding in different ways.

The first visit was by The Right Honourable Baroness Amos (now CH and PC). If memory serves me correctly, Baroness Amos visited Accra in an official capacity at least twice during my three years in Ghana. Once as an FCO Minister and secondly as a Cabinet Minister – Secretary of State for DFID or Leader of the House of Lords, or whatever. It did not matter. I had the privilege of working with her (including lunch, drinks and dinner) on these visits. She was a delight (and, no doubt, still is) to deal with. Professional and personable, she knew her stuff as well as how to engage with people from all walks of life. She had a good sense of humour and took time out at an official diplomatic reception to meet my Mum and Dad, who were visiting. No need to say more, really.

The second outstanding visitor was the biggie; no, not Her Majesty the Queen, but the Right Honourable Anthony Charles Lynton Blair, Prime Minister, instead. He visited in 2002. Part of his one and only Great West African Tour. Or his Temporary Great Escape from his Greatest Critics tour.

As usual, the FCO delivered a Rolls-Royce service for the PM. I was charged with the organisation of his visit out to a cocoa cooperative some ninety minutes' drive out of Accra (the Presidential and Prime Ministerial motorcade did it a lot faster than that).

My part of the visit worked, but we all learnt one lesson from such VIP visits, ignore the Ghanaian Chiefs, through whose land one has to travel at one's peril. That is not to say that it was perilous travelling through the land of a Chief. It probably was centuries ago, but in the 21st century, no matter the dignitary, one had to show courtesy to the Chief (especially Paramount Chiefs), call on him and oblige him with various courtesies and, of course, the obligatory bottle of schnapps. We never discovered the penalty for ignoring paying homage to the Chief, but it was noticeable that even the President of the country could not waive this protocol. Perhaps he would lose votes in the next rigged election or worse, male members of his family would lose the procreative parts of their anatomy. Who knows (this is rhetorical – do not write to me)?

But back to the schnapps. When approaching the Chief, one has to refresh the Gods by pouring onto and into the dusty dry earth of the village a small part of the bottle. But not too much, as the Chief gets to have the bottle and no doubt keeps it in his award-winning collection of schnapps. I have, to this day, no idea why schnapps is the beverage of choice. My suspicions would lead me to suppose the Dutch influence from previous centuries, but who knows? A cold party-eight Heineken would have been much better, not to pour on the ground so much, but to drink afterwards. But Mr Blair came and went. I wonder whatever became of him; hopefully, his demise was partly caused by his decision to decommission The Royal Yacht. But anyway, I preferred Baroness Amos.

It was not all work, visits, cultural exchanges, diplomatic receptions and Brie cheese on the beach. No, there were parties to attend. None more so than an illustrious member of the Diplomatic community whose Christmas parties were the highlight of that particular season. Expatriates from the boondocks were all invited to a massive buffet, free bar and, generally, a very festive time. Alas, on one occasion it all got too much.

I had had another engagement to attend to on this particular party night and so was unavoidably late. My late arrival (along with Leone and Inspector Higgins and Her Majesty's Consul) heralded a scene reminiscent of fans wanting a piece of Kylie Minogue or some other superstar (Kylie, pay me now). As Kylie was not in the neighbourhood (or probably not even in Africa), my first instinct was that this was a massive, uncontrolled attempt to persuade me to audition and play the panto Dame. But, unfortunately, that was not it. The host had had an accident and I, apparently, was now the most senior person at the party and was expected to do something.

Apparently, our host, whom I knew quite well, had fallen into the fridge whilst attempting to reach down for a beer or perhaps a vintage schnapps. In doing so, he had dislocated his shoulder. As described to me, he had then proceeded to climb out, in agony, and when someone tried to help by touching his (as yet undiagnosed) dislocated shoulder, his scream had projected his false teeth onto the perfectly manicured lawn. He had then promptly fainted, or collapsed or died or gone into a coma or plain passed out from his exertions of preparing for the party. Suffice to say, he was not dead, but he was incapacitated and, without his supervision, the party had taken a wild turn for the worse. Wine and spirits were being drunk from the bottle; those that were not being imbibed down throats as fast as possible were being stashed away in handbags, rucksacks, African baskets, holdalls and any other container capable of holding loot for separate Christmas events. The food was heading the same way. And the more ingenious guests were snaffling knives, forks, spoons, table decorations and linen. These expat volunteers were determined that Christmas in their villages, miles away from home and civilisation, would be one to be remembered.

I remembered that Inspector Higgins had a background in Law and Order. I was particularly keen on the Order bit. So he was duly despatched to round-up friendlies already at the party and bring it back to a modicum of sanity. I, in turn, went to another bar far far away. No, I did not. I went to see how our host was coping. When I found him, he seemed to be coping quite well. He was either asleep, passed out, unconscious or in a coma. Not dead, as I could see he was breathing. This was not down to some expert medical training I had done in a previous life, but because I noticed the rhythmic rising and falling of his false teeth perched atop his undulating belly. And I could not help but notice that one of his shoulders was not quite where it should have been. In non-medical parlance, it was about six inches adrift from the ball and socket joint that had been created to keep his shoulders close to the body. And it was at an uncanny angle, a very uncanny angle.

Whilst I stared at this medical conundrum, Inspector Higgins duly brought the party back to order, confiscated the misappropriated beers, wines, furnishings and even some other personal belongings that should have stayed with their rightful owners – but all is fair in West African Christmas Parties that go wrong. He then dutifully entertained the remaining party-goers with his world-famous Elvis impressions (he is currently a singer in residence at the Savoy in London). That hastened their departure.

Meanwhile, I dutifully escorted our injured host to hospital and stayed with him until he threw up over me and the lampstand. The lampstand took it very well. I, on the other hand, decided to leave, without consulting the duty doctors (who had promised me that they would fix his shoulder, re-engage his false teeth and generally get him to a better state of health than the one he was in) to meet my colleagues to conduct, over a few wines, a non-medical post-mortem on the events of that Christmastide night in the tropics.

The Ghana years passed quickly. Leone was happily working in the visa section. So happy that once, when she was working as the cashier, she accepted photocopied money instead of real money. Not a bad idea, I thought. However, shopkeepers in England seemed rather put out when I tried it.

Benny and Adele went to a traditional African school. When it was not raining, the lessons were outside underneath a magnificent Baobab tree (the upside-down tree). It was a tree from prehistoric times, which can live for over a thousand years. Adele came back to England with a Ghanaian accent – odd for a white, half-Lithuanian, quarter-English, quarter-Irish blonde-haired girl who was born in Saudi Arabia. Benny came back with lots of Ghanaian souvenirs, including a real bow and arrow. I had bought it thinking it was a toy, but it was real and is now safely stored in the loft. But if needed, it can kill up to a distance of fifty yards. Not the bow, but the arrow unleashed from the bow.

As usual, I went about my work in a planned and methodical way. I methodically planned to be not in the office as much as possible. The business bods back in London thought this was good; I was out and about touting for business for UK plc. Others in the High Commission wanted to see more of me, believing that my lunches in and visits to the hotels and bars in Accra, Kumasi, Akosombo (the southernmost point of Lake Volta – a lake that can be seen from the international space station, if ever you are passing that way) were more for pleasure than work. They might have had a point, but I was having a pint in the service of Her Majesty's government. Annual visits to Togo were also part of my not being in the High Commission regime.

At first sight, Togo looks desperate. The first thing you see is a sea of humanity queuing at the Ghana/Togo land border. To this day, I am not sure how anyone gets across within their lifetime. To my untrained eye, it looked like two or three generations of numerous families had been born and raised in the queue whilst waiting to get their travel documents stamped. Fortunately, I had a 'fixer' and a Diplomatic passport. Much to the annoyance of the multitude, I was across in a relatively short hour. But Togo, or at least its capital, is deceptive. Behind the derelict walls and dilapidated yards, guarded by rabid ridden dogs, the French had secreted some very Parisian style and a number of Parisian quality restaurants and bistros. Of course, these were in desperate need of British goods and services, so I had to spend many hours frequenting them, practising my French, trying out their food and beverages and, all the time, tirelessly working to persuade them to buy from Britain. The UK/Togo trade statistics did not reflect all my hard work.

In between all this hard commercial work, I endured a four-day official visit to Johannesburg. Separately, the whole family spent one Christmas day in a Cape Town vineyard. A week later (on New Year's Day 2002), we flew in a private helicopter over the Cape of Good Hope and, in between, we lunched in the magnificent Two Oceans restaurant at Cape Point to celebrate my forty-fifth birthday, with great family, great friends, great food and even greater South African wine.

Cape Point, incidentally, looks over False Bay – the Bay where Captain Bligh and the *Bounty* stopped for repairs in 1788 and reprovisioning en route to Tahiti and thence, into British Naval History. And some 223 years later (not later from the lunch, but later after Captain Bligh's visit), I would be inextricably linked to that bit of history. Destiny again you see.

All the time whilst I was slaving and travelling on behalf of the British government, I was wondering when the FCO people in London would find my file and summon me back to the Mothership in Whitehall. I would soon get that call.

Part Nine

London

June 2004 – March 2006

Chapter 25

London – North Korea, South Korea and Buckingham Palace

I had been abroad for so long (fifteen years, and four substantive postings, including a ten-week stay in the Seychelles), it was not really a surprise that I did not really fit in back at HQ in Whitehall. The story unfolds thus. Prior to leaving Accra, I had picked up a job in a brand new (and obviously management consultant created) Directorate called the Directorate of Strategy and Innovation (DSI). It seemed to be full of bright young people thinking outside the box. I (unwisely with hindsight) thought this would be a good wheeze and duly signed up.

In mid-2004, I found myself in the Innovation team, a team of about six or seven, none of whom I knew or whose names I even recognised, but whose credentials included postings in Europe, Africa, Asia and the Middle East. This was good, I thought, plenty in common here; a vast amount of experience covering most of the globe. A team with that experience should be able to innovate and strategise (no such word in case anyone noticed) to the content of our collective heart and the improvement of the FCO lot. As I was introduced to one and all, I politely asked in which posts they had served. To a man and a woman, they all said that they had never been on a substantive Posting. Two had visited a couple of posts in Western Europe.

The outward facing blurb, for the rest of the FCO to admire, was that the Innovation Team had such a wide variety of Postings and overseas jobs and experience under their belts, it was in existence to help one and all with any corporate governance, human resource and operational issues that any of the home departments might have. But the penny dropped. I, me, myself… I was that wide variety of 'Postings and overseas jobs and experience'. From what I could gather, the other innovators were in steady well-embedded jobs that had very little to do with innovating anything. One young lady was doing a key job reviewing small posts. This lady was bright, young and very intelligent but had never been abroad, let alone served in a small post. My offer of assistance was turned down with the spurious offer that much more exciting things were coming my way.

Days and weeks passed where the only exciting thing to come my way was my regular meet-up on Friday evening with the other lost souls struggling to find a niche in this Brand New World called the Foreign Office of 2004. My frustration and boredom began to show. To alleviate that and to try to prevent my departure (which would have meant revamping their advertising slogan), I was sent on missions to sit in on meetings being held by my Human Resource, IT, and Estate and Security colleagues. There were probably other departments too, but I cannot remember now. This was not too bad. I saw some familiar faces and old friends and caught up with the gossip, old news and new news.

It was one of these old friends who after a particularly excruciating meeting on integrating diversity with leadership, asked me what on earth I was doing in the Directorate of Strategy and Innovation. That was probably the most sensible question I had been asked in my first six months of my home tour back in London. A sensible question to which I did not have a sensible answer. Actually, I had no answer at all. He went on to explain that none of the other departments I visited (it seemed to be only me from the Innovation team visiting other departments and sitting in on their meetings and contributing nothing) knew what DSI was doing. Again, I could not help with the conundrum. He even went on to say that someone, who shall remain nameless (like most of the people in this book), had nicknamed DSI the Stasi – the East German secret police, as was. That was not a good sign.

The straw that broke this camel's back happened at a regular meeting of senior officers, chaired by the very senior Chief Clerk. Actually, it was not 'chaired'; one new innovation, from America, was that we all stood for these meetings (some three years hence, I was to work in the USA and everybody sat for meetings and laughed when I told them about our vertical meetings). The idea of vertical meetings was to keep them short and succinct. That worked until a new very senior officer decided she would sit, so tradition returned, as did meetings that went on and on and on and on.

My job at these vertical assemblies was to write-up the decisions of the group on a whiteboard, get everyone to agree that it was what was agreed and later circulate them in draft form for final approval by one and all. Once I circulated everything for final approval, it was at that point everyone agreed that we had not agreed on these decisions as written up by me and a whole new round of correspondence began. That was not the proverbial straw. That came when a nice senior officer brought in from another government department (whose experience of overseas was probably a school day trip to Boulogne) asked me how I felt being the 'Teacher's Assistant'. No disrespect to teaching assistants, but for me, it was time to move on. And I did.

I, as an Innovation Officer, innovated myself out of a job. I only lasted six months – not a good start to three years in London where one was expected to work three years in one department or two times two years in two departments before going abroad again. I noted a little while later, and not without a little smirk, that the Innovation team had quietly disappeared and no longer existed. Not long after that, there was no such Directorate of Strategy and Innovation. Civil Servants 1:0 Management Consultants.

I am sure that at the time of the DSI's demise, there was somewhere in a Whitehall pub, a senior management consultant crying into his beer, before he went home to his £4 million house in the stockbroker belt paid for by the taxpayer.

This self-sacking from DSI was the start of a somewhat nomadic time in London. I was hastily drafted into the Freedom of Information team in our Knowledge Management Department (KMD). The job was to try to manage the man who was trying to manage the spreadsheets that were managing the mass of Freedom of information (FOI) requests landing in the FCO post box at an alarming rate – hundreds. Our job was to try to keep a track of all these requests and to gently let departments know when they might be getting close to breaching the statutory time limits for replies to be sent. Bearing in mind that this was all additional work, our nagging of departments was not well received. The requests covered everything under the sun. The Africa Directorate stopped doing bilateral work and just answered FOI requests. Other departments also complained about being overwhelmed and blamed us. "Do not blame us," I replied. "We did not pass the FOI Act. That was part of the Labour manifesto and Ministers laid it before Parliament, it was voted in, Her Majesty the Queen approved the Act, it became law and lots of people wanted information based on that piece of that law."

I settled into trying to manage the man who was trying to manage the spreadsheets that was managing the mass of Freedom of information (FOI) requests landing in the FCO postbox at an alarming rate (yes, repetition I know, but I like the rhythm to it). The only problem (think 'poisoned chalice' here) was that the man

I was supposed to be managing was never there. There were regular morning meetings when I was supposed to update everyone, based on information from the spreadsheet being updated by the invisible man, which covered the number of incoming and outgoing requests, what was trending and what was slowly slipping off the radar. Bullshit can only work so many times, so I thought I should ask the obvious question of my direct boss. Where is the invisible man? The enigmatic reply was that he was not well and did a lot of nocturnal work. Not the ideal defence when the Permanent-Under-Secretary (PUS) needed statistics to explain to Ministers why they were not getting the FCO Rolls-Royce service they had become accustomed to. I could see a big blame train coming, a blame train coming around the corner and it was coming directly at me. But there was divine intervention. Or to be precise, it snowed all over East Kent, and continuing the railway allegory, the trains stopped. I could not get into work.

All over Europe – West, Central and Eastern; throughout the Rockies of America and Canada; throughout the plains of Siberia, and all over the upper and lower foothills of the Himalayas, their societies cope with snowflakes. Big snowflakes, huge ice storms, blizzards, avalanches, to name but a few snow-related nouns. But we, here in the South-East of England, cannot. Let us panic with a capital P. Let us declare a state of emergency. Let the economy lose a few billion. Let this slight dusting of snow cause mayhem. But to me, the fact I was not able to get to work (I suspect the invisible man had the same problem), gave me thinking time. I sent off a couple of emails looking for other jobs. I was picked up for a couple quite quickly, too quickly. The hiring managers assumed that I had discussed my imminent move with the driver of the blame train. I had not. I was unceremoniously moved from dealing with Freedom of Information into no man's land. Two jobs down in eight months. Not looking good.

By the way of a postscript to FOI, if you were to ask any Minister (of whatever political persuasion) or any senior Civil Servant (of whatever political neutrality), the vast majority would privately say that they wished the Freedom of Information Act did not exist. But that was not my problem. I was going to Pakistan.

I must have been good at something. I did not have long to wait for another job, literally forty-eight hours after the snow had melted, I was asked to help with a one-off eight-week British passport project. This involved some innovative (not that word again, I was thinking!) detection of fraudulent immigration and embarkation stamps in

British passports. I trained, I understood, I delivered (a management consultant would be paid thousands for those six words – I will take £20.00 for this book) and I headed for the passport section in our High Commission in Islamabad. My stay was all too brief.

In Pakistan, if one wanted to enjoy a glass of beer or wine with one's evening meal at the hotel (and I certainly did after the long flight to Islamabad), one had to become an alcoholic. This did not necessarily mean:-

(i)   You had to consume vast amounts of beer, wine and spirits over a prolonged period of time and...

(ii)   during that time, have many blackouts, and...

(iii)   deceive one's partner by lying and stealing their money and...

(iv)   going missing for days on end and losing one's job and...

(v)   eventually getting divorced and never seeing the children again.

(vi)   And then you try rehab and Alcoholics Anonymous, but you eventually stop going to the meetings.

(vii)   You relapse. And then, as if all that is not good enough for you, you end up shacking up with an equally down-and-out bar person from the worst pub in the United Kingdom (which is near Dumfries, by the way), whereupon the whole unseemly cycle starts again.

No, you do not have to do all that in Pakistan. To be an alcoholic there and avoid all the aforementioned drama, you merely fill in a form. Yes, it is that easy.

At the reception desk of the hotel (which was later blown up by terrorists – the whole hotel, not just the reception desk), one is very subtly asked if Sir or Madam would require an alcoholic beverage with one's meal. If the reply is yes, a form is handed over which, upon completion, declares to anyone who cares to ask that the person named on the form is medically an alcoholic and needs to have alcohol (to us in the West, a rather unconventional way of dealing with the problem). And so I became an alcoholic. I was not alone. The hotel restaurant was full of alcoholics. Actually, you could not see them as all the tables were in booths, which were segregated from fellow drunks, sorry, diners, by dark heavy curtains. Not really conducive to a happy meal. I did not tarry long – but just as an aside, the wine was delivered in a teapot.

I spent a week in Pakistan, mostly working in the High Commission. I managed a mini-tour around Islamabad. A bit like Dhaka, once you're away from the diplomatic enclave, it was a teeming mass of humanity. Prior to leaving for Pakistan, I had heard about the town of Murree in the Murree Hills or, to be accurate, Murree is in the Pir Panjal range of mountains. Murree is at about 7,200 feet and I am pleased to say that, after this rapid rise from 1,600 feet to 7,200 feet in a rather broken down taxi, I did not suffer altitude sickness and join the local band. Instead, I bought a carpet (which was to cost me more in customs duty than the actual price of the carpet itself – I still have it) and a pashmina shawl for my wife – she tells me she still has it, but I have not seen it for a while, a bit like most of the presents I buy her. Murree is a pleasant town – but in reality, you are probably better off spending your money on a long weekend in Paris. I had a nice lunch and headed for the airport.

Whilst I was away, the talent spotters were on the hunt for a brilliant mind, a keen thrusting, ambitious officer, a go-getter, a problem solver, a man or woman of steel to take on the role of 'Team Leader' for the Korean peninsula and Mongolia. Instead, they got me.

And so it came to pass (I like that phrase, it saves me thinking of different ways of starting a new phase of my peripatetic life) that I would manage a team of two and all three of us would be dealing with South Korea, Mongolia and (fanfare) North Korea or, to give the country its proper title, the Democratic People's Republic of Korea (DPRK). Before I get into the job and the travels, has anyone noticed (I expect that they have) that when a country puts 'Democratic' in its title, it is, in fact (there are exceptions, but not many) a basket case? For example, the Democratic Republic of the Congo – authoritarian regime, wars, child soldiers, corruption, female genital mutilation, human rights abuses. I could go on but I might ruin your lunch. There was the former East Germany, the German Democratic Republic, neither democratic nor a Republic. Others off the top of my head are Algeria (authoritarian regime), Ethiopia (authoritarian regime). In fact, all of the countries with 'Democratic' in their name are not, according to the Economist Intelligence Unit Democracy Index, democratic. And the worst is (fanfare) the DPRK, which was now under my jurisdiction – the late (evil) Kim Jong-Il might have disagreed with my jurisdiction, but let us not quibble about that.

I shall deal with the three countries, not in what happened chronologically, but as entities in their own right. That means there might be some overlap between South Korea and North Korea, which obviously there isn't in real life. Whilst the countries are only yards apart in places, that gap, in reality, could be measured in light years. Or if you look at the satellite picture of the Korean peninsula at night, for North Korea it could be measured in dark years.

I do not know much about Mongolia. We have an Embassy there, and we also had one there back in 2005. We probably had one there for many decades prior to that – perhaps just to keep an eye on what was happening in the Eastern half of the Soviet Union. If that (the Eastern half of the Soviet Union) had not been there, we would probably not have bothered to open this embassy. But we had one, and if we had one then, by default, we needed a 'Desk Officer' in the FCO in London so that Embassy staff in Ulaanbaatar (Capital of Mongolia, if you did not know) could write to somebody and feel loved and wanted.

Our Embassy in Seoul (Capital of South Korea, if you did not know) was, on the other hand, big and important. It was important because it bought lots of things from the UK, strategically it was (and still is, a key ally) in an area dominated by China, and it was very very close, probably too close for its own liking, to North Korea.

The UK bilateral relationship with South Korea virtually ran itself and so the Embassy only contacted us if they wanted to blame London for something or they needed something trivial. We occasionally drafted briefs that were then rewritten by those in Seoul – cut out the middleman or woman was my battle cry, little did I know that someone was listening. Otherwise, the big boys just talked to the big boys and life went on.

However, one day, it must have been a slow day, I was told that a senior Royal was going to pay an official visit to South Korea on behalf of the UKTI (the trade and investment arm of HMG), Obviously, I knew about the visit, but UKTI had taken the lead and we, the FCO, were politely watching from the sidelines. But now HRH was definitely going, the powers that be had decided that I should sit in on the UKTI briefing at Buckingham Palace. Having been inside Number 10 Downing Street, the Cabinet Office, the House of Commons, the House of Lords and Deal Town Council Chambers, here was my big chance to achieve the full house of British governance buildings. I was not going to miss out on that. The meeting was arranged and, some twenty-four hours beforehand, I was reminded that, as the FCO was responsible for everything beyond Dover and I was the FCO official responsible for South Korea, I would lead the delegation of three (myself and two from UKTI). No problem. And so, on the following day, we met outside the Palace and were duly escorted to HRH's office.

HRH had his team there and, after the usual courtesies, the meeting commenced. It was all going rather well. I had the trade statistics off pat, briefed HRH on the major sectors, the political background and the key objectives of the visit. All of which was academic because as soon as HRH had landed, he would again be briefed, somewhat differently, by Her Majesty's Ambassador on the ground. But be that as it may, for the moment. As I said, all was going rather well until one of HRH's aides gently intervened to inform HRH that I had been not only to South Korea, but also to North Korea. Not many people go to North Korea, even less live to tell the tale, and for obvious reasons (or if they are not obvious now, they will be when I come to the bit about the DPRK), no member of the Royal family in the past has trodden on North Korean soil, and will not for a very long way into the future. HRH was curious, and I took time out of the South Korea briefing to enlighten him on the dark side of the Korean peninsula. This all went well and I answered the questions, but I realised that time was passing and I needed to get back to the South Korea brief. I politely said to HRH that perhaps we could get back to the matter in hand, to which the response was something like, "I will decide what we will talk about." HRH 1:0 Kevin. And probably that is why, amongst a couple of other things, I ended up in Siberia.

As we concluded the meeting, I wished HRH *bon voyage* and looked forward to briefing him on his trip six months hence to Mongolia. Not a good move. His officials had not yet built up the courage to tell him about that particular overseas visit. There followed some chaotic conversations, glares at me and, as we bid farewell, I could hear HRH saying to his team something along the lines of "Mongolia! You cannot be serious".

And now to the basket case that is North Korea. Probably the worst human rights record in the world, it has gulags holding some 200,000 political prisoners, and tortures and kills many of them. The population is brain-washed into thinking that they have to put up with starvation, poverty, working all the hours sent and adoring their dictator because the Korean War was still being fought and the people need to make sacrifices in order to prevent the country being overrun by the imperialist Americans to the South. The economy is non-existent. Very few people are allowed to leave the country. Fewer still have access to outside radio, TV or (today) the Internet. The dictatorship controls everything. And, of course, the dictator and his acolytes live in the lap of luxury. If anyone detracts from anything the dictator says, then it is Goodnight Vienna and probably not very quickly.

In normal circumstances, we would not touch such a country with a bargepole. But North Korea has nuclear weapons and a really big army. If you add to that the fact that the USA and South Korea do not have diplomatic relations with the DPRK, it is good news that a serious member of the United Nations has an Embassy in Pyongyang.

The bad news was and is that North Korea did and does not take any notice of anyone whatsoever. It keeps testing its nukes, it keeps repressing its people (and still does, more and more harshly, it seems to me) and has lately seemed determined to annoy a volatile President of the USA.

But back to 2005. As a good husband and father, I liked to tell my wife and kids what Dad was doing in London all day long. I got into the habit of calling the North Koreans the bad guys. As did my son Benny, who was then aged nine. And so, one day, I came home and announced to the family that I was going on a familiarisation trip to North and South Korea via Beijing. I would be away for two weeks. It has to be said that you do not get many jobs like this. It was not well paid – but the travel and adventure easily made up for that.

I should say that, as we had diplomatic relations with North Korea, I met occasionally with the second in command at the North Korean Embassy in London. I cannot say these meetings were friendly. The British government policy was to try, at every opportunity, to point out the errors of this errant state. Be it human rights, nuclear weapons, the parlous state of the economy, its ever-increasing belligerency towards anyone and any country (except idiot allies like Libya and Syria) and its breaches of UN resolutions. I could go on. Suffice to say that the North Koreans did not take kindly to me putting across, in a somewhat forthright way, the views of the British government. In my meeting with the North Korean number two prior to my departure for the Far East, he was trying to convince me that as soon as I had visited his paradise land, I would be convinced of the error of my thinking and, what's more, convince the whole of the British government that they had got North Korea all wrong. How wrong was he to be.

Just before I left, I was told they were thinking about completely restructuring the whole of the department and my thoughts on the matter would be gratefully received. I thought nothing more of it.

After a long journey to Beijing, and a couple of days to get over my jet lag, I headed out to the airport to get the flight to Pyongyang.

I was travelling on the DPRK state-owned airline – Air Koryo. It left on a Tuesday and returned to Beijing on the Saturday. No matter what happened, I would be in the country for four nights and five days. If the North Koreans had had anything to do with it, I would still be there now – in a gulag.

I was in Air Koryo business class. The seats were, quite literally, like 1930s sofas. Four wooden legs, six inches long and sticking into the base of the seat; the upholstery had seen better, much better days. The chairs did not appear to be securely fixed to the cabin floor and moved about. Of course, in Air Koryo's business class, the food was to die for. Literally, you could die if you ate it. It was, to a morsel, inedible. Normally on a jaunt (sorry, 'official visit') like this, one is very well fed and watered. Not to North Korea – I managed to lose about three kilos in as many days. I was met on arrival and, at that point, I realised that I had my own private mobile telephone with me. This was not allowed and so gamely I handed it over, was given a receipt and the phone (duly tampered with – though they did not publicly advertise that) could be picked up on my way out. So off I went to the Ambassadorial residence to freshen up and have dinner with some North Koreans. Apart from the food, that went well.

After dinner (a very loose description), I asked if I could call home and, of course, the Ambassador said yes and then mimicked microphones and listening devices to let me know that the North Koreans bugged everything. That was common knowledge. I duly called the UK and could actually hear the North Korean listening gear cranking up. After the usual familial pleasantries, my son came on the telephone to ask, "Dad, have you met any of the bad guys yet?" For obvious reasons (there were gulags some two hundred miles to the north), I tried to change the subject rapidly. But my son was not to be deterred. Eventually, I had to say that I had to go and wished them all a fond farewell, hoping, but not saying, that I would see them again soon and with my fingernails where they should be.

The following day was taken up with meetings, the last of which was with the Human Rights Department of some Ministry or other. I had said in the car on the way there that the Ministry must have been the Ministry for the Contradiction in Terms. That remark (duly passed on by the driver or interpreter or any North Korean in earshot) along with the ill-disguised discussion with Benny about the bad guys, ensured my reception at this meeting was cold, ice cold. Indeed, when I mentioned the fact that the whole of the civilised world thought that the way that North Korea treated its citizens was the most uncivilised treatment in the world, to a man (they were all men) they all stood up, shouted and left. *That went well*, I thought (not!). The Ambassador sat quietly – *less than helpful*, I thought, but then again, he had to live there. Not me (although, had it not been for my diplomatic immunity, I might have spent a few years living in the gulag).

The next few days were taken up with the obligatory tour of the city – it was grey, it was Soviet, the people were grim, it was decaying, and the cult of personality was everywhere. Massive, really massive, pictures and statues of Kim Il-sung (the first dictator of North Korea and still called the Head of State – that should be the Dead of State, as he had been dead for years) and his, son, the equally evil, Kim Jong-Il (now deceased). I was shown an 'art gallery' and, apart from the massive – really massive – pictures of the father/son duo dictatorship, there were lots of paintings of flowers. I asked the name of the flowers and apparently, there were only two names; the Kim Jong-ilia flower and the Kim Il-sungilia flower – I kid you not. Outside the city, the countryside was equally bleak; I noticed a distinct lack of birds anywhere – I suspect that, in the famines that regularly occurred (caused by the regime), all the birds and other animals had been trapped and eaten. North Korea is not a nice place.

On the Friday, prior to my departure on the Saturday, it was time for the proper propaganda to kick in, and I spent a whole morning on the North Korean side of the Demilitarised Zone – the DMZ. The Z is pronounced Zee and, as I read somewhere, very correctly I might add, "There ain't no D in the DMZ". Poetry.

The DMZ was, and still is, the most heavily militarised, fortified, mined bit of real estate on the planet. The North Korean colonel briefed me on where the Americans could and would attack. How they (the DPRK) had the best army in the world and would easily beat the USA in any fight. I had the tour of the Panmunjom and Joint Security Area. Of course, we could clearly see the South Korean and US military from our side, as they could see us from their side. It is worth remembering here that I was only about fifty kilometres from Seoul, my next destination, but to get there I would have to go back to Pyongyang, fly to Beijing, change flights, fly out to sea and then land in – guess where – Seoul international airport.

Just before I departed the DMZ, I heard loud booms, not unlike explosions far away. I asked my North Korean host what the noises were. He denied hearing anything. He clearly did not want to tell me that these loud booms were not the Americans invading, but factory manufactured noises to convince the poor North Korean peasants in the vicinity that there was a war on. Such was (and probably still is) life in that very bizarre, unreal godforsaken country. I hope in our lifetime that the Kim family is removed, brought to justice and twenty-two million people can see the light.

There is a lot more I could say, but enough for now. I headed to the airport, picked up my mobile telephone, and got to Beijing. It had been opened. It was an old mobile, so I took out my SIM card, kept that and threw the phone in a large rubbish bin. The North Koreans are probably still monitoring to this day some landfill somewhere to the south of Beijing, wondering if I am dead. They are probably hoping I am dead after they read this.

The best part of the second leg of this official visit was my guided tour of the DMZ from the South Korean side. Whilst on the North side, I had deliberately worn a khaki coloured linen suit that was easily identifiable. I had said to the North Korean colonel (all via an interpreter) that I hoped to see him Monday. I was not on his thoroughly regimented programme for Monday so he shrugged.

On that bright sunny Monday morning, with my nice linen suit freshly hotel cleaned, I toured the South side of the DMZ. And at a certain lookout point, with the aid of binoculars, I set my sights on my erstwhile hosts of the previous week. The 'mirrors' on the opposite side picked up their binoculars and stared back. And there he was, my favourite North Korean colonel, staring incredulously back at the man in the linen suit who had somehow escaped the clutches of the North and crossed the DMZ to now smile and wave greetings across no man's land. He did not reciprocate. He seemed intent on getting to a telephone as fast as he could. Indeed, that particular exchange took some explaining to some of my UK/USA entourage, who had not been told that I had come from the Dark Side.

After an interesting four days in Seoul, I flew back to Blighty, had the weekend with my family, and went into work prepared to delight one and all with the memoirs of the man who had crossed the DMZ. Nobody seemed particularly interested; they were all looking at the proposed restructuring of the Department. I quickly noticed that my job was no longer there. I went to find my boss and he was staring at the new restructuring. I said that my job appeared to have gone. He pointed out that his too had disappeared. Then our colleague from the Hong Kong desk joined us – his job too had gone. We all had something in common; we were in our late forties/early fifties, male and white. I will not bore you, dear reader, with the bureaucracies of our moves, but for me this was to be a massive blessing in disguise – a restructuring that would enable me, for the next eleven years, to run my own posts with no bosses in the immediate vicinity. Bliss!

As I left the Far Eastern Department and the delights of the Korean Peninsula, I registered with a department of Human Resources that dealt with officers without a substantive job to do. It was called the Corporate Pool (others called it the Cess Pool, but that was a bit harsh, I thought). That was on the Friday. On the Monday, I got an enigmatic call, asking if I had experience of small posts (yes) and would I be available for a short stint overseas (a yes from me and a quick, too quick agreement, from my darling wife). I had signed up for seven months in Yekaterinburg, 1000 miles east of Moscow in Siberia.

And so it came to pass that since I had arrived back ready for work in the summer of 2004, I had (in summary) spent six months in the Directorate of Strategy and Innovation as an Innovation Officer – I had innovated myself out of that job; I had spent a few weeks dealing with Freedom of Information (invaluable for some work later in life), but did not last long there; worked on a one-off project management job involving a week in Pakistan and, from there, viewing (again) the mighty Himalayas from the mini-Murree hills just outside Islamabad; and, thereafter, I had travelled to China, North Korea and South Korea; all the time experiencing new travels, new knowledge and new friends (and OK, a few new beers, restaurants and clubs). Of course, I had enjoyed the privilege of being inside Buckingham Palace and had a charming conversation with HRH Prince Andrew, the Duke of York. Little did either of us know then that we would meet again in Siberia.

This all sounds good, but having four different jobs in less than two years was not good. But all that was to change.

Sadly, and not to be forgotten, I had lost a very good friend during my freewheeling stint in London, and was about to lose another.

I think of Phil and Dave often. Taken from us well before their time.

With fond farewells to my lovely wife, Leone, and my two children, I headed east – to Siberia.

Temporary Duty:
Yekaterinburg (Russia)

I arrived in Yekaterinburg in late April, very late at night and with a five-hour time difference from the UK. The flight was Lufthansa on its way to Tashkent and stopped only briefly in this once-closed Soviet city, formerly named Sverdlovsk. Ominously, I was the only one to disembark. But as you will have seen from the section on Lithuania, I was not the first person in my extended family (that is my dear mother-in-law) to be sent to Siberia. However, I was here under much more pleasant circumstances.

I was met by the Deputy Consul General (DCG) and the Consulate (my) Russian driver. The DCG told me that the driver did not speak any English; neither of us believed that for one second. It was better the devil you knew than the one you didn't. I was taken to the fully-furnished CG's flat (in a building adjacent to the Consulate, on the fourth floor and above the Czech Consulate General). The American Consulate General was next door to us and I would soon make the acquaintance of my US opposite number. I tried to sleep. As it was only about 2000 hours in the UK, I could not, so I unpacked. My predecessor had basically packed up everything and there was very little with which to amuse myself, so I stared into the dark Siberian night, later falling asleep only to be awakened by the Deputy Consul General knocking at the door. It was 0930 (0430 my time) and time for the first day in charge.

The job here was to be Consul General (CG), the big cheese in a subordinate post. Some might say that, if they knew that I was in charge, it was probably an insubordinate post (but look out for Auckland for that). The previous Consul General had had to leave in haste for personal reasons and the Ambassador in Moscow needed somebody quickly to hold the fort for a few months whilst the new CG learnt Russian – a linguistic skill that is much needed in this part of the world. Very few people speak English East of the Ural Mountains. Fewer speak French and even fewer speak Lithuanian. But my lack of knowledge of the Russian language was not going to prevent me from doing my job and enjoying this new adventure. It did not occur to me at this juncture that I had now spent time in some very tough Posts (Dhaka and Riyadh), been in North Korea and now Siberia – perhaps the Human Resources people were trying to tell me something.

On my way to Yekaterinburg, I suggested that I should transit the Embassy in Moscow for, perhaps, at least a morning for some quick briefings, but rather interestingly, the polite reply was no; there was no need. (To be fair, I had had quite substantive briefings in London – but not many, if any, of those people had been to this post or this part of the world).

The UK team at the Consulate General consisted of the Deputy CG (FCO) and two ladies from the Immigration Service (IS), who were on temporary duty for the summer visa rush. The rest of the staff were Russian nationals. In addition, there was, under the umbrella of the Consulate but not managed by me, the British Council with three staff.

I know, dear reader, that on your mind is the obvious question; why on earth is the British taxpayer paying for a Consulate General in the middle of nowhere in the middle of the biggest country on Earth? Well, I shall enlighten you. Of course, I might not enlighten you, you might already know. In which case, jump a few paragraphs.

The city was founded in 1723 and named after Peter the Great's wife, Ekaterina. It was the strategic gateway between Europe and Asia. It was a mining area. During the Soviet era, strange things started to happen. A lot of strange things started to happen in the Soviet era, but as I have – on average – only about another 20 years on Earth, there is not enough time for me to explain Soviet thinking before the Good Lord (at least I hope it is the Good Lord, rather than the other guy), clutches me to his bosom and says: "That was a hell of a book you wrote, Kevin. A shame no one published it or bought it," and duly opens the Mother of Pearl gate (austerity has hit Heaven and God has sold the original twelve gates made from a single pearl) and lets me pass. But back to those strange Soviet things, rather than my thinly disguised appeal to end up in Heaven.

Russia, prior to the creation of the Soviet Union, had Oblasts, which were simply regions. Under the Soviets, these Oblasts became administrative districts with an administrative capital. And to go with these administrative districts and administrative capitals, there were lots and lots of name changes. But the one we are interested in is Yekaterinburg. And Yekaterinburg became Sverdlovsk, named after one Yakov Sverdlov, a former communist party leader.

It also became a big industrial city. During World War II, many strategic industries not only moved into the city of Sverdlovsk, but also into the region and the surrounding Oblasts. The Americans did the same with the Cheyenne Mountain in Colorado – only they had states, not Oblasts. And later on, after World War II, the Soviets decided to enrich uranium very close to Sverdlovsk itself – in a city then named Sverdlovsk 44 (now Novo Uralsk). We all know what enriching uranium means, do we not, boys and girls? Nukes. And not just nuclear-related weaponry was produced, the city produced conventional weapons. In addition, not far away from Yekaterinburg was Izhevsk, still a major producer of the ubiquitous AK-47. I went to the factory, but more of that later. Of course, amongst those weapons-making factories, I am sure there were cheese and milk factories, toy factories, chocolate factories, cheesecake factories, beer and wine factories and everything else that is needed to keep our Soviet hobbits happy in their idyllic life in their Soviet shires.

The Soviet authorities, of course, did not want all this happiness to spread to those unlucky masses that were not privileged enough to live and work in these hidden paradises. And so it came to pass that many of these cities near to Sverdlovsk (Yekaterinburg), became closed cities. Nobody, I mean nobody, could enter these cities. Indeed, for a considerable time, Sverdlovsk itself was off-limits to foreigners.

I am sure that the citizens of these closed cities all lived very happily with their three-headed dogs, as the sky gave a lovely green radioactive glow, day and night, with no one from the outside world to disturb their idyll and no need for the residents (without a permit, which was never issued) to visit elsewhere. Oh, Brave Nuke World!

After the collapse of the Soviet Union, lots and lots of cities reverted to their old non-communist names and, in 2006, we were back to Yekaterinburg. Lots of the factories (not all, by any stretch of the imagination) had been converted to civil use, closed cities reopened (not all, by any stretch of the imagination) and normality had returned to the Soviet (now Russian) shires; if you believe that you will believe anything in this book.

That is my very potted and potty history of the Sverdlovsk Oblast and surrounding regions. It is probably totally inaccurate, but I do not have time to correct it all.

And so back to the Consulate General and the job in hand. Yekaterinburg was/is Russia's fourth largest city. Thus, for the UK Plc, there was the possibility of trade and the possibility of opening up Siberia to our Western values. People from the region would need visas to visit and study in the UK and it would be plainly easier to administratively deal with the citizens of the West Siberian plains from Yekaterinburg than Moscow. And so the powers in the FCO in the early nineties decided it would be a good wheeze to open a Consulate General in the Ural region. For the sake of balance, I am assuming that the Russians agreed as well (they probably would not do so today). I for one am glad they did. The consular district was probably the size of the old Western Europe. To me, this was manna from heaven, more chances to get out and about in a part of the world that few get to see.

I spent the first few days getting to know the team. One of whom still lived in a closed city some forty miles to the North of Yekaterinburg. He needed a special permit to travel in and out. He was probably spying on us, but so too probably were the rest of the Russian staff. But such is life in certain countries and we live with it.

It was very early May 2006 and one of my first representational jobs (these were tasks formally representing either the government as a whole, the Prime Minister, Foreign Secretary, or indeed, Her Majesty the Queen) was to lay a wreath on behalf of Her Majesty's Government at the 9th May Victory Day (the Soviet victory over Nazi Germany in 1945) remembrance ceremony. This is a very important day in the history of Russia. Everything needed to go smoothly. It would be the first time that my CG colleagues met me and the Sverdlovsk authorities had a chance to introduce themselves. We got lost.

We went to the wrong cemetery, and to add to my woes, it was – believe it or not – snowing on 9th May. With minutes to spare, we made it to the right place. As calmly as I could pretend, I solemnly took my place, with my wreath, in the official line-up. As I had not been there for the usual pre-ceremony diplomatic chit-chat (and, for me, much-needed introductions), I did not know who was who. I surreptitiously checked out the flags of the various officials; all male and white, it has to be said. I was looking for my American colleague, and I found the flag on the wreath and its owner was perched behind it. And lo! What a small world it was; he was a former colleague from the US Embassy in Vilnius. I did not know him well, but I knew him.

Ceremonial duties completed, I reintroduced myself to my USA opposite number and we agreed to meet over coffee later that week. I tried for lunch or post-work drinks, but to no avail. Then, I remembered from our Vilnius days that my colleague (a great guy, an academic and a Russian and Ukrainian speaker) was a very cerebral man and small talk and drinks were not his style. Nothing wrong with that. I only really saw him again on official business a few times over the coming months.

I soon mastered the work of the Consulate and now wanted to master the roads, avenues and alleyways of the city of Yekaterinburg. I had a pedometer and was determined to do 10,000 steps a day. And in so doing, I would, of course, partake of the local restaurants and hostelries. Thanks to globalisation, the two nearest bars/restaurants to the Consulate were an Uzbek one and (yes, it is true) an Irish bar. In my early days, I frequented both; the Irish one only because I liked the Health and Safety sign outside: 'Beware, drunks crossing'.

Walking throughout Yekaterinburg is fascinating (if you like that sort of thing). One must first visit the 'Plotynka', the dam or weir crossing the river Iset in the middle of the city. The river should have had a health and safety sign on it. The water was rusty brown. I would hazard a guess that this colour was not from oxidising metal. Unless it was a heavy metal, and here I do not mean (i) loud rock music or (ii) innocent metals that weigh a lot but, instead, the more evil metals of cadmium, mercury and lead. Poisonous, deadly poisonous, and probably in the river from some upstream unregulated industrial factory still locked away in those aforementioned idyllic closed cities. Amazingly, people were fishing and I occasionally witnessed some sort of alien species, about the size of a hand (similar shape, but badly arthritic), being caught. I hope those fishermen did not take them home for tea – the life expectancy in the Urals was already not that good.

Everywhere in the city were massive statues and monuments (I was to notice this in other Russian cities as well), including a twelve-foot Lenin, his left hand outstretched pointing to the birthplace of the 1917 revolution in St Petersburg (later to become Petrograd, Leningrad and then back to St Petersburg – no wonder people got lost). Actually, I think he was pointing towards the Irish pub, but that is just my opinion. I found some other monuments to times gone past – from the Decembrists of 1825 to, my favourite, a giant statue of Marshal Zhukov on his gallant steed just outside a 'sanatorium'. Zhukov – rhymes with Fuckov – which is literally what he told the Nazis. He defeated them at Stalingrad (now Volgograd) and led the Russian/Soviet attack on Berlin (now still Berlin). To this day, the Russians and probably others think he was Russia's greatest military figure. He must have been pretty good; he survived the wrath of Stalin – unlike many millions of others.

And of course, talking about death (not of millions, but of a well-known family), Yekaterinburg was the death place of the whole Romanov family in 1918. They all were shot in cold blood (probably directly on Lenin's orders) in the basement of Ipatiev's house, just around the corner from the Consulate. The bodies were then taken out to the woods, burnt and buried. All the remains of the Tsar and his family now have been recovered and reburied much more respectfully. Ipatiev's house was destroyed in 1989 on the orders of the Governor of Sverdlovsk – one Boris Yeltsin. Whatever happened to him? And in the place of Ipatiev's house stands the quite magnificent Russian Orthodox Church, the Church on the Blood. I strolled around it on many occasions. And paid my respects to my late young friends, Phil and Dave.

All was not always nice and comfortable on my strolls around the city – a great city, I might add. Most of the time, I managed to grab a beer and food by looking at pictures on the Russian menus. But gradually, relations between the UK and Russia deteriorated because of the presence in London and the public utterances of a poor unfortunate soul called Alexander Litvinenko (who died whilst I was in Yekaterinburg). I knew I was being followed by the FSB (the successor to the KGB). I suspect that they became more and more frustrated as this intrepid diplomat walked and walked and walked, popping in and out of bars, restaurants, museums, shops and more bars, and took lots of photographs of heroes of the Soviet past – I am sure they would have preferred it if I had not walked so much and had entertained myself, in a compromising manner, in the numerous girly bars dotted across the city. But that was not to be. They had a job to do. And as they could not compromise me, in revenge, they played tricks with my food orders and the good order of my bowels.

On one occasion, I ordered and pointed to, as a lunch starter, smoked salmon with a little topping of caviar. I knew how to treat myself. But the FSB sous-chefs in the kitchen also knew how they wanted to treat me; they changed my rather succulent order to a bowl of slightly off-brown fried fish skin (complete with scales), probably from the most polluted part of the river Iset. I declined to eat it, but paid for it.

However, on another occasion, I am convinced to this day that the FSB put the world's most powerful laxative in my borscht (which must, in my opinion, always be complemented with a good powerful Georgian red wine – not the laxative, the borscht). However, the FSB had not reckoned with the fact that, in my previous life, I had chased would-be immigrants around villages in the North-East corner of Bangladesh, miles away from any civilised sanitary conveniences, and that twelve-hour bowel clenchings were the order of those halcyon days. And so, whilst I was acutely aware of major movements in my lower intestine, I walked and walked, not giving in for several hours until I reached a nice hotel and pebble-dashed the nearest civilised loo – which happened to be for the ladies. No females were about, I hasten to add; the only other people around were two rather serious dark-suited gentlemen who looked desperately disappointed and desperately in need of easing themselves even more than I. I am inclined to think that the FSB officers involved are probably convinced to this day that I am in *The Guinness Book of Records* for bowel control. Kevin 1:0 FSB.

Let us move on (pun intended) from my bowels. The Consulate trade team of two delightful ladies – one from the West of Ukraine and the other, I do not know where (spot another potential spy) – was keen to get me out and about to promote UK goods and services. I was thus privileged to travel, mostly on the slow but efficient Russian train network, including the Trans-Siberian Express, to such weird and wonderful places as Perm, Ufa, Chelyabinsk, Izhevsk, and Magnitogorsk. On the train, I had my own compartment and very nice it was too: personal service, beer and wine and food. Most journeys took over ten hours. Travelling at about forty miles per hour, I really did get to see the real Russia through my own personal first-class compartment picture window. A magnificent expanse of woods, forests (is there a difference?), snow-covered villages (and that was just in the autumn), as well as bleak grey Soviet towns and cities, smokestacks belching out who knows what, agricultural practices from the days of Constable and the Haywain. It was all very Dr Zhivago-esque and the train to Yuriatin – believed to be Perm, believe it or not. In another of life's great coincidences (at least in my life), the old teacher I met in Geneva many chapters ago was Mr Pasternak and, of course, the author of Dr Zhivago was one Boris Pasternak.

The only downside of the trains was the loos at the end of the carriages; they were of two designs – on the old trains, everything went on to the tracks and on the new trains, it did not. Quite simple really. I preferred the new trains. Whilst travelling, I realised that I was an alien in a completely different culture and, for some unfathomable reason (months in Siberia might be one answer), my brain came up with this rhyming couplet:

> "I am an alien vulture,
> In another man's culture."

I cannot get it out of my head to this day. Maybe some forensic psychologist can make something of it.

All of these Siberian travels, towns and cities had their own interests and peculiarities. Perm and Magnitogorsk were originally closed cities, and fascinating for a foreigner like me. There were grandiose statues of a time long past – I am sure I saw one of Stalin. Everywhere I visited, I called on various businesses interested in trading with the UK – and these meetings were very agreeable, convivial and at times laden with vodka. There were others who only agreed to appointments with me because they had never met anyone outside of a forty-mile radius.

In one city, I lunched with the visiting Papal Nuncio (the Ambassador from the Vatican). He took the view that the miracle of water into wine meant that we Catholics should consume wine in vast amounts whenever possible. I have never consumed so much red wine in a single sitting. The Papal Nuncio was determined that neither of us should leave the table until such a time as we had drunk all of the blood of Christ – eight pints. Luckily my hotel was next door – he had his carriage waiting to take him to an evening meal out in the Tundra somewhere. I hope he made it.

I visited schools, orphanages, opera houses, a gold factory where I lifted a piece of gold bullion worth £228,000.00 (too heavy to put in my bag), and various seats of administration. At times, I would be shown photos of previous diplomatic visitors. Regularly, I was pleased to see a former chain-smoking Private Secretary from Lord Carrington's days. He had made it to the top. It was nice that I, far from the top, was following in his footsteps across Siberia.

As winter approached (temperatures were easily approaching minus ten, fifteen and twenty centigrade), I decided, as a parting shot, to go for lunch at a monastery some three hours north of Yekaterinburg. Why? Because the Abbot had written to me about a letter he had received from Buckingham Palace. I was curious. We were heading away from the taiga (forest) to the tundra (freezing cold without forests). Siberia in the winter has to be seen to be believed. Everywhere, there was deep snow covering everything; the land, the lakes (all frozen) and the peasant villages. Everyone in the villages was either hibernating or drinking vodka. I had a very pleasant lunch with the Abbot and his assistant. We discussed the merits of Tolstoy (I had read *War and Peace* whilst in Yekaterinburg) versus Dostoevsky (*The Brothers Karamazov* – which I had not read but my interpreter from the Consulate had, and thankfully translated my attempts at bullshitting the Abbot into a reasoned exposition of the book). Much more interesting was the claim that this particular monastery was the one where the Tsar had rested up in before his final and fateful transfer to Yekaterinburg. I think I might have known about that. Maybe the Abbot was bullshitting me now. The letter from Buckingham Palace was just a simple thank you acknowledgement for a previous letter. Still, I am glad it was sent – it enabled me to go on this very unusual and perhaps unique visit.

Talking of Buckingham Palace (as one does!), and before we leave Siberia, I was informed whilst in Yekaterinburg that HRH the Duke of York was on his way back from Mongolia (remember that conversation?) to London and would refuel at Yekaterinburg airport, and could I go out to the airport and do the honours? (That is, make sure there were no hitches.) HRH was not expected to disembark. He did. And we had a pleasant chat for about ten minutes. Just before he reboarded the flight, he looked quizzically at me and said: "The last time we spoke, you had been to North Korea and now here you are in Siberia. What on earth have you done wrong?!" I am not sure I had an answer.

Prior to leaving Siberia for London, I saw a nice Consul General Job coming up in Denver, Colorado, the US of A. For whatever reasons, the Ambassador in Moscow thought that I had done a splendid job (luckily, he did not see me failing badly in my attempt to outdrink vodka with two Russian Red Army colonels!). He recommended that I should get the Denver post, and when one of these top Ambassadors pronounces something, it happens. And so it came to pass that I and the family were headed out West.

Part Ten:

Denver (USA)

May 2007 – July 2011

Chapter 26

A British National in the Court of King Colorado

And so it was that we headed west, to the Wild West. In days gone by, it was the cinematic domain of John Wayne, Clint Eastwood, James Stewart and Gary Cooper. In non-cinematic days gone by, it was the land of Buffalo Bill, Geronimo, Sitting Bull and Lt. Colonel George Armstrong Custer to name but a few. My original parish as Consul General was just Colorado, but it later expanded to also cover Wyoming and New Mexico. And within my dominion, there were such famous place names as Cheyenne, Laramie, the Hole in the Wall (hence the famous Hole in the Wall gang – Butch Cassidy and the Sundance Kid), Fort Collins, Cody, Durango/Silverton, Santa Fe, and the further afield Tombstone and Deadwood. Not only was there all that, but also the High Plains of New Mexico and, in our backdoor in Denver, the magnificent Rocky Mountains. For those of you who are not fans of the Westerns, cowboys and Native Americans, panoramic unbelievable scenery, gunfights, steaks and burgers, your reading time, holiday time and money might be better spent in Blackpool or Bognor Regis.

The Consulate General was in downtown Denver, the state capital of the great state of Colorado. It was a mini-consulate, just the two of us. Me as the Lone Ranger with my sidekick, Tonto. And before anyone gets uppity, my sidekick was indeed part Native American – the inestimable Lona McCollum. Not a very Native American name, but with war paint on, she was a twenty-first century Buffalo Calf Road Woman – the Native American warrior who is rumoured to have knocked Custer off his horse before he died.

What did we do all day long in the Consulate? A good question. Apart from covering the politics and economics of the Mountain West, we covered Climate Change, Trade and Investment, the odd Consular case, the media, relations with the state government, relations with the two state senators and the five congressmen and women in Washington. Of course, we also arranged and catered for visits from Ministers, very senior civil servants and, for one week, we hosted the Democratic National Convention (DNC) at which a certain Barack Obama accepted the Democratic nomination to run for President of the USA – whatever happened to him? Just for clarity, the British Consulate did not host the DNC; 1776 had happened and we Brits were precluded from deciding who would lead America. A shame I know, but we all have to move with the times.

Having worked on all that, I did seem to spend an inordinate amount of time, once a year because of budget cuts, writing papers justifying the existence of a London-based diplomat being paid to live in a mansion in a fantastic city miles away from anywhere. I succeeded. Unfortunately, my successor did not and sadly there is no longer a London-based presence in Denver and I think the Consulate is now a trade office. So be it. I, Leone, Benny and Adele all had a great four years there.

Our first major adventure in Denver was admiring and getting lost in our three million dollar home (rented, I should add). It had a basement half the size of a football pitch, which included a pool table, massive TV, comfy area, and a second area as a fifth bedroom with en suite. The ground floor was more impressive, with a completely separate sophisticated dining area for official guests, our own more informal open plan area, my office (the size of a small bungalow), decking, a garden, triple garage, and our own driveway. Upstairs, there were four bedrooms, two en suite (the one in the master bedroom was the size of a small detached cottage in rural Kent), and through the front upstairs windows, on a clear day, were views of the Rocky Mountains. And there was an official car. This was the life for us.

Prior to heading for Colorado, my uncle Michael had told us that we had some very distant Lynch relatives in a place called Fort Collins. And so, one crisp blue Colorado morning, we headed north to meet our distant cousins. We found the address and, with some trepidation it has to be said, knocked on the door. It was opened by the double of my sister Angela – over generations and oceans, the gene pool had not been too diluted. We were made very welcome and, cryptically, they said that they had organised a surprise for us. We would be out and about for about three hours (no alcohol – which sounded worrying) and then have a leisurely late lunch. I am not one for surprises, especially surprises not involving beer or wine, but who were we to get back in our car and drive away? What a mistake that would have been.

We all piled into a big twelve-seat van (their family consisted of two adults, three teenage children, with another joining us for lunch) and drove out of the city. Using my massive intellect, I was determined to work out our surprise; no alcohol hinted at perhaps shooting things (not really my thing) or driving go-karts (another pet hate) or canoeing (it was getting worse). Imagine our surprise when we turned up at an old airfield. And imagine our bigger surprise when, walking towards a hangar, we were told to beware of the rattlesnakes sunning their lithe long bodies in the grass. And, indeed, this was true. We saw one snake that was about four foot long and heard the distinct rattles of others as they warned us to keep away – which we did. Our hosts seemed to be oblivious to our imminent instant death. Indeed, we met our first real cowboy – Stetson, cowboy boots, Levi jeans and jean jacket, large leather belt with an even larger buckle made out of Texas Long Horn. Referring to the rattlesnakes, he kindly informed us: "They will not bother us if we do not bother them."

Well, far be it from me to differ, but I do not really know what bothers rattlesnakes (apart from the obvious: treading on them or their young). He (the rattlesnake) might be bothered that we have built an aerodrome on his home; he might be bothered about the latest news to come out of North Korea; he might be bothered (fast forwarding to the present) about President Trump's latest tweet. There are a whole host of issues that might be bothering Mr Rattlesnake and, in being bothered, he just might want to bite the nearest non-snake thing. Just in case anyone had not noticed, we humans – after thousands of years of evolution – have forsaken any built-in mini, major or mass weapons of destruction. On the other hand, most of our fellow inhabitants on planet Earth decided, wisely, to keep on their person, large teeth, talons, claws, poison for spitting, hooves for kicking, horns for horning and a whole other array of attack and defence mechanisms. These are solely for the purpose of using when they are bothered about something. And restating my case, we really do not know everything that could possibly bother the non-human species. We live in the hope (or die in the mistake) that the non-human life surrounding us is not having a bothersome time and that, between us, we can make it through to the following day.

Saying all that, we made it to the hangar alive (making it to the hanger not alive would be a pointless journey, in my opinion). And there we were informed that we were going gliding.

Gliding, we were going gliding! I had to think for a minute. We had only just met our long-lost cousins. We were in the land of serial killers, bizarre murders and internecine feuds that lasted through the generations. How was I to know whether there had been some strange family rift many years ago that caused this Colorado branch of the family tree to flee to the US of A? And that to this day, they were harbouring revenge against any member of the Lynch family who crossed their path. The rattlesnakes had failed in their part of the plan and plan B was to drop us from a great height onto to some very hard rocks. So I did the husbandly and fatherly duty, protecting my family was paramount. I said that Leone should go first.

But "Death on the Rockies" was not to be the next lurid British tabloid headline, and our long-lost relatives are indeed a fine family. We are still in contact.

In front of the Southern Rocky Mountains, covering the great states of Colorado and Wyoming, is a mountain range called the Front Range. It is the first set of mountains one meets when heading west from the East Coast, across the Great Plains to wherever on the West Coast (but avoid South Los Angeles if you can). And so it was that each of us individually got to glide alongside the great Front Range. Heading North on our left were the great 14,000 feet peaks of various Rocky mountains and to the right were the vast expanses of the Great Plains, all the way to the Mississippi River – that was too far to see, of course, but what a great start to our USA posting. Lunch later consisted of the great American tradition of burgers (best I have ever tasted) and beers.

Of course, it was not all gliding and burgers and beer; mostly, but not all. I had to get out and meet the politicians, the media, the influencers, the opinion formers, the business people and the bar owners (the excellent Noel Hickey and his family). Coloradoans, be they native born to that great state or having settled there from further afield, are to a man and a woman, wonderful, friendly warm human beings, always ready to help and give sound advice. And lots of them still loved the English accent. On one occasion (to do with a small accident and pain, I should say, first of all), I had the occasion to say the F-word aloud. My American colleagues laughed and informed me that even when we Brits swear it does not sound angry, more quaint than anything else. Even so, I did not make a practice of swearing (quaintly or otherwise).

Like most of us (except perhaps some poor Bangladeshis living in the rice fields of West Bengal), I have travelled in various lifts, be they in the UK or anywhere else in the world. Mostly they are cold, silent inhumane places wherein everyone studiously avoids each other until their floor and only then do we hear a begrudging, "My floor, excuse me, please." And sometimes not even that – just a nudge to get one out of the way. But not in Denver, where lifts are thriving social centres of politeness and pleasant conversation, ranging from the weather to the latest shenanigans in Washington DC. That 'Lift Life' as I like to call it, transfers itself into everyday encounters. The Mountain West people are polite, engaging, interested in you and incredibly helpful. That is up to a point. They do have the 'Make my Day' legislation in place. More of that later.

At the beginning of my tour, I was out and about meeting with the Governor of Colorado, the State Representatives in Washington DC, the members of the Colorado General Assembly (from both the Senate and the House of Representatives), representatives of the Native Americans, lawyers (lots of lawyers), oil and gas men and women, and more bar owners. Later on, I did the same in Wyoming and New Mexico. These early meetings paved the way for further, more substantive meetings and, occasionally, the odd difference of opinion on UK and USA policies. Even though I was a Consul General miles and miles away from the bosses in the Embassy in Washington, I was still expected to try to influence those worth influencing on matters of particular importance to my masters in Washington and their bosses in London. There was a broad brush remit on trade and investment: get the Coloradoans and Mountain West to buy British and invest money in the UK. On the more specific issues, it was to try to convince the climate change naysayers that they were wrong (in the land of oil and gas and ranching) and that the death penalty was wrong (in the land of the 'Make my Day' legislation – a reference to Clint Eastwood as Dirty Harry).

On the latter, I approached a senior State official with my lobbying notes to see if the State legislature would be willing to remove the death penalty from its statute books. Think of Daniel walking into the lion's den – but with not such a good outcome. But as I say, Coloradoans are nice people and the senior official gave me the diplomatic equivalent of a pat on the head (rather than a kick up the ass) and at the same time asked me if I had been drinking the 'Kool-Aid' – a kindly expression politely telling someone that whatever they want is not going to happen.

He then went on to tell me about the Colorado 'Make my Day' legislation – legislation that basically means a gun owner can legitimately kill an intruder or intruders on or in their property, no questions asked. Well, maybe one or two. Even if the intruders are unarmed, they could be killed. Basically, do not enter a Coloradoan house if you are not wanted. There are not many burglars in Colorado.

But it does not have to be a robber or a burglar. In one case, a man shot dead a drunken woman who had walked into his bedroom at three in the morning. He was not charged. Forgive me for saying so, but if I were single and living out on the Colorado plains and a drunk woman entered my bedroom on a cold snowy night, I am sure that shooting her would be the last thing I would do. But perhaps that is just me and my libido.

Continuing with my death penalty lobbying exercise, I thought – logically it seemed to me – that if the Colorado legislature had decided to listen to this humble messenger from the former colonial power requesting the removal of the death penalty from the statute books, the unintended consequence would have been more 'Make my Day' deaths. If people were not going to be executed by the state, why not do it oneself? I never raised the subject again, and strangely enough, no one ever again asked me to do so.

On the former issue of climate change, I was sent with a climate change script to give a speech at an oil and gas meeting in Colorado Springs. Someone somewhere, either in Washington or back in London, had it in for me. This is not Dan the Man into the lion's den. This is Kevin the Consul General on his way to the bottom of an oil and gas filled pit.

Colorado Springs, to the South of Denver, is one of the most conservative cities in the whole of the USA, if not the world. There is huntin', shootin', fishin', cigar smokin' and clubs where women were completely banned (probably still are). Colorado Springs was where Democrats were subject to the 'Make my Day' law without having to trespass anywhere (probably still are). Climate and change are two words that are never in the same paragraph, let alone sentence.

The venue for my speech was the top hotel and conference centre in Colorado Springs. It is called the Broadmoor. A very nice place, apart from the unfortunate name for those of us in the know in England. In a small corner of a foreign field in Berkshire, is the United Kingdom's most secure, psychiatric hospital for the criminally insane. It too is called Broadmoor. When it became public knowledge that I was going to give a speech on climate change to a bunch of red-necked Republican oil and gas men and women at a place called Broadmoor, well, the laughter only just outweighed the pre-death condolence notes.

The reception from the organisers was friendly to the point of hysteria (as in hysterically funny). They had only just heard about the subject of my speech. My able sidekick Lona had immediately picked up the vibes and offered to get me out by the back door, but none of that for our intrepid (foolish) diplomat. The show must go on, but not before I had drunk a couple of large chardonnays. Predictably, as I started my climate change speech, the climate changed to very cold; some people walked out, others quietly reholstered their pistols after being told that I was English and had mistaken Colorado Springs for Florida Springs (the springs of Florida affected by climate change). Whilst other speakers received ovations, my delivery to a crowd of some 200-250 was met with a stony silence, until a large Texan voice boomed, "Man that was brave." Thunderous applause echoed throughout the Broadmoor; no one took any notice of the climate change science and policies I had been advocating but I, for a short while, was the toast of the bar rather than just plain toast.

Alongside delivering speeches and pontificating on the death penalty, counter-terrorism, radicalisation, the legalisation of marijuana (Denver has now legalised marijuana, it is now known as the Mile High City for a reason other than that it sits at 5,280 feet above sea level) and various overseas conflicts in which the UK and USA were involved, I had to attend numerous breakfasts, lunches and dinners.

Over the years, the FCO has, in my humble opinion, drifted away from its core work – getting to know Johnny Foreigner and (of course, in these days of political sensitivities) Jane Foreigner and all LBGT foreigners. If we are to influence foreign countries, we need to get out and about – meet the people, learn the language (if foreign, if English, at least to make sure we are intelligible, both in the spoken and written word), study the culture and history, travel and report honestly and accurately. Too often I have seen stuff that reflects what the author thinks his readership wants to hear rather than the unvarnished truth. To do all that, we need to stop surveying ourselves in order to see how diverse, acceptable, gender-balanced and corporate we all are. Get out and about.

In Denver, the breakfasts were many, the lunches not so many and, thankfully, the evening receptions/dinners were not that many at all. These political and economic repasts ranged from the excruciatingly boring to very interesting (a rarity, I might add). The lunches invariably started with a discussion about the demise of the 'Three Martini' lunch. The Three Martini lunch was a tax-deductible perk and people back in the day took advantage of that. They had lots of Martinis or their alcohol of choice and wrote that expenditure off as tax deductible. Not a bad idea.

However, the stormtroopers of the God of Work decided to bring in all sorts of hurdles to prevent taxes from being drunk rather than going straight to the Treasury, so they brought in fitness for duty rules, a decrease in the tolerance of drinking during working hours, different taxes (not to the benefit of the Martini men and women) and less leisure time. None of this affected me or, indeed, stopped me. Much to the amazement of my US colleagues, I would regularly order a glass of nice wine with my lunch – I paid for it myself, I was not going to have a splendid luncheon spoiled by tap water. I started a mini-revolution; not one to compare with the American Revolutionary War of 1775-1783 (we lost, apparently), but a revolution by any other name. Soon, after my taboo-breaking glass of Californian red, my fellow diners started to follow suit. But only on a Friday. Fair enough. However, it soon came to pass that Fridays became the preferred day for working lunches. Some of these extended lunches extended well into the afternoon, the evening and, on the odd occasion, the following Tuesday.

The one place where a glass of red was not going to happen was in America's most secure prison. Nicknamed the Supermax, it is the Alcatraz of the Rockies; its official title is the US Penitentiary, Administrative Maximum Facility. And wearing my Consul General hat, alongside the Consul from Houston, we needed to visit the Supermax. The US Department of Corrections had notified us that there was a Brit (at least, they thought he was a Brit) in the Supermax who would be released eight years hence (nothing like thinking ahead) and he would be going straight back to England. The corrections people just wanted us to officially recognise his British nationality as soon as possible. Arrangements were made for an early visit. And visit we did.

The Supermax is not a nice place. It could be, I suppose, if they shot all the inmates, moved the cells above ground, refurbished and enlarged them; built a swimming pool, spa, bar and gym; dismantled and unpowered all the electric fences and wires; made sure the razor wire was safely pulled down and destroyed; ensured that everyone had a their own key to their own room rather than some sort of foolproof central locking system; and then persuaded the corrections officers that not all the guests were potential killers, terrorists, madmen or disgruntled and disaffected youths with a penchant for stealing three pairs of crocs in a row, thus entailing a 'three strike' life sentence. Yes, I suppose if all that happened and a few other things, the Supermax could be nice. But it is not. And the reality is: it is not supposed to be nice. It accommodates (I use that word loosely) some, if not all, of the most dangerous men in incarceration in America. In, in, in, I like that – read the previous sentence again. You do not get to see that in the great literary works of our age. Some might say they are not surprised.

In the interests of not ending up in the Supermax myself, I will not go into the detail about its entrance or layout, nor our exit from the prison. My colleague and I duly met our man below ground in the very very secure visiting rooms – at least ours was a room. He was on the other side of some very thick glass, his wrists and ankles shackled. There were two windowless walls and a door behind which we could just see two Corrections Officers standing guard.

Now to the job in hand, was our man British? We had some background papers, but not much to go on – no proof of US citizenship, just a statement he had said some years ago that he was originally from Manchester. I should note here that there is one Manchester in England and thirty-one in the USA, and so we had odds of 31/1 that our man would not end up near me and my family on my retirement in this green and pleasant land. Not bad odds for me and my family.

Saying that, we had yet to fully establish how this nondescript man in front of us had ended up in the Supermax. But I would have given odds of 31/1 that it was not going to be pretty. His original sentence was for four years for robbery. He had now been behind bars for twenty-six and was due to be released in a further eight. It did not take a genius in maths to work out that somewhere along the line another thirty-four years for in-prison misdemeanours had been added to the original sentence. Either that or someone had lost his file.

Being fully trained members of the Consular Corps, we had prepared the best we could. But we could not master our opening remarks. We tried, prior to the meeting, to do some roleplay to see where that would take us. I played the inmate of unknown origin (IUO):

Consular Corps: "How are you?"

Inmate of unknown origin (IUO): "Well, after thirty-four years in jail, can't complain."

Or, he could have replied: "Well, after thirty-four years in jail, I have a list of complaints I would like you to resolve."

Or, he could have replied: "How would you be after thirty-four years in jail?"

Or, he could have replied: "Enough small talk, get me out of here."

Not a good start for us, unless he stuck, very unlikely, with the first answer. We thus decided to try the old weather favourite:

Consular Corps: "The weather has been good for this time of year?"

IUO: "How would I know, I only go outside for one hour in every twenty-four, if I am lucky."

No, not good either. We tried many scenarios and the best we came up with, and the one we used, with diplomatic delicacy, profound caring and with as much general prison-like bonhomie as we could muster was this:

Consular Corps: "What the f*** have you done?"

IUO: "Oh dear, I was hoping you would ask me about the weather or life in prison or my nationality, but since you asked..."

And so it transpired that our man in the Supermax had, as we originally knew, been sentenced to four years for robbery back east. But whilst in a Federal Correctional Institution (FCI) in Kentucky (actually the FCI in Kentucky is in a place called Manchester. The plot was thickening, either that or I was), he had attacked a guard with a Scrabble board. No, I kid you not. Through the microphone and thickened glass (and believe me, I would not have said this face to face without bulletproof glass protection) I said (wittily, in my opinion): "And so they hit you with the full letter of the law." I thought it was good. Ignoring my brilliant, off-the-cuff wit, our IUO replied that another four years had been added to his sentence. Not being idle in changing the subject from a scrabble scrap, I opined that we seemed to be missing another thirty years.

Our inmate then kindly elaborated. In another prison, in a twin cell, his cellmate had died The death had occurred at night. The cell door fully secured and, according to CCTV, no one else but our man and the deceased had been in the cell. Nothing out of the normal there, he seemed to think. Suicide was a common occurrence in some prisons.

On the other hand, the authorities had a few problems with the fact that the deceased was covered in blood and bruises, and had had his hands tied behind his back before (according to our IUO) hanging himself whilst our man peacefully slept. That was until a late night cell check caused the prison authorities to notice a body hanging up where it ought not to be and thereafter woke up our prisoner who, soon afterwards, received an additional thirty years to his original sentence.

Our inmate could not seem to understand why the court did not accept his defence against murder. His defence being that, if allowed, he could make the Judge bloody and bruised and, with both hands tied behind his back, make the judge commit suicide. Apparently, contempt of court was a secondary issue in the verdict. He was transferred to the Supermax.

He maintained his innocence on the hanging, admitted the robbery and the scrabble board scrap and, to our astonishment and the trepidation of all scrabble clubs in the North of England, admitted to being born in England. What was more, he had evidence to that effect. So be it, he was English and, if he had not further extended his time in the penal institutes of the US of A, he might be playing in a scrabble club near you. While all this was going on, another inmate next to us was irately engaging with his solicitors. The visiting area was, for a prison like this, slightly open plan.

Our now confirmed Brit pointed very discreetly to the irate inmate in the next visiting cell. This inmate was dressed in a very dark red jumpsuit – the 'worst of the worst'. Our man made a cut of the throat sign, pointed to himself and then made the sign of four. *All very interesting*, I thought – as one does. Diagonally, through the bulletproof glass, I could actually see the other inmate. Our eyes met. Not in a Barry Manilow-type way, more like a shocked stare way. No one stares down the British Consul General, I thought. And he did not – to be honest, I think he got bored. He was probably well practised in staring competitions, but this one did not seem to interest him.

Just in case I am wrong and thus bring a very horrible death upon myself, I am going to use the word 'alleged' a lot in the next few sentences.

I had allegedly tried to stare down the alleged Tommy Silverstein, alleged killer of four people inside jails and alleged leader of the alleged Aryan Brotherhood gang in US prisons. His alleged lawyers next to us were allegedly showing him some of his alleged drawings, discussing alleged prices. And allegedly after my alleged stare, we were asked if our alleged business was concluded. It was. We left.

After all this penal excitement and the conferencing, speaking, lunching, dining, meetings and the occasional consular case, I had to get out and about throughout the three states to get to know my parish. Through a very dear friend, I had been introduced to the Churchill Cigar bar in the Brown Palace Hotel, opposite the Consulate. This bar, although a bastion of Republicanism, was a broad church. Although not that broad, during the Democratic National Convention in 2009, the Churchill bar succeeded in having a total exclusion zone that denied access to any Democrat, no matter what their standing was. All taken in good spirit (and wine and beer), I might add. Here in the Churchill bar, with sage advice from the inestimable Roger Hutson, the late great Gary Boyce and various Republican, Democratic, Academic and Legal Colorado A-listers, I would plot my visits to the far corners of the Mountain West.

These visits were to working ranches where one, as a matter of course (usually, the first one) gets to eat slices of a bull's bollock. Should you ever visit Colorado (and you should), do not be fooled into thinking that Rocky Mountain oysters bear any similarity to a saltwater bivalve mollusc that, when eaten, will somehow improve one's sex life. No, in fact, you are eating the thinly sliced sex life of an erstwhile happy bull. I went to many ranches with my family for pleasure rather than work. Amazing, beautiful places.

And when my young intern from the UK arrived, to assist for three months, my standing went through the roof. My intern was one George Bush! Really. Doors opened fast! He is still a good friend to this day.

On other visits, I would go to small towns with populations of around 10,000-15,000, where I would hold forth on the greatness of the United Kingdom, eat some more bollocks of bull, drink Coors Light and, on one occasion, make headlines in one local newspaper. Not because of some strange antic or heretical prophesy (like Obama would be the next President of the USA) or even eating rattlesnake mousse, but because I had visited the town. Nothing more, nothing less. The article can still be found on the Internet – *The Fort Morgan Times*. Fame at last! Fame at last – a Kevin Lynch headline in *The Times*.

On a visit to Cheyenne, the state capital of Wyoming, I called on the chief advisor to the Governor. After the usual pleasantries, I was left to my own devices and wandered around the state capital building. In the west wing, I came across a full-size bison standing on a plinth. Fortunately, it was dead. Of course, one would not expect to find non-indigenous species housed in a state seat of government. Well, maybe not. And, to be honest – my memory is a bit hazy here – but I am certain that I found, tucked away in a corner in this very same building (I hope they are still there), two Emperor penguins; unfortunately, dead and stuffed. Apparently, they were being brought back from an expedition to Antarctica (where else?) and, believe it or not, did not survive. People in Wyoming have a penchant for putting strange dead animals in strange places.

On a visit to the University of Wyoming in Laramie, I was to be introduced to Big Al. That sounded ominous, especially as I had just had lunch in a Wild West saloon, where I had asked about the provenance of some bullet holes in the wall behind the bar – I was expecting some tales of a nineteenth-century gunfight involving Butch Cassidy and the Sundance Kid. Nope, that was not the case. The offending bullet holes were the result of an over-exuberant birthday party the previous Friday night. Anyway, it turned out that Big Al was an Allosaurus. A large dangerous carnivore predator from the Jurassic age. Fortunately, he too (like the bison and the penguins) was dead and only his skeleton exists. But an interesting exhibit in a university if ever there was one.

Travelling way down South into New Mexico, I found the wonderful artistic state capital of Santa Fe, the oldest state capital in America. The Santa Fe Opera, the art galleries, the adobe buildings, the governor's palace, they are all worth a visit. Whilst all this art and culture was good for my soul, I was about to see something extraordinary and out of this world. I was going to look into deep space.

As part of our UK/USA scientific relations work, I had been invited to see the Very Large Array (VLA) at Socorro in New Mexico. One of the world's top astronomical radio observatories and thereafter, a flight on the Governor's helicopter up to Magdalena Ridge to look into the future. My boss in Washington, Brian F should have done that. Unbeknownst to him, some eight years later, he would buy a house round the corner from me in Deal! Two former bosses now in Deal. I think they are stalking me for ruining their careers! I digress.

Magdalena Ridge sits at 10,600 feet and hosts the Magdalena Ridge Observatory. From inside their laboratory, I was privileged to see meteors twenty light years away from Earth, space debris and my Mum's house in Deal (not really). The scientific stuff was interesting; here were the real Bruce Willis types from the film *Armageddon*. Here, they kept an eye out for the kind of asteroid that hit the Earth some 66 million years ago and caused some minimal destruction – massive climate changes, mass destruction of land mass, mass extinctions and a power cut in Horsham.

In answer to the obvious question, these scientific Bruce Willis-types said it was inevitable that the Earth would be hit again by something big (cancel all those insurance policies, they will not be valid), but for the moment, homo sapiens might be able to deflect or destroy the offending inter-galaxy large rock, depending on the size, speed and trajectory and (crucially) if there was enough notice. We could use thermo-nuclear weapons – either a direct hit or an explosion nearby or (and I am not sure if this was a joke) we could coat one side of the planet killer with a thick resin so that there would be a slightly different gravitational pull on the side without the resin, which would make the offending comet/meteor turn or move slightly in space. This slight movement way out in space would cause the rock to miss the Earth by tens of thousands of miles. With hindsight (and wondering which painting and decorating firm would bid for such earth-saving work), I think I might have been mocked. But a good story, nonetheless.

Alas, amongst the many great memories of the great state of New Mexico, my other, much more down to earth memory is of a stay in a hotel in Albuquerque. After a hard day's visits, including to what was then the prospective site for Richard Branson's Virgin Galactic spaceport, I settled down to dine, write my reports, order my dinner and drink a bottle of wine. The wine and two glasses duly arrived. I said that I was alone and there was no need for an extra glass. Wow, did that cause a stir. Apparently, in this part of the world, one is not allowed, if one is by oneself, to order a whole bottle of wine. One could become drunk or an alcoholic. Bad morality for a state that is partially crippled by the manufacture, distribution and use of crystal meth. But not wanting any crystal meth, I explained that it was about six o'clock in the evening and that I would be working and dining at the table until about ten o'clock. My thinking was that a bottle of wine with food over four hours was not going to turn me into a monster, raving, demented alcohol-fuelled mass murdering demonic history-making killer of half of the population of New Mexico (an asteroid would do that stone-cold sober). And so after some negotiation (in view of my previous sentence, all very pleasant, I should add), we came to a good compromise. Just in case the local Sheriff came in, I would have two glasses on my table, one for me and the other one (with a small tincture of wine therein, for the sake of reality) to avoid breaking a bad local law. And, hence, the worldwide award-winning series *Breaking Bad*.

Of course, life in the Mountain West was not all visits, weird stuffed animals in weird places, ranches, burgers and beer and fun meals out. My darling wife was hard at work being the partner, the pillar and the mainstay of Her Majesty's Consul General. Amongst lots of other roles, Leone had been anointed the Honorary President of the Daughters of the British Empire (Colorado Chapter – and no, it is not a chapter of Hell's Angels – although, thinking about it, it might have been). The DBE, as it was known in shorthand, was a wonderful group of ladies (and a few of their male partners) who still had ties back to the Motherland (England, not Russia), but had made their lives and homes in Colorado. They did many good things for charity and other organisations. And quite often they all came round for tea and cake. At least, it started as tea.

My job at these events was to support Leone (a Lithuanian Honorary President of the DBE – I loved that) by serving tea and cakes and making witty speeches about the USA and UK. During such events, bearing in mind that I do not drink tea, I noticed the male partners who attended with their wives (to a man, involuntarily) looked enviously at my cold Coors Light beer. Being a generous soul, I offered my colleagues beer and, to cut a long story short, these pleasant, dignified, English heritage *Downton Abbey* afternoons morphed into cheese and wine and beer parties with taxis for all. "No taxi without beer and wine," they would shout. It took me a while to realise they were corrupting one of the great slogans of the American War of Independence – "No taxation without Representation."

Whilst it was rather nice way out West, away from the hurly-burly of the big boys in the Embassy in Washington DC, I, alas, like my other Consuls General dotted around the USA, had to go to Washington on regular occasions for briefings and to pay our respects. I did this quite regularly by plane, but once I decided to cross America by train – the famous Amtrak. From Denver to Chicago, twenty hours, change in Chicago and then another nineteen hours to Washington. I had booked my own berth and so, late one Tuesday evening, I left Denver train station for my cross-country rail adventure. The first part of the journey was across the Great Plains, through Nebraska, Iowa and into Illinois for Chicago. That would be fascinating, but it was dark and so I went to sleep. I missed the first stop out of Denver; it was Fort Morgan. If I had disembarked, I am sure another headline would have been written. Later, I awoke to miles and miles of Nebraskan prairie and grassland. And, of course, my fellow passengers in the dining car. No, I had not been walking in my sleep to the dining car.

The conductor directed me to the dining car and, thence, to a table (no one gets to eat alone). No one took any particular interest in me and so I hurried my breakfast and headed for the observation lounge – more prairie and grassland. I have the propensity to stare out of windows at the ever-changing (well, on this part of the journey, never-changing) world beyond my window for hours on end. The bar was open but I held out until 1201. And then I gazed out the window with a drink in my hand. Much better.

My fellow passengers were either families of four interested in keeping their children from going stir crazy with boredom or, to be honest, very obese people who would probably find flying anywhere very uncomfortable. Naturally, these people enjoyed the freedom of not having miniature airline food; instead, they were tucking into almost everything on the menu. Time passed and we stopped occasionally – I thought for passengers to get on and off, but the reality was that the stops were for the obese people, continuing with their health regime, to smoke as many cigarettes in fifteen minutes as humanly possible. The high spot of these fourteen stops was Ottumwa – not many people know this, but Ottumwa was the birthplace of Radar O'Reilly from *M*A*S*H*. I have been there, so there. *M*A*S*H* reappears later, if you have got this far. And so, on to Chicago.

I had booked a Business Class lounge in Chicago Union Station for three hours for my transit. A bad move, as it did not have a bar. And so I had a pleasant three hours with some equally pleasant people in the Junction Pub in the station. We even swapped emails and never heard from each other again.

The Chicago to Washington leg took me through Indiana, Ohio, Pennsylvania, Maryland, West Virginia and into Washington DC. Apart from Gary, Indiana (I would not recommend going there and I only saw it from a train window – no wonder the Jackson Five left), this journey was much more picturesque, unless, of course, you like prairies, in which case this journey is not for you. The route is much more densely populated, with admirable views of the various admirable towns and cities. We followed some rather splendid rivers through some rather splendid woodland.

Some of the passengers were not so splendid. My physically challenged travelling companions from the Denver to Chicago leg had alighted at Chicago to, I assume, feast on some well-earned worldwide famous Chicago pizzas (extra-large, if you please). They, not all, I should add, had been replaced by some more insalubrious types. This became obvious when police with drug dogs boarded the train on more than one occasion and removed various fellow passengers from the carriage. Not because they were travelling without a ticket, but because they were moving drugs across state borders. Not a good thing and I suspect most of them who were removed from the train are still in a state prison somewhere deep in the backwoods of Pennsylvania wishing they had never heard of crack cocaine. Or they could be back in Gary, Indiana, which might be worse.

I arrived in Washington refreshed and better educated about America. Looking out the train windows with guidebooks for every state is a marvellous way of learning and getting around. Apart from the drug smugglers, I would do it again.

Chapter 27

Wild West Travels, True Grit and the Pink Hummer

People, friends and places are interesting. At least, I hope so; otherwise, I am writing all this for nothing. I have found and met lots of interesting people in interesting places. I have made interesting friends in interesting places. But it has to be said that some of my friends have never visited me in some interesting places. Not many, if any, came to Bangladesh, Senegal, Russia or the Kingdom of Saudi Arabia. Even my elderly mother-in-law, who had spent time in the snows of Siberia, came to the sands of Saudi Arabia. But I do not blame my friends – they could equally accuse me of not visiting them in Beirut (excuse: there was a civil war going on), the Falklands (excuse: we did not know it at the time, but the Argentinians had designs on this far-flung outpost of the British Empire), East Berlin (no excuse), Wellington (excuse: far too far away, in those days), Kinshasa (no excuse: but never go there). I could go on, but that is enough for now. Suffice to say that we had lots of wonderful visitors in America, which enabled us to see more of Colorado and the USA than we might have done.

Steamboat Springs is a name with which to conjure guests. The Richards family (Steve, Tracy and Steph) had come for a visit – their first, I think. Steamboat is renowned for its adventurous skiing, but even getting there is an adventure. You arrive over high passes and the continental divide, close to the wonderfully named Rabbit Ears Pass – if you ever go this way and need to ask why a pass is so named, you need to invest in a new optician, or get out of the house more. As I say, Steamboat Springs is renowned for its skiing. We went in the summer. But that was not going to deter us from getting up to the summit of the main mountain via the ski gondola. How we got down proved interesting. From the summit, we had admired the magnificent views and eaten the obligatory ice cream. We then ignored the signs about bears in the woods and decided to walk down the mountain, back into town and head for another wonderfully named American attraction – Fishtail Creek.

From on high, the walk looked easy, downhill all the way and no bears to be seen.

We, the Magnificent Seven (me, Leone, Steve, Tracy, Benny, Adele and Stephanie), headed for the creek. Down and down we went, following the path. Everyone was chirpy, happy, blissful, enjoying the majestic wonder of the Rockies. Through the brush and down the dale, our happy band wandered. Songs cheerfully emanating from our voice boxes, eulogising our happy lives and happy holidays. All that came to an abrupt halt in the middle of some tall thick brush. There it was. Right in front of our two families. Right in our path. Poo. Warm, steaming, recently deposited bear poo. The guidebook says something about what to do if you actually come across a bear – do not run, walk backwards, do not attack its offspring, talk to it (no chance), and make lots of noise – screaming counts, I think. But it says nothing about discovering very recently deposited bear poo with not a bear in sight. We improvised. We ran and ran. We threw the children over our shoulders – not on them, but over them – so that we economically-productive parents could survive and perhaps live another day to procreate again. And we made it. The children managed to get a lift from a nice mountain ranger who was not too impressed with European parenting skills. The bear was never seen and, to be honest, probably defecated on hearing our singing and then ran for his life.

We had many holiday adventures with the family Richards; they will reappear in New Zealand.

On another holiday outing, this time with the Babilius family from Lithuania (my sidekick Mida, her husband and two children); we covered some three thousand miles and only really saw the heart of America. Four adults and four children headed North through Wyoming, cut across into Nebraska and spent our first night in South Dakota. This first night of our eleven-night Grand Tour of the Mountain West had been booked on some dodgy website and entailed the eight of us staying in someone's small woodshed surrounded by Hell's Angels bent on revenge on the English for the pre-1776 times. I found it extremely interesting that all my travelling companions now conversed in Lithuanian and left their Lithuanian passports by the torchlights. Being the optimist, it could only get better.

South Dakota is interesting. Sioux Falls is a city well worth visiting. It is in Minnehaha County – Minnehaha means 'Laughing Water'. How nice – a shame that she died in a very cold winter. Do not despair it was only a story, part of Hiawatha, but visit Sioux Falls if you can.

We moved on across the North of Wyoming, heading for Cody. En route, we overnighted at two smaller woodsheds. I am not sure, to this day, for whom these woodsheds had been built. There was nothing inside the sheds save beds (I use that term very very loosely) that had to be unchained from the wall; no water, WC, carpet, or heating. A mini-bar and room service were out of the question. Nor was I sure why they had been built where they had been. According to all the signs, the place was full of bears, wolves, more Hell's Angels, snakes and Native Americans offering Bed and Breakfast fifty miles away (we should have taken up the offer). Our Lithuanian visiting family slept in the van. I did not blame them.

I risked my life by going and finding a loo in the middle of the night. The kids did not sleep, convinced that they could hear bears breaking open whatever could be broken open in their search for food. Leone found it difficult closing her eyes, probably due to the rattlesnake family curled up in domestic bliss beneath her unchained bench. We survived.

We moved on to Cody and Yellowstone National Park. The accommodation improved. The scenery and wildlife were spectacular, but my mind was now focused, laser-like, on the five-star hotel that I knew we had booked in Las Vegas – about 900 miles away, but it took longer because we got lost in Utah. Stopping in a town with a population of eighty (yes eighty) in the middle of Utah was bizarre. Everyone in the diner looked at us – I am not sure that they had ever seen such a diversified gene pool. We looked at them and I am not sure that I had ever seen such a small undiluted gene pool. Once the bargaining for our women started, we left. I was on the point of some serious negotiations, a double cheeseburger, fries, salad and a dessert for my daughter did not seem such a bad deal. But I was overruled.

Viva Las Vegas, where we refreshed in massive rooms, massive showers, massive beds and mini-bars that were the size of the woodsheds now very far to the North and a distant memory. The hotel lobby was bigger than the town of eighty in Utah (I wish them well). Mida broke the bank at the roulette table and returned to Lithuania later to put a major deposit on Poland (historically and to this day, the Lithuanians have always wanted to put a major deposit on Poland, but not with money).

After two days in Vegas, we headed North East, back towards Denver via the Hoover Dam (impressive); the Grand Canyon (very impressive, apart from the early morning hogs who luckily were not hungry and left Leone, Adele and Benny intact – I was sleeping); the Four Corners where Colorado, Utah, Arizona and New Mexico all meet (semi-impressive); the Mesa Verde Cliff Dwellings (impressive, but to be honest, we, in England, were living in big castles in the thirteenth century). The Mesa Verdeans – I know that is not correct, but it will do for a collective noun for the moment – all left to go and live elsewhere. I hear there are still some in Dover Castle in Kent, England.

And so back to our mansion in Denver.

So there we are, around the heart of the mid-West in five paragraphs. A bargain if you have paid for this book. If you have borrowed it, go and buy your own copy, I need the royalties; I am being sued by a very small town in Utah.

During our various outings in Colorado and the Mountain West, we must have crossed the Great Divide in different places at different times of the year. Everybody should do it. It's indescribable in places, but best described by Bob Seger in *Roll me Away*. Because of copyright, I cannot reproduce the exact verse here, but listen to it – which is probably better than my just writing about it!

Your heart will sing as you cross the Great Divide. Coming from the East, you will have the vast expanse of the Great Plains behind you and the Rocky Mountains before you and beyond that the mountains, lakes and flatlands, all leading to the shore of the great Pacific Ocean and Los Angeles, but never mind that (Los Angeles, not the shore of the Pacific Ocean).

I should not leave my own self-opinionated local travel guide without two further mini-adventures. The first concerns a pink Hummer and John Wayne and the second a Christmas mountain rescue from the ski slopes of Vail, Colorado.

A pink Hummer and the late great John Wayne? What on earth is that about? For those over the age of sixty, you might recall *True Grit*, the Oscar-winning 1969 film with Big John starring as US Marshall Rooster Cogburn. One of the closing scenes is of John Wayne taking on four bad guys by riding his horse, reins in his mouth, and firing, swinging and swirling rifles from both hands. Fantastic. That scene (and many others from many other great Westerns) was filmed in Colorado in a place called Deb's Meadow, near the summit of Owl Creek Pass, near the town of Ridgway. Too good a place not to visit. And so with another best mate, Inspector H of the Yard (he of Accra fame), we headed off to hire a car for our adventure into South Western Colorado. The only drawback was that we had decided just to hire a car on spec on the day of our travel. And the only one suitable for our escapade was a pink Hummer. Needs must, and so off we headed into the Wild West, in a pink Hummer.

Ridgway has a population of about 1,000 people and two Brits arriving in a pink Hummer did not go unnoticed. Nor did the fact that we wanted a double room, proclaiming, perhaps too strongly and loudly, our need for two single beds. Luckily, they had one such room. And off we went to join the cowboys and cowgirls in the True Grit café. Once we had ordered beers, large beers, in deep voices, flashed around our wedding rings and shown everybody within five miles photos of our respective wives and children, we settled into a night of steaks, beers, bar stories about the old West, the filming of *True Grit* and how pink Hummers were popular this fall. Ridgway was a great town with great people. Of course, we paid homage to Big John at Deb's Meadow, where the two of us re-enacted that famous scene. It was not quite the same without five horses, guns and rifles, Robert Duvall, Dennis Hopper or, indeed, John Wayne. But job done and so we move on.

Somewhere in Colorado, most of the time, one can guarantee a white Christmas, but not for us any old white Christmas. One year, the Christmas was straight out of the movies. But the week did not start well. Friends from England would arrive on 23rd December and so, the day before their arrival, we set out for a quick skiing trip to Vail for the day. Leone and Benny and Adele had all been taking lessons. I had learnt many moons ago on the slopes of the Swiss and French Alps and so, accompanied by a good friend, a long-time resident of Denver and somewhat of an expert on skiing in Colorado (better than France and Switzerland), we headed to the beautiful resort of Vail where we were reliably informed the 'Green' ski slopes were supposed to be easy. However, it did not take long for the skiing population of the pistes of Vail to notice a mother and daughter who might be a little bit out of their skiing comfort zone. The father was busy trying to collect skis that, after several falls, had decided to break free from their respective owners. Benny was nowhere to be seen. Fortunately, one helpful gentleman took pity on the whole sorry snowy saga and called up the Vail and Beaver Creek (wonderful name) Ski Patrol. They arrived and duly plucked our ladies from a potentially pitiful snowy mountain grave. I grabbed the skis and poles and made my way down the mountain, looking like I had just mugged some poor family for their ski equipment. A happy ending. Not. There was one thing wrong with this picture.

We had arrived as a family of four, now we were three. Benny had headed off with the son of our companion and was nowhere to be seen. To make matters worse, a blizzard had just started and everyone, bar Benny and his friend, was coming off the mountain at a rate of knots. The Ski Patrol was back in action, but within minutes Benny and his friend could be seen expertly skiing through the snow towards the resort, oblivious to the helicopters, skidoos, wailing mothers and a father in desperate need of a drink. We did not go back to Vail during our four years in Colorado.

After the Vail event, every cloud had a silver lining, or in our case, more snow than you can shake a stick at. Our friends duly arrived, but to a dull grey Denver. However, the weather front in Vail was slowly heading for the Mile High City. Weather-wise, Christmas Eve was dull and grey, a slight covering of snow. But what Coloradoans do know about (and they know about many things, except how to grade the difficulty of ski slopes) is the weather. I called my sidekick, Tonto Lona McCollum, and she guaranteed a winter wonderland. I was not so sure. She was right. I am not sure if we notice in England, but when a thick blanket of snow falls, the sounds are absorbed. And waking up on Christmas morning in 2008 was like waking up inside a cotton wool ball. Everything was eerily quiet and muffled. A peek out the window revealed why; a magnificent White Christmas, about two feet of snow had fallen during the night.

Our Residence was in a small cul-de-sac. Not your normal cul-de-sac, this was the cul-de-sac for the very rich. Outside was a massive shared driveway (now completely undrivable except for the city snowplough), gardens, old oak trees, a view of the magnificent snow-clad Rockies, a view of the prestigious Cherry Creek Country Club and Golf Course (magnificently covered in snow). And someone had kindly constructed a snowman, complete with tray and four chilled flutes of Christmas Champagne – courtesy of our collective children. Not a bad start to Christmas day. It would end with the police calling in for a chat.

Christmas day had started well; lunch went well, the drinks (adults only) went very well and the opening of presents went well. One present for our well-built guest was an orange jumpsuit imitating (too closely as we were later to discover) the in-prison dress for those prisoners with medium risk criminal convictions who, at any given time, were supposed to be under the jurisdiction of the Colorado Department of Corrections. That is locked away and not enjoying champagne outside four very nice houses in view, via our select gateway, of passing snow ploughs. Snow ploughs that our man in orange brazenly waved away so as not to disturb our own perfect, brilliantly white, two feet deep virginal snow.

Alas, unbeknownst to us, one of the drivers of the snowploughs had become somewhat worried. He mused about a big fellow in an Orange County Jail jumpsuit, with a strange accent, with a glass of champagne in one hand who had, with his free hand, denied access to a legitimate snowplough driver going about their lawful duties. In effect, the big fellow in the orange jumpsuit had ensured that no one entered the millionaire cul-de-sac. A cul-de-sac, to be fair, on the balance of probabilities, where one would not expect to find on the day of the birth of Our Lord, a man in an orange Department of Corrections jumpsuit directing traffic. After a mulled wine at home and musing with his wife, the driver of the snowplough called the police.

They arrived in force. They surrounded the house. They called on us to open the door, come out, lie down and generally behave ourselves. We did all four at breakneck speed, wondering what the problem was. Once it transpired (just slightly before frostbite set into our faces that were buried in what had been hitherto been very nice snow) that the man in the orange jumpsuit was a visiting policeman from London merely enjoying his new Christmas present in the best White Christmas ever, the SWAT teams were stood down, and guns were holstered. The children were calmed and reconciliatory coffee was made and drunk; and we, the Lynch family and friends, went about our business of enjoying the rest of our Christmas behind the safety of a Monopoly board. The police, I am sure, went back to the station with a funny story to tell. I did not report the incident to my superiors.

I could write a whole book on Colorado (others might say that I have difficulty writing a whole sentence, but be that as it may). I have not covered American football games. The Denver Broncos lost every time we went to see them and, after we left, they won the Super Bowl. I have not covered baseball matches. The Colorado Rockies got to the final of the World Series after we left. So it's best to leave sport alone. Suffice to say, though, they were great days out for all the family. The Americans really know how to do big sporting events.

On the work – rather than fun – front (although as a highly visible Consul General, one is never really off duty), we had visits by the Ambassador and a visit by Lord Digby Jones – UK Business Ambassador for UK Trade and Investment (he was not the Ambassador). He was a quite brilliant representative of the UK and, quite rightly, thought that lots of Civil Servants should be sacked – I do not think he included me. We also had many Lords, Ladies and UK Parliamentarians descend on us for the Democratic National Convention (at which time the future High Commissioner to New Zealand and Governor of the Pitcairn Islands – my future boss – stayed in my basement for a week). There were numerous others, including my old neighbour from days gone by in Dhaka Bangladesh – he had risen meteorically to be our Consular man, covering the whole of the USA and the Caribbean.

I covered my three states well and did not neglect such fine world-renowned institutions as the National Renewable Energy Laboratory (NREL), the National Oceanic Atmospheric Administration (NOAA), Boulder University, the Colorado School of Mines and the Celtic Tavern School of Poker.

By early 2011, the FCO had found my file and decided that it was time for me to move on. I and Leone had given a lot of thought to calling it a day, but there then appeared on our job website, the enchantingly entitled job 'Consul General Auckland and Deputy Governor of the Pitcairn Islands'. It had my name all over it. But in 2011, the system had changed – actually, it had changed some years ago but I had managed to avoid this particular new process. Staff now had to submit papers dreaming up ideas as to why they, and no one else, should get any particular job. These papers would be sifted by their future Line Manager and a couple of his or her friends, and then there would be a shortlist of four or five called for an interview. For difficult posts, these so-called "bids" were not thick on the ground – the people who were bidding might have been thick on the ground or anywhere else for that matter, but that was not my concern. I knew that, in my early fifties, and in my right mind, I would not be bidding for the likes of Kabul, Baghdad, North Korea, the Middle East or anywhere else vaguely uncomfortable. I had done my bit, so I threw my hat into the ring for the Auckland/ Pitcairn job (apparently, so did twenty-eight other people). I was shortlisted for an interview.

The FCO is a global service and so getting an interview panel and job applicants together in the same building on the same day at the same time is a little difficult and expensive, so interviews were mainly conducted by telephone. In my case, telephone inks were set up between the High Commissioner in Wellington, the current Deputy Governor in Auckland, the Deputy Head of Overseas Territory Department in London and me in Denver. But it worked. At least it worked for me – I got the job.

So after a fantastic four years, Her Majesty's Consul General, Kevin Lynch, Leone, Benny and Adele Lynch left Denver on 4th July 2011 (yes, the Brits were leaving America on 4th July). Many many friends had been made and, as Arnie Schwarzenegger once said, we told everyone we would be back. And we have been.

One final note on Colorado. Too many friends to single out, but four must be mentioned.

Many thanks to Neil Peck for all his guidance and friendship and, likewise, to Roger Hutson. Many thanks to Noel Hickey, his wife Wendy and their family for their great friendship (and especially to the Celtic Tavern). And, just in case Lona has got this far, I have already mentioned you, Lona!

Plagiarising from somewhere, I was not born in Denver, but I got there as fast as I could!

Part Eleven

Pitcairn (Overseas Territory)

August 2011 – Dec 2011

Just to explain here that for this part of my memoir, I am going to combine my ninety-day stay on Pitcairn, with my subsequent five visits back to the island and my work on Pitcairn matters whilst I was in Auckland, Wellington, Tahiti, New Caledonia and Fiji.

I will be condensing five amazing years into the following pages. After the Pitcairn bit, will come the Auckland bit. But in real-time, the two were intertwined. If you understand that, you are a better person than me.

Chapter 28

Preparation for Pitcairn

When I applied for the Auckland/Pitcairn job, I did not notice the small print. Somewhere amongst the plethora of papers detailing this double-hatted job, I had not noticed a minor detail; the Deputy Governor would have to, prior to taking up residence for five years in one of the most liveable cities on the planet, reside for three months on one of the remotest inhabited islands in the world. When I did notice, I thought (being the wily old fox that I believed I had become): "No problem, I will get away with a month or six weeks on the island." How little I knew.

Pitcairn does not have an airport. It is serviced by a supply ship once every three months, and when that ship visits, one can stay on Pitcairn for four days, eleven days or three months. The three-month sojourn was a new innovation (and, it has to be said, a good innovation) to the Deputy Governor (DG) job. All part of the training, they said. However, I am getting ahead of myself.

As I say, we left Denver on 4th July 2011. I had a lot of training to undertake in England before getting out to Auckland for further training by 25th August and being in Pitcairn by 5th September. I then left very late in November and had returned to Deal by 5th December 2011. Eventually, the whole family was to be in Auckland by 28th January 2012. Whilst all that was happening, we had to move back into our house and get the kids into boarding school. (That did not last long, thankfully; it was not a good move on behalf of the Lynch parents. Benny and Adele were with us for our time in Auckland – excellent). Whilst I was on Pitcairn, Leone would be busy with the house, kids, and the move to the other side of the world. Not many people have jobs like this. To be honest, not many people would like a job like that, or perhaps be able to cope. Each to their own, live and let live, and all that.

The history of Pitcairn, *The Mutiny on the Bounty*, Fletcher Christian and Captain William Bligh, and the subsequent 228 years of Pitcairn Island life is well documented in books, films, *The Pitcairn Miscellany* and various other publications. Indeed, a good friend from the Churchill Bar in Denver had written his PhD thesis on the early days of Pitcairn. In view of all these other masterly writings on the subject of Pitcairn (and for the reason of brevity), I will not rehearse Pitcairn's history, at least, not all of it here.

The Pitcairn Islands (Pitcairn, Henderson, Oeno and Ducie) are a British Overseas Territory. Part of a group of fourteen territories under the jurisdiction and sovereignty of the British government. In the UK, they are managed by the Overseas Territory Department of the Foreign Office in London and funded by the Department for International Development in East Kilbride (DFID), coincidentally probably one of the remotest inhabited Civil Service outposts in the UK. Overseas, the Pitcairn Governor is based in Wellington, New Zealand; the Deputy Governor in Auckland, New Zealand, and the Governor's Representative is on Pitcairn (a twelve-month diplomatic posting). Then, there is the Pitcairn Island Council and the Mayor of Pitcairn.

To add to that mix, the EU in Brussels (because of EU funding) has an interest and that interest has been delegated to their man in Noumea (New Caledonia, another South Pacific Island). And then we also have the Pitcairn Island Office (PIO) in Auckland, close to the Deputy Governor. There are all sorts of Non-Governmental Organisations (NGOs) who have, in various sectors, ongoing interests in the Pitcairn Islands. It is complicated and the good old Deputy Governor has to try to pull it all together and to try to keep it all together. That is, try to keep Pitcairn together rather than keeping him or herself together. Or maybe it does mean the latter.

As with all the previous postings and jobs, there was the usual round of briefings. As an experienced diplomatic hand with numerous postings under my belt, the FCO and DFID briefings were none too onerous. The NGOs presented their none-too-onerous views. I met those FCO staff, who had been to Pitcairn and were still sane (very few). Curiously, they looked at me sadly and wished me well.

The bulk of the work done on Pitcairn before, during and beyond 2011 revolved around the legacy of the serious child sex crimes committed there by the majority of the men over several years (and probably generations). This was and still is the dark side of Pitcairn. It is the elephant in the room and I need, for the purposes of this book, to deal with it early. 'Operation Unique' was an investigation by UK police into the serious allegations of widespread child rape on Pitcairn. Several men were convicted of serious sex crimes against children and were jailed on Pitcairn; two pleaded guilty and one was found not guilty.

In 2011, nearly the whole island (its local population then was about fifty-two) detested the fact that Her Majesty's Government had brought these men to justice, brought back the rule of law to an island that had hidden its dark secrets away for far too long and installed various non-Pitcairn professionals to ensure that such heinous crimes would never be repeated. More generally, HMG was trying to bring Pitcairn back from *The Lord of the Flies* island it had been on the brink of becoming, and thence moving it on from its erstwhile reputation as the Alcatraz of the South Pacific to becoming a fully-fledged member of the law-abiding international community. Or as near as an island that is the world's smallest and remotest democracy can be.

Alas, that did not last long: one of my final jobs in 2017 was to oversee the reconstruction and staffing of Her Majesty's Prison Pitcairn in order to imprison the former Mayor for very serious child pornography crimes. It was as though my working life was coming full circle – from Her Majesty's Prison Canterbury to Her Majesty's Prison Pitcairn. But that is for the future.

In a nutshell, HMG policy was to try to help bring this important piece of British history back in line and thence to a bright sustainable future. Of course, the majority of the Pitcairners did not believe a word of all that and merely thought that HMG (and anyone or any institution that was vaguely touched by HMG) was spying on them and secretly trying to close down the island – not a bad idea but, in reality, not so. But no matter what HMG said to disabuse one and all of this closing down notion, a hardcore majority of Pitcairners were convinced that closing Pitcairn was our ultimate goal. They would not be swayed and they had created a toxic HMG/Pitcairn relationship. The situation was far from helped by the then-Mayor (and subsequently re-elected Mayor) being charged with possession of the worst kind of child sex abuse pornography.

By 2017, I am pleased to say that that toxic relationship is no longer the case. I believe (and I don't care what others think) I might take some credit for that turnaround.

All of the above leads me back to the bulk of my training that I did between leaving Denver and getting to Auckland airport on 1st September to start my journey to Pitcairn. Naturally, aside from the FCO and DFID, there were the obligatory calls on the NGOs, the EU officials and others. The most striking thing about those calls was that no one was willing to bring up or address the serious sex crimes against Pitcairn's children. Not for them to sully their hands on the big pile of elephant dung in the middle of the room. No, that was all left to the inestimable Lucy Faithfull Foundation (LFF).

When leaving HM Prison Canterbury, which is now some forty years behind me, to join Her Majesty's Diplomatic Service, I would never have thought that I would be dealing with the theory of paedophilia and be in day-to-day contact (on Pitcairn) with convicted paedophiles. But hey, "What is this life, if full of care if we have no time to..." deal with child sex abuse on one of the world's remotest inhabited islands. An island so remote that surely nature never intended it for human habitation. And (in the eighteenth century) a human navigational plotting error should have meant that Pitcairn would never have been rediscovered at all. Fletcher Christian has a lot to answer for.

I spent two weeks at the LFF, and there with me was the next Governor's Representative (GovRep) who would spend twelve months on the island. The idea, to repeat myself, was that I would spend three months on the island and be replaced by the GovRep and her husband. Such is life in the FCO, the new GovRep was the wonderful Carol S and her husband. Carol and I had worked together in Lord Carrington's Private Office some thirty years earlier.

Together, we went through various Pitcairn Child Safety Reviews, learnt about internet child pornography, met convicted paedophiles, met with the social services, met with the police and met with a very strange man who believed in 'boy love'. He was about seventy years old and under police observation. In a classroom setting, we did the theory and met up with the inestimable Mike Sheath: he had been to Pitcairn and knew the island's dark side and light side inside out. He would be our lifeline if we needed child safety advice whilst on a two mile by one mile hostile island in the middle of the vast Pacific Ocean. A key learning point was the ability to look out for, in ourselves and in our other professional colleagues, 'Professional Accommodation Syndrome'. That did not mean begging your professional colleagues to share their accommodation with you. It was a variation of the Stockholm Syndrome – developing a benign emotional attachment to one's captors. On Pitcairn, it meant that, as in *Star Wars*, one had been turned, or was being turned, by some Darth Vader-like Pitcairners to the dark side. In essence, it meant that those sent to safeguard children had been convinced that the heinous crimes of the past were cultural, consensual and that no one was hurt. And that HMG were the real bad guys. All four ideas were and are absolute rubbish, of course.

After all this training, it was time to head to Auckland and a few more training courses, briefings and then to the Pit, as I had quaintly decided to call my new place of work. Unfortunately, when some Pitcairners later learnt of my new jargon for Pitcairn they took great exception to it. I think they felt that if Pitcairn was the Pit (and that was bad enough) then they must have been the Pits. I am not sure why they got so upset.

So, I left my home, family and friends and headed to Auckland and, after Auckland, spent three months on Pitcairn. I was flying Air New Zealand, via Los Angeles to Auckland. Door-to-door it was about thirty-three hours. Fortunately, I was in Business Class. Late at night, about ten hours into the first leg of the flight, bored out of my mind, after I had watched all the films, eaten too much and could not face another New Zealand Sauvignon Blanc (but that would change on the next leg), I switched on the flight map. Bad move. We were flying over Denver and the Rocky Mountains. Seven miles below me was a fantastic city with great friends, all probably eating steaks, tucking into the best cheeseburgers in the world, smoking big cigars, playing poker and generally living the American (if not global) dream. And me, well, I was on my way to what one person in England had called the modern-day 'Devil's Island'. Quite probably, this was the only time in my FCO career when I thought what on earth (or at least at 38,000 feet above the earth) was I doing? Plagiarising Dorothy in the *Wizard of Oz*, I thought to myself: "Kevin, I have a feeling we're not in Colorado anymore."

But after many hours, I went onwards and downwards into Auckland airport, into a taxi, into a hotel, into jet lag (bad jet lag) and into bed in a rather grotty hotel, I am not sure how long I slept. It could have been seven minutes, seven hours or seventeen hours. But I awoke. I had deliberately arrived on a Saturday so that I could at least have the weekend to get over the jet lag. If anyone has ever flown England to New Zealand, they will know better than I that it takes much more than forty-eight hours to get over the twelve-hour time difference. It takes about a year. But here I was, wide awake – it was light outside but very quiet. *Time for a stroll*, I thought. There was no receptionist at the grotty hotel, so I was unable to establish time, date or planet. Outside, my worst nightmare hit me. I must have caught the wrong flight. I was in either Seoul, South Korea or Tokyo, Japan. All about me were Korean or Asian restaurants, shops and people (not many people, it has to be said). There was sushi, kimchi and Bulgogi for sale everywhere. And for me, the big giveaway to being again on the Korean peninsula was the sight of some restaurant owners who seemed to be secretively negotiating the price for a very nice large dog.

But do not fret dear reader, I was indeed in Auckland and over the next five days, I was to learn how to ride a quad bike (an ATV if you like), undertake Powerboat Level 1 training in Auckland harbour and become a 'First Aider'. And, of course, meet the Governor, the incumbent Deputy Governor, the great Evan and Shirley from the Pitcairn Island Office, the two people who really know and run Pitcairn from 2,500 miles away and various other Pitcairn stakeholders (I hate that word, but it serves a purpose. I shall try not to use it again, ever, in this book or during the rest of my time on Earth).

Summing up my training, in five days, I had certificates that enabled me to crash my quad bike (see later on, when on Pitcairn) and thereafter fix or heal myself, and if I was ever given control of a powerboat again (highly unlikely), and it crashed and sunk (highly likely with me at the helm) and I were to drown, I could resuscitate myself. Just on quad bikes again (or in my case, mostly off them, lying on the ground) for a moment, did I mention that they are mad machines with minds of their own whose sole purpose in life is to wound, maim or kill the rider? Minor points, I know, but worth remembering if you want to buy one.

Anyway, what more training could a man ask for? Was I ready for Pitcairn? Was Pitcairn ready for me? The answer to both questions was, and probably still is, a resounding no. But it was time to find out.

As if to rub salt into the various wounds I had received during quad bike training, on the way to the airport, I could not help but notice that I was, singularly, the only person heading to the airport and in the check-in lanes; the only person heading for and sitting in the departure lounge. Something was afoot. A quick look on the internet (one of my last for three months) gave the game away. Not only had I signed up for three months on Pitcairn with very limited ways of leaving once the supply ship had left, but I was also actually leaving New Zealand whilst most of the civilised world was either coming here or would be riveted to their TVs watching the 2011 Rugby World Cup (no TV on Pitcairn). I should have noticed that! But in the end, perhaps the God of Rugby was on my side, I would be far far away when the French beat us in the quarter-finals.

Chapter 29

Travel to Pitcairn: Not for the Faint-Hearted

Pitcairn is not easy to get to (nor indeed to get back from), apart from staying in a five-star hotel in Tahiti for three nights on the way there and one night on the way back. Now I know that some people would dream of three nights, all paid for, in a five-star hotel on Tahiti. But in exchange, would three months on Pitcairn be OK? That would give many people pause for thought. By 2017, after my three months stay and five subsequent visits to and from Pitcairn via Tahiti, I was overheard to say 'Not Tahiti again'. Well, bless my soul, you could have heard a pin drop. The looks of incredulity directed towards me were incredible. I was glad *The Daily Mail* was not in earshot: 'British Diplomat bored with Tahiti' would roar out from the front page and some very senior people in London, who were negotiating with HM Treasury for more money for the FCO, would be roared away from the negotiating table with nothing to show for their efforts. And the roar would eventually come back to bite me. Still, it was not to be and, anyway, I digress (again).

To fly to Tahiti from Auckland is approximately a five-hour flight. Nothing wrong with that. Except that you take off on a Sunday afternoon and arrive on Tahiti on Saturday evening at 9.15pm. In the past week, I had travelled across far too many time zones and now this – crossing the international dateline backwards. It was all too much. Whilst disembarking at Fa'a'a (yes that is a place name), international airport on Tahiti, I think I saw myself through a hole in the space-time fabric of the universe, embarking on the Los Angeles-Auckland flight some six days earlier.

I needed to lie down, so I did. In my five-star hotel, with a lagoon outside the window, French Polynesian islands, mountains on the horizon and Albert Einstein on the next balcony formulating theories on jet lag, the space-time continuum and my recently acquired insanity.

It was not all lagoons and laziness for the next three days (two Sundays in this particular week). I had to pay a courtesy call on the

French authorities; it was they who were a key part of the lifeline to Pitcairn. They allowed our supply ship to disembark passengers on to their small island on Mangareva, a forty or fifty or sixty-hour sea journey from Pitcairn. The length of the journey depended on the weather. But I shall come to all that.

On my second Sunday of the week, commencing 4th September 2011, I toured Tahiti. It took six hours. There is only so much surf and blue sea a man can take (said he heading off to a small island in the middle of a very big ocean). The Gaugin museum is small but good, but even he decided that Tahiti was not for him and headed off to the Marquesas, where he died in 1903. And so after I had doffed my cap to the French Authorities on my first and only Monday of the week (who wants two Mondays in any week anyway) and paid my respects to the various memorials to firstly, Captain Cook and then later to the Bounty at the wonderful Matavai Bay, I was off to the airport again.

This flight was not to be compared with Business Class on Air New Zealand, nor the Tahiti Nui flight from Auckland to Fa'a'a which heads onto Paris. Nope, we were now getting down to the nitty-gritty of inter-Pacific island travel. This was a twin-propeller plane, sixty seats, no Business Class, extremely limited trolley service (at times non-existent), no seat allocations, a baggage allowance of twenty kilos and not one gram more, and very important this, not enough fuel to get us all the way to our next stop, Mangareva.

Of the sixty-six seats, only fifty-five were allocated to passengers – apparently eleven extra souls might have affected fuel consumption, and instead of sixty-six people arriving safely in Mangareva there would have been regular air and sea rescue operations mounted for sixty-six souls bobbing about somewhere in the South Pacific – all 63,800,000 square miles of her (although it might have looked a bit odd if the air-sea rescue people were searching in and around the holiday resorts of Fiji).

In a somewhat bizarre coincidence with some of my fellow travellers on the trans-America train, many of my travelling companions were, shall we say, corpulently challenged? But there was no train to Mangareva and with these flights frequently full, it was scary to think that one such lady or gentleman would squeeze in next to one for the next five to six hours. Frequently, I did not escape. And I am not the smallest person on the planet. Uncomfortable is an understatement. But, to be fair, crunched up against the window had its advantages, giving one fantastic views of the islands and atolls of the South Pacific.

As alluded to earlier, fuel was a problem and we had to refuel on one of two atolls in the middle of nowhere. Some people actually left the aircraft on these atolls: I think they were professional plane refuellers, who did six months shifts. I hope they were paid a lot. One of the two atolls was Hao, you would not have wanted to have been here in the seventies – lots of nasty nuclear stuff being shipped to the French atomic testing site of Moruroa. And in the mid-eighties, the two French intelligence officers involved in the blowing up of the Greenpeace ship *Rainbow Warrior* in Auckland harbour were detained here. Not for long, but I will not go into that for fear of undermining our current pleadings with the French to be nice to us after we leave the EU.

And so, on to Mangareva, heavily squashed in my seat but my spirit soaring as I was getting to the end game of this particularly long journey from Deal to Pitcairn. We landed on an airstrip on Mangareva. Or rather we did not. One thousand miles from Tahiti, we landed on an island called Totegegie, five miles from Mangareva. Nobody mentioned this bit of fun and games. Mangareva could not support an airstrip and so the nice French government built an airstrip on one of Mangareva's reefs. The nice French government built many things in French Polynesia – airstrips, black pearl farms, roads, hospitals, schools etc. How kind. But, oh, I forgot, the nice French government had been using their particular portion of the South Pacific as a test site for their nice nuclear weapons. Fair exchange, I say: radiation, nuclear pollution, atolls and islands blown to smithereens, fish that are inedible due to radiation poisoning: all that in exchange for a few schools and pearl farms. What's the problem? There goes my offer of a Legion d'Honneur (Chevalier). And any hopes of Her Majesty's Government getting a good deal from the French. It is all my fault.

Back to my plight – how to cross the five miles of sea from Totegegie to Mangareva to pick up the boat to Pitcairn. Luckily, over the years, the Mangarevans had thought about this problem and ensured (it was probably those nice French people) that a boat was on hand to transport us intrepid travellers to Rikitea the main village and harbour. As soon as I knew that I would not have to swim for land my spirits soared again. And so we headed across some quite rough seas to Rikitea.

In the harbour was a 400-odd ton hunk of junk ship that had seen better days. I could not see its name, but my immediate thought was that it had been abandoned and the poor old Mangarevan authorities knew not how to dispose of it. My soaring spirits collapsed when I saw its name: the MV Claymore – my lift to Pitcairn Island.

Prior to boarding, I took some time – about fifteen minutes – to tour Mangareva (an island five miles by six miles with a total population, including from the surrounding islands, of about 1,000). One main street, one neo-gothic Cathedral. (This is internally splendidly adorned with Mother of Pearl and black pearls and well worth a visit, but then again so are Notre Dame in Paris and Westminster Abbey in London, which are a lot older, a lot nearer and probably a lot more accessible). In addition to the Cathedral, there are two shops, a few people and lots of dogs.

After this feast of deep South Pacific culture, I boarded the MV Claymore. A working supply ship: far removed from luxury yachts, cruise ships and any other type of pleasure cruiser. Way back in 2011, I had only three other travelling companions. But today, thanks to the magnificent efforts of the Head of Tourism on Pitcairn, there is normally a waiting list for the twelve bunks. And, to be fair to the crew and owner of MV Claymore, it is perfectly comfortable on board for the traveller who does not want luxury – be it high end, average or mediocre luxury. And travelling on the high seas to and from Pitcairn is, in my humble opinion, one of the last great adventures.

I was to undertake this trip five times in five years. Each journey was different, very different. There were times when the South Pacific sea behaved as though we were in a remake of the musical *South Pacific* – as flat as the proverbial pancake, the sea an unbelievable turquoise and everyone out on the decks in shorts and T-shirts singing, 'There is nothing like a dame'. On other occasions, the wind howled, the waves crashed against the hull and the ship rocked and rolled (and not in the musical sense). During these voyages, most travellers stayed in their bunks, the majority feeling seasick. One travelling companion from the British government was not seen for the whole journey. When she emerged to disembark at Pitcairn, she was so desperate to escape her floating nightmare, we had to stop her from diving in and swimming for land (where she would have met an untimely death being hurtled by high waves against immoveable rocks – but in the state she was in, that probably seemed preferable to another nanosecond on the ever-moving deck of the MV Claymore). The poor lady looked like the young girl in the *Exorcist* about three days after the Devil had taken over her body. The only thing lacking was that this British government envoy could not swivel her head through 360 degrees – well, at least, I think not.

'Was I seasick?' I hear you ask. If you go back to page one, second paragraph, you will get a hint. No, I did not get seasick. Perhaps presciently, about thirty-seven years ago on the cross-channel ferries, I had mastered my seasickness. And that was a massive bonus, to me, when it came to travelling to and from Pitcairn. I always hoped for rough seas (sod the others) because that way, with everyone ill, I did not have to listen to complaints about how the British were running Pitcairn, listen to weird and wonderful ideas about improving Pitcairn (a golf course, an extreme mountain bike track, a helipad, to name but three) and generally get earache from the thoroughly ill-informed. I am sure that, at times, even the crew, from Bob in the engine room to Neil on the bridge, wished that I would succumb to seasickness or any other debilitating illness. In my more bored moments, I would sit and pester them with inane questions about seamanship, Master Bates and nothing of interest to them whatsoever.

And so, some fourteen days after leaving Deal, I heard the anchor drop. Climbing up to the bridge, I saw a big volcanic rock sticking out of the vast blue ocean: my home for the next eighty-eight days, seven hours and twenty-five minutes. In the distance, through binoculars, I could see the famous Pitcairn longboat heading out in the rough swell to bring us ashore. Standing on the tiny forward 'deck' was Pirate Paul, legs wide apart, shirtless, landing rope in one hand and Pitcairn flag in the other, ready to join the longboat to the MV Claymore. Depending on one's point of view, this was an impressive sight, a sight to bring fear into any new visitor to Pitcairn, a sight to arouse any homosexual visitors, a sight to arouse any lady heterosexual visitors, or just a sight.

Previous travellers have quite rightly described the transfer from the Claymore to the longboat as the most dangerous thing they have ever done. Others have described it as a spiritually uplifting near-death experience, others as the thrill of a lifetime, and still others as, "What is the big deal? They have not lost anyone yet." To me, the key word here is 'yet'. We shall leave it at that. Of course, on calm days, this transfer was a walk in the park.

Someone somewhere ideally described the transfer as the "Leap of Faith". As the new Deputy Governor, I knew that everyone would be watching how I fared with the Leap of Faith. And I knew that some of those watching from either the longboat or from ashore would be hoping that I would be the one to break their unbroken record of not losing anyone. They did not reckon on Deck Boy Lynch. I threw my worldly possessions onto the deck and then, like some dynamic Olympic high jumper, threw myself into the air and just managed to miss the millions of square miles turquoise blue ocean before landing on the massively undulating longboat. And now the real work was starting.

Chapter 30

Working on Pitcairn: Councils, Elections and the Boor

The timing of my handover with the incumbent Governor's Representative (and husband) was dictated by the fact that the Claymore having to unload supplies, do some maintenance and get back to Mangareva to meet the plane that would take the Pitcairn and Mangarevan passengers in a reverse journey to Tahiti. In short, the Claymore would leave on Sunday and I had arrived on a Thursday. Too long a handover but nothing to be done about that.

Once the Gov Rep and her husband had left, I had eighty-four days and three hours and fifteen minutes to learn all about the reality of Pitcairn. With hindsight, it would take anyone a hundred years to learn about the reality of Pitcairn. And so on Sunday 11th September 2011, life and learning on the Pit began in earnest (or as earnest as I would make it – I am not a very earnest chap).

The fact that the Deputy Governor (DG) of the Pitcairn Islands was spending three months on Pitcairn as the Governor's Representative (GovRep) was new and complicated – worthy of Sir Humphrey in *Yes Minister*. Both the DG and GovRep were unelected members of the Pitcairn Island Council. Their job was to try to ensure that the Council did not try to pass laws that were out of sync with British Government policy, such as bringing back hanging (which with hindsight might not have been a bad idea); in addition, the FCO's finest had to try to ensure that the Council behaved in a manner befitting any Local Council in any district in the UK, and generally seeing that normal standards of good and corporate governance were upheld. For whatever reason (presumption of innocence springs to mind) we, the British government, had failed miserably on that latter point. The Mayor and, therefore, the Council Chair had been charged in 2010 with the possession and downloading of very serious child pornography. He would not stand down, and was even re-elected with those charges hanging over him (five later years, he was convicted and imprisoned for his heinous crimes, but more of that later).

In addition to that Council role, the DG/Gov Rep had to help oversee the four Division Managers who were responsible for the maintenance and upkeep of Pitcairn. Basically, I was the Head of the Civil Service, an unelected Councillor, the eyes and ears of the Governor and, thus, the whole of the British government. I was an advisor to the Council, an advisor to anyone who wanted advice – or in reality, the person that a lot of Pitcairners would like to see make mistakes, big mistakes. There were those who would stop at nothing to set traps for the unsuspecting me and many future Governor's Representatives. Of course, I should not forget that, as a member of the British Civil Service, I was viewed as the enemy by a significant majority. So nothing much to do then but sit back and enjoy Paradise Island. Incidentally, in 2011, Paradise Island had no beaches, bars, restaurants, cinemas, TV (although there were enough real-life soaps on this island to fill the British TV listings for the next fifty years). There was no radio, nor mobile phone connections. The electricity was switched off between midday and five o'clock and from ten o'clock in the evening until eight in the morning. The Internet was the slowest on the planet, when it worked – in 2011 the alleged downloader of child pornographer was the IT manager, I kid you not. And in my house was a shower in which one had to run around in in order to get even slightly wet.

The workforce consisted of about thirty-eight people who had multiple jobs. Councillors could be cleaners and vice versa. Everybody had fancy titles: Division Managers, Heads of Department, Store Manager, a Nursery Manager, the list went on and all of these managers and departmental heads had assistants of some sort or another. If memory serves me correctly, there were some ninety-one jobs divided up, very unequally, and not without some family bias and family malice, between the thirty-eight men and women of the Pitcairn workforce.

One of my early duties was to deal with a case of bullying in the workplace. The offender simply hung himself by his own petard when, in reply to a question, he insisted that it was perfectly OK to shout and scream at employees and that some people deserved to be humiliated, publicly, whilst at their desk. During the formal disciplinary inquiry, the offender decided that he would outstare me. Ha! Ha! Unbeknownst to him, I had stared down an alleged mass killer who was also, allegedly, the leader of the white supremacist, neo-Nazi, organised crime ring operating in America's toughest jails. And so I won this particular contest; but I was starting to get worried that I might be getting a reputation for staring down criminals – did I mention that this chap on Pitcairn had convictions for child molestation? Must have slipped my mind.

There were two semi-happy endings to this sorry saga: one, we threw the disciplinary book at our offender and two, he did not speak to or acknowledge me for the next five years (whilst living on Pitcairn and in later annual visits). That was very pleasant. This man was (and probably still is) acknowledged by the majority on Pitcairn, and further afield, as an obnoxious loutish, rude oaf. And no one in their right mind in the non-Pitcairn world would want to hang out with him at anytime, anywhere.

An unintended consequence of all this eye contact is that I can no longer lock eyes with anyone for more than a nanosecond – which for my interlocutors is a rather disconcerting habit.

In the meantime, I held the keys to the prison and, on a weekly basis, had to allow access to ensure essential maintenance – the hot, humid and rainy climate on Pitcairn ensured the fast deterioration and the even faster takeover of buildings by mould, plants and insects. On my first Monday, a Pitcairner came to my office and asked for the keys. Absentmindedly and not really looking to see who was asking, I handed over the keys and, making conversation, asked, "Do you know where it is?" I was actually thinking of the generator when I asked. But it came across as if I were asking this particular Pitcairner amongst the indigenous population of fifty if he – on a one mile by two-mile island, on which he was born and had lived most of life – knew where Pitcairn's most infamous building was to be found. Add to this fact that he had been locked up in there for over two years for child sex crimes and was still on parole, and you will understand why he gave me a rather strange look, grabbed the keys and headed off to tell anyone who would listen that the real Deputy Governor must have been thrown overboard on the journey here and an idiotic impersonator was now amongst them.

I should point out here, just in case you were wondering, Her Majesty's Prison Pitcairn had been decommissioned with the proviso that the British government could recommission it (code for reopen and reuse) if and when needed. And in 2016, it would be needed again. But that is for the future.

My days consisted of getting to know the people on Pitcairn – not really hard considering that you saw all fifty-odd of them virtually every day (and some of them were odd indeed) – as well as getting to know their work and working practices. Absurdly, perversely and wrongly, in my opinion, one man with very serious child sex abuse convictions was allowed to work in the shop selling sweets to the island kids. In the UK, he would probably have still been in jail (but that is another story). He ignored me – hating the presence of those he deemed to be responsible for his incarceration on Pitcairn.

Council meetings could be civil, uncivil, childish, adult, humorous and vindictive. But what astounded me was that, despite the various factions or individuals having completely opposite points of view, when it came to voting on a particular issue, invariably it was 7-0. Always unanimous. This was one of the many ways that Pitcairn pretended to the outside world that, in 2011, all was harmonious on this somewhat dysfunctional island. One of the ways to ensure that outsiders did not see any disharmony was to ensure that visitors/tourists to the island did not get to see the internal internecine politics of Pitcairn was by ensuring their non-attendance at the Council meetings. Visitors were told that the meetings were boring and taken on 'trips' to try to ensure that no one would leave with a bad impression of Pitcairn – alas, some got through the net. One visitor described the place to me as a "poisonous cesspit of depravity and desperation." But before I go on, by 2016 things had changed for the better. Much better.

I suppose the Council meetings could have been worse, and not all of them were totally bad – they could have emulated the cabinet meetings of Madman Hussein of Iraq. It was rumoured whilst I was in Iraq that one Minister had the temerity to complain about the number of deaths during the Iraq/Iran war. He was taken outside and shot and his deputy immediately promoted. No more was heard of the death toll in that particular bloody war. There were occasions on Pitcairn when it crossed my mind, fleetingly of course, that a shot in the dark might not have gone amiss.

A lot of stuff was deliberately brought to the Deputy Governor/GovRep for decision or advice. All that stuff was a lose-lose game. Whatever decision or advice was handed out, within seconds an opposing party, family, relative, friend, victim or other ne'er-do-well would be on the doorstep complaining. For me, schizophrenia became a common daytime condition. I did not sleep much and still have insomnia. Night time after ten o'clock, when all the lights went out, was mostly taken up with admiring the amazing South Pacific night sky.

Election times were particularly fraught. With an electorate of about forty-two every vote counted. Let me repeat that; every vote counts. And there would be all sorts of shenanigans by those on both sides – basically, the Christian clan and the Warren family – trying, legally or illegally, to ensure that certain people did not get to vote. At every election, all the issues surrounding voting rights were brought to the door of Her Majesty's Government, then to Auckland and then to legal advice from across the planet. The idea being that whoever 'lost' the election or their seat on Council could then blame HMG. *Oh, what fun.*

The various electoral protagonists ensured that overseas relatives, still with the right to vote, were back on Pitcairn; places and dates of birth were endlessly re-examined; parentage scrutinised (on Pitcairn, that was not always a good idea) and even coercion and bribery were not unknown. All this was happening in the world's smallest democracy. And in 2016, it coincided with the Trump election. Did you not read about the Pitcairn election at the same time? Shame on you – the Pitcairn one was much more devious and interesting.

Chapter 31

Pitcairn Leisure Time (PLT)

Whilst there was no TV, radio and other distractions on Pitcairn, there was enough to, occasionally, take one's mind off work. I memorised the names of all people in the graveyard and, just to add to my mental exertions, I memorised the names of the living as well – not too hard, just think Christian, Young, Warren and Brown and success. If anyone turned up with names like May, Hammond, Johnson, Mitchell, Nithavrianakis, Podenas, Scantlebury, Bradley, Bedford, to name but a few, they would sow the seeds of confusion. They would need, by Pitcairn deed poll, to change their names to Christian, Young, Warren or Brown. And insanity would then prevail again.

Amidst all these names, I had heard that people had various nicknames (Blondie, the White Witch, Duvet Pete, Mouth on a Stick, Egypt – someone who was in denial – in de Nile), and more importantly, there was an internal Pitcairn Honours system. The Order Of Fletcher (IV Classes):

(i)   The Lower Order Of Fletcher (LOOF)
(ii) The Higher Order OF Fletcher (HOOF)
(iii) The Grand Order OF Fletcher (GOOF)
(iv) The Royal Order OF Fletcher (ROOF)

Make of this what you will. I am not commenting further.

I walked a lot on Pitcairn. This is known as travelling by stealth, as no one can then hear the arrival of the gas-guzzling, fume-emitting, climate-changing, deathtrap quad bike that most people use to get from A to B, even if A to B is about three feet. There were rumours that the Pitcairners knew the sound of different quad bikes – to me they just all sounded loud, old and in need of the breakers yard. But as I walked to most places and, thus, by their definition in "stealth", the darker characters spread the rumour that I was trying to catch them out. As everyone had told everyone for years now, the bad stuff had stopped, so why did they have to worry?

On my strolls, I also tried to memorise the place names on Pitcairn, at the bottom of various cliffs. There are such gems as Robert Fall, Freddie Fall, Where Dick Fall, McCoy's Drop, Johnny Fall, Lin Fall, Martin Larson Fall, Dan Fall and Nellie Fall – lots of falls, but mostly by men. There is a rock called Hard Rock – go tell the restaurant chain, I am sure that they would be interested in that. My favourite is Big Stone Break My Hip. After my quad bike crash in late 2017, I was hoping that there would be a spot called Kevin's Drop or Deputy Governor Break Arm, but I am reliably informed that it ain't gonna happen. My other favourite is NoPubHere; if you believe that you need to seek professional help.

During my stay, there was, for a few brief Fridays, Christian's Café. A bar/stroke restaurant where the freshly caught lobster was second to none – it would beat anything from any Michelin starred restaurant in the vicinity. It was a place for a cold beer and a laugh, but we 'off-islanders' were still in the Pitcairn goldfish bowl. So, until my last night on Pitcairn in 2011, temperance was the name of the game (and a rock just around the corner from St. Paul's Pool).

There was also the one surreal, very surreal, disco in the house at the highest point of Pitcairn. Here, cigarette smoke drifted across the dance floor and caught in the light of the 1970s mirrored disco ball. Here, a convicted child molester imitated for the whole three minutes and thirty seconds of *Night Fever*, every move by John Travolta. Here it was that, without irony, almost to a man and woman, the Pitcairners en masse performed *In the Navy* by the Village People. And here it was that I decided to slide off home, and leave them all to it. As I trundled down, torch in hand, towards my house, I looked back and the party house eerily struck a striking resemblance to the house of the mother behind Norman Bates's hotel in *Psycho*. And eerily, the music that was now quietly riding on the wind sounded like the soundtrack from the film *The Shining*.

But even though there was a paucity of entertainment, there was, of course, fishing. For reasons of my sanity and an inescapable desire for self-preservation, I did not go out onto the vast, temperamental South Pacific Ocean in the tiny one or two-man vessels that others did. I went on the big longboat and we caught Wahoo – an amazing game fish: very fast and similar to a barracuda. We caught five or six, about five feet long and weighing in about thirty or forty kilos. What a day that was. Not for the fish, of course, they had their brains bashed out and their flesh removed for future consumption.

Mostly, I made my own entertainment on Pitcairn: reading, walking, looking out to sea to ensure that it was still there; photographing the magnificent waves breaking on Bounty Bay, thinking about my wife and children on the other side of the planet. And most of all, losing weight by my inability to cook, the lack of pubs and restaurants and, try this at home, walking up and down the aptly named 'Hill of Difficulty' some seventy-six times in my eighty-nine-day stay.

Chapter 32

Pitcairn from Auckland

After living on Pitcairn, I then transferred to Auckland and became the fat remote controller. I was the NASA equivalent of the commander of the lunar (or looney) command service module in Auckland, trying to look after successive Pitcairn Governors' Representatives and later Administrators (a bureaucratic name change that, in my humble opinion, meant nothing). My job was to support and advise, 24/7, 365 days a year, our diplomatic colleagues on Pitcairn. I was supported by the Governor(s). Two in my time in Auckland. Pre 2015, that job was tough, very tough, but post "Goat Wars" (see more below), life on and off Pitcairn became easier, not as easy as living in Paris or New York say, but easier.

From early 2012 to late 2016, no year was the same. Actually, no day was the same. All the GovReps/Administrators were magnificent. I take my hat off to all of them for lasting twelve months on Pitcairn. Some with no or minimal leave. All the time, they were under the microscope from the locals. All the time, they were problem-solving. All the time, thinking about problems or perhaps all the time thinking about flagging down a nearby ship (nigh on impossible) and getting the hell outta Dodge. The latter thinking was more likely.

On top of all that thinking, they had to manage our non-Pitcairn professionals (and their partners) on the island. There was the butcher, the baker and the candlestick maker. No, that's not right. There was the policeman, the doctor, the teacher and the social worker. They were mostly New Zealanders or Australians, and all of them started out with good intentions. The majority survived. Others were corrupted by the child sex crime deniers, others saw crime in every nook and cranny, others drank too much, others tried to hibernate their way through their twelve months and still others, many others, got on with their jobs and went fishing and came back, outwardly, unscathed. As one said to me, years later, "Had I known what I was getting myself into, I would have rather gone to Afghanistan for twelve months." In my five years there, between myself, the team on Pitcairn and the Governors, we managed the problem that was Pitcairn. A problem that is now vastly improved.

Back in Auckland, there was, and still, is the magnificent Pitcairn Island Office. The logistical genius is Shirley, who solves crises from storm damage to airline strikes, from overcrowding on the supply ship to supplying KFC and other delights, ensuring that every three months everyone gets what they need from New Zealand. She has successfully managed several medical evacuations, and when Shirley growls, people act. With Shirley is Evan, the Head of the PIO, the money man, the contract man, the negotiating man, the man who understands it all and stops us silly diplomats from doing silly things. Most importantly, Evan was my other drinking partner when it was needed – quite often, as it happens. Without these two stalwarts, Pitcairn would probably slowly sink deep into the Pacific Ocean – do not even think about it.

Still, in Auckland as Deputy Governor, it was my job to cover every aspect of Pitcairn so that if the Governor, the Foreign Secretary, the Queen, my Mum, or anyone else asked about EU funding, DFID funding, Child Safety, repopulation, Council activities, court cases, Pitcairn prisons, logistics or even the price of a beer in downtown Auckland, I would know (I would certainly know the last one). A great and busy job, but back on Pitcairn it was not all work. On Pitcairn, one man was not doing his job – or at least in the very recent past, had not been doing it. He was going to single-handedly bring Pitcairn, once again, into disrepute.

Chapter 33

The Trials and the 20-Month Celebration

I am not sure of the exact date or dates, but in 2010 the then-Mayor, Michael C Warren, was charged with possessing child pornography – both images and videos. Some of these were of the most serious kind. He was also engaging in vile sex chats with a girl or girls he knew to be very young. All this just after eight men, one-third of the island's male population, had been convicted (two had entered guilty pleas) of serious sex crimes involving children. One was already a previous Mayor, and now this Mayor who, at the time of downloading serious child sex pornography, had child safeguarding responsibilities. If Pitcairn had wanted to put the previous sex scandal behind them, this was not the way to go about it.

Warren engaged a lawyer and, in 2011, a seven-year trial was about to start. A trial where the British taxpayer was going to pay for the prosecution and the defence. I do not know the exact cost but I suspect that it was more than £1million. And I and many others would be in the thick of it.

Warren's lawyer decided that his defence, before the actual substantial criminal trial for possessing child pornography, would be that Her Majesty's Government did not have the legal right to govern Pitcairn. He (or rather Warren instructing him) was going to spend the next seven years trying to attack and dismantle almost every facet of the newly created 2010 Constitution. If any particular part of the Constitution could be knocked down, then the Defence would argue that Warren could not be put on trial (if a lawyer is reading this, it is very simplistic, I know, but it's best to keep it that way. If anyone else is reading this, thanks for buying the book and getting this far).

On the Pitcairn prosecution side, we would have the Pitcairn Attorney General (two in the time of the trial), their assistant, and our QC prosecuting solicitor; all inestimable good people and good friends to this day.

Unbelievably, some of the previously convicted men thought that if this trial failed on constitutional grounds then their earlier trials would be reopened, the verdicts overturned, compensation awarded and everybody (on Pitcairn) would be happy. I know that Pitcairn is remote, but it is not on another planet. There was no chance of that happening but, as I say, some lived with that pitiful hope. Their motivations were not only the possibilities of compensation and clearing their name(s), but also that they would then have the ability to easily move around the globe, from country to country, either for pleasure or changing residence, without being held up at borders or their visas being denied. Then (and now) international travel was, quite correctly, somewhat difficult for those with serious child sex convictions. Some would claim to me that they were sentenced to life on Pitcairn. Well, I say tough. Think of the victims and not yourselves.

I would be called as an expert witness on behalf of Her Majesty's Government and spent two and a half days testifying and being cross-examined (way above my pay grade, I might add). In addition, I think I attended over ninety per cent of the hearings. I attended two hearings, via video conference, whilst on Pitcairn and many others were by video link from the courts in Auckland. Finally, the appeals in May 2018 ended up going to the Judicial Committee of the Privy Council in London – the court of final appeal. Basically, the Privy Council is that side of the highest court in the land, the Supreme Court, which deals with, amongst other things, the Overseas Territories (if a lawyer is reading this…). We won!

Over the seven years of this trial, we, as HMG, had to be very wary that we were not seen or heard doing or saying anything that might in any way jeopardise the court proceedings. Bear traps were set by the supporters of Warren – they tried to engage HMG staff in conversations about the hearings. They hoped that we would say something that could be detrimental to the defendant, so that they could then seek cause for a mistrial: when briefing visitors to the Island, I advised that the correct response to such seemingly innocent enquiries was the equivalent of, "No comment, the matter is sub judice, before the courts." Too legalistic for me. And so I came up with the much more succinct: "Why don't you f*** off and mind your own business." That seemed to do the trick.

Having said all that, the criminal trial is done and dusted. There was a conviction, several convictions, as a matter of fact, for possession of child pornography. But before we come to that, we had a problem.

Whether one likes it or not, in our legal system there is the presumption of innocence. As each constitutional argument and challenge was rejected (and dismissed at Appeal), we inexorably headed towards the child pornography criminal trial. A conviction that could result in various sentences, including imprisonment. For complex reasons, the defendant could not be moved to either England or New Zealand for trial. Nor, in the event of a guilty verdict and a custodial sentence, could the defendant be persuaded to serve his sentence in England or New Zealand. And so, what to do if there was a custodial sentence handed down? Because of the presumption of innocence, we (HMG) could not make the necessary preparations, repairing and recommissioning Her Majesty's Prison Pitcairn. The defence lawyer would have torn us apart.

However, with the potential problem of possibly incarcerating the former Mayor, we had to take advice from anyone willing to give it. Legal people and IT forensic experts advised us that there were very few defences once the offending child pornography had been discovered on a defendants computer, laptop or other device. IT experts could (and would) inform the court or courts where the imagery had come from, when it had been viewed, when and where it had been filed and any efforts to conceal its existence. And indeed, the depths to which any defendant had gone to conceal the illegal material.

If memory serves me correctly, Warren had so much pornographic imagery (not all illegal) that if he worked eight hours a day and slept eight hours a day and then watched pornography for the remaining eight hours, it would have taken him over five years to fully review his sad and distorted cleverly curated collection.

If anyone is remotely interested in a very short summary – my version – of the defendant's defence as to why he had downloaded the vile child pornography, here it is. He argued that he had done so because he wanted to understand why some of his fellow citizens had been previously imprisoned and why now, every two years, the island was subject to in-depth Child Safety Reviews. Nobody believed that – especially, and most importantly, the court.

After the guilty verdicts and a custodial sentence of twenty months, a failed appeal and then an instruction from the judge that the defendant would be on bail for precisely six months, the British Government had to recruit Corrections Officers from the New Zealand Department of Corrections (which was already overstretched at home) and get the mothballed HM Prison Pitcairn back up to standard in order to house its one and only inmate for ten months. (The other ten months would be on conditional release).

How we did that was, and in my mind still is, a mini-miracle. But we did it. 'We' being the many people not only involved in the logistics of reopening the prison, but also the people fretting and funding it all. Then there were the lawyers from the Pitcairn bar and the NZ Corrections people, and we must not forget the Judges, the police and others. Of course, there were also the Pitcairners, some of whom were former inmates, who helped reconstruct the prison. People who, to be fair, when hearing about Warren's crimes, completely disowned him.

For what it is worth, I arranged my last visit to Pitcairn (in September 2016) to coincide with the start of Warren's prison sentence. It had been a long time coming. The New Zealand Department of Corrections would not (wisely, I suppose) let me stand by the prison gate to clap him in. But back in my accommodation, quietly by myself, I raised a large glass to everyone involved and partially imbibed a very nice vintage red wine brought onto Pitcairn especially for this occasion. It was a very good feeling and, all in all, a job very well done. It took over five years but, again, a job well done. And great praise goes to Paul Rishworth, Simon Mount (now QC), Danielle Kelly, Kieron Raftery QC and many others at the Pitcairn Bar (the legal bar, not the pub).

Chapter 34

Pitcairn and the Year of the Goat

I have no doubt that there are many milestones in the history of Pitcairn: the arrival and departure of the original Polynesian inhabitants; Fletcher Christian and the arrival of and subsequent burning of the *Bounty*; the total emigration to Norfolk Island in 1856, the return to Pitcairn; the Seventh Day Adventists; the island running out of money in the 1980/90s and then gaining financial support from the British taxpayer; the criminal trials; the advent of European Union funding or the day that the Deputy Governor took a magnificent diving catch in the annual Pitcairn cricket match.

However, some might add that the key milestone of the twenty-first century was the finale of the 'Pitcairn Goat War'. A war which took place, sporadically, between 2013 and 2015. Let me elucidate.

The EU had awarded Pitcairn 2.4 million Euros to build, on Pitcairn, an alternative harbour. In reality, this alternative harbour was a jetty, or to be even more realistic, it was just a wharf; in true reality, it was and probably still is the world's most expensive fishing promenade. The idea behind the alternative harbour was to boost the economy and even increase the rapidly declining population.

When the South Pacific Ocean decides to put its angry face on in the vicinity of Pitcairn, it is impossible to land cruise ship passengers, yacht passengers and any other income generating maritime travellers at Bounty Bay. So some wise person or persons unknown came up with the wheeze that if it was too rough at Bounty Bay, then passengers (for which read money) could be landed on the leeward side of the island at a place called Tedside (which means in the Pitkern dialect/language, 'the other side'). Then there would not only be a boost, via tourism, to the aid-dependent economy, but also visitors might be convinced that the island would be more accessible than hitherto, Allowing them to settle, thus boosting the increasingly shrinking population.

As the Deputy Governor of Pitcairn, I was – on behalf of the EU – the Territory Authorising Officer (TAO). This meant that I had strategic and operational responsibility for the whole project.

Incidentally, TAO in Chinese means the 'way' or the 'path'. *A good omen*, I thought. The EU funding would help Pitcairn on their way to the path of righteousness. What a load of rubbish. Who wrote that?

Anyway, back to me being the Big Cheese on the project. The EU managerial bureaucracy and paperwork was a nightmare – there was too much, it was too complicated and there were far too many people who could and would use the EU project just to get to Pitcairn and tick a box on their bucket list. Whilst ploughing through the forests of documentation that would enable us to get the Euros into the Pitcairn bank account, buy the material and heavy equipment for the alternative harbour, and pay the salaries (extra money for the boys and girls) to build it, I found an EU clause which stipulated that any work disrupting the environment should be mitigated. Wow, that was a showstopper.

We had plans to blow rocks out of the sea and out of the land. We wanted to bulldoze through what dense vegetation there was still left near and around Tedside. We would be crushing rocks and making concrete. It would be a bit like building anew a few hundred yards of the M25. All that to do without impacting the environment – not a chance. And then, of course, it suddenly dawned on me that the environmental NGOs would be watching. What to do?

I knew, I knew, I was so glad that I knew. An independent environmental impact assessment that would also recommend mitigation measures. I was a genius. Masterminded with Evan from the PIO, we found an environmental island expert who was willing to go to Pitcairn at short notice. And go he did – the wonderful Matt B. And I went with him. Not for the EU stuff, Matt had to be totally independent. So concerned was he about the neutrality of his role that he was seasick all the way to Pitcairn and did not leave his cabin. On Pitcairn, I went about my business for four days and Matt went about his. So dedicated was he to his work, that he forgot the electricity went off at 2200 hours, whereupon he found himself in the darkest dark of the darkest night that you can imagine – every night after 2200 hours was like this – about a hundred yards from his house. It took him over an hour to crawl, from memory, along the dirt path to the safety of his garage and a torch. That feat alone should put him in the annals of the history of Pitcairn. But I digress, slightly.

Back in Auckland, Matt produced his report. An excellent study of the flora and fauna of Pitcairn and he professionally detailed the environmental 'damage' the EU project would cause. Matt expertly concluded that any 'normal' environmental damage, past, present and future could be mitigated by the mass culling of the hundreds of goats on Pitcairn. And that is where the Goat War started.

Most small island nations in the twentieth and twenty-first centuries have been trying to eradicate goats from their lands. Goats, originally, were not native to these islands – an invasive species is, I believe, the technical term. Goats are mightily destructive and goats on Pitcairn were no different. The feral goats on Pitcairn had, over many years, destroyed a lot of the vegetation to the point that they were almost eating plants (lantana) that were poisonous to them. This destruction of vegetation could easily be seen after it had rained. After the strong rain, the island would be surrounded by a ring of brown water where loose mud and other debris, which was no longer held by plant roots, had been swept down the steep hills and cliffs into the sea surrounding Pitcairn. As if that was not bad enough, a marine biologist posited the thought that the mud and grit settling around Pitcairn could damage the coastal ecosystem. And so it was a no-brainer to most of the human race – cull the goats, have a harbour and save the land and sea environments.

The team back in Auckland put together the A team of the G(oat) team. We had recruited the Southern Hemisphere's top goat expert – Big Jack C. He, in turn, had recruited a crack team of goat cullers and together we pulled out the stops to get them all, including guns and dogs, to Pitcairn. Unfortunately, there were those on Pitcairn who had no brains.

An informal, secret anti-goat cull committee had been formed, which argued that our estimate of there being several hundred goats was completely wrong. They claimed that the number was a manageable 150. They further argued that the goats were directly descended from the *Bounty* and, therefore, had some sort of historical protection. Best of all, they went on to state unequivocally that the goats had 'Goat Rights' akin to Human Rights.

We, of course, countered that 150 was 150 too many; we were not going to cull pets; after much research by me, a *Bounty* logbook showed that Captain Bligh had left Tahiti on his last ill-fated voyage on the *Bounty* with thirty-three goats (how nerdish was I), and if thirty-three goats was good enough for Fletcher Christian and his eight mutineers and eighteen Tahitian men and women way back in 1789, then 150 goats now was far too many. In order to protect my sanity, I did not get into a debate about the existential rights of goats. At times, I held back from saying out loud that the really dangerous invasive species on Pitcairn was the humans and that maybe shooting them and leaving the goats to their own self-destruction might be the best solution for the conundrum that is Pitcairn.

Of course, the real reasons why some Pitcairners were against the goat cull was because a good idea had been thought up, not by their own people, but by the big bad British. More importantly, they were thinking that, if someone were to take a close look at the environment on Pitcairn, they might conclude that the Pitcairners themselves had been seriously neglecting their paradise island for many decades. Not only that, but they had also been adding to its environmental decay. God forbid that that would come out into the open.

The battle lines were drawn, and over the next few months, claims and counter-claims about the number of goats on Pitcairn were exchanged. The number of pet goats increased by about fifty per cent. Photographs of these pet goats were sent to environmental Non-Governmental Organisations with the claims that big bad Kevin was going to, in the most hideous way possible, kill all their pets, including 'Petal', 'Blossom' and 'Tweety Pie'. Fortunately, the NGOs knew about goats and took all this rubbish with a large lashing of salt. And talking of salt, suddenly, the modern-day food that was regularly being imported from New Zealand was an abomination. Goats were needed for food. Goat curry for breakfast, lunch and dinner. And prior to the arrival of myself, big Jack C and the hunters, we had heard very discreetly from pro-cull Pitcairners that several members of the community, including community leaders, had been secretly rounding up goats and were hiding them; turning them into pets overnight and generally preparing to undermine the cull.

At that time, we were we getting clandestine goat reports from anti-goat Pitcairners. On Pitcairn, we had the magnificent GovRep Pete Smith and his equally magnificent wife, Cynthia. Pete and I had been together in Bangladesh many moons previously and were (still are) good friends. Pete regularly updated me on goat captures, goat movements (after dark, quad bikes could be heard zooming all over the island, collecting goats from homemade traps) and goat strategies. If this had been a real conflict, military historians today and in the future would have endlessly examined the tactics of both Pitcairn and Her Majesty's Government in order to set difficult exam questions at Sandhurst Military Academy. Or, if the truth be told, nobody in the real world would have given a shit.

On my arrival on Pitcairn, the 'Battle of the Goats' was in full swing. The best thing about arriving to conduct the cull was that I had a ready-made, highly-trained, heavily-armed close protection team – the hunters. No matter the pre-arrival shenanigans, we were here and the cull was going to go ahead. On the first day, 144 feral goats were humanely destroyed. That seemed, in no small way, to undermine the claim that there were only 150 feral goats on the island. And interestingly, there were not many takers for the abundance of edible goat meat. There were many attempts by the anti-cull clan to release goats back into areas that had been cleared by the hunters and their dogs. These were unsuccessful. As the days went by and the Claymore sat quietly to take the hunting party back to New Zealand, hundreds (over four hundred) of goats were humanely destroyed. And that should have been that. But it was not to be.

Big Jack C and the hunters told me that the dogs had indicated there were numerous goats being hidden on private property. Probably about seventy on top of the pets. That would leave about a hundred on Pitcairn. Big Jack C predicted that such a number would mean escapes into the wild and, in five to ten years, we would all be back to have another cull. It goes without saying that this cull came at quite a hefty EU price. In vintage Foreign Office fashion, I called a conference, or in this case, an emergency Council meeting – deliberately called on the same day that I and the team would be reboarding the Claymore and getting away from Pitcairn.

Prior to the meeting, I was approached by several Pitcairners who confirmed that many goats had been hidden, re-released or indeed that some Pitcairners had tried to resuscitate dead goats. These pro-goat cull Pitcairners advocated that the anti-cull clan needed a good "head punch". I discussed tactics with Pete. I could not get hold of the Governor nor the EU man in Noumea (how convenient was that?). A head punch was a good idea, but I was reliably informed by the policeman on the island that, even on Pitcairn, it was illegal. I had another idea. At the Council meeting, after listening to waffle and other tripe about our cruel and allegedly illicit actions, I calmly announced that, as the TAO, I was cancelling the alternative harbour – Euros 2.4 million – because the cull had been undermined and was thus far unsuccessful at mitigating the environmental damage that would be caused by the construction of the alternative harbour. I calmly left the meeting and then ran all the way back to Pete's place and drank a large cold beer in one go.

Pete too walked out. We would not take any representations. People were trying to call the Governor. I was trying to bring forward the departure of the Claymore. Half the island loved the 'head punch' idea, the other half would have loved to punch my head. The New

Zealand police officer arrived and agreed to escort me to the longboat and insisted that he would come all the way out to the Claymore in order to ensure my safety (*a bit over the top*, I thought, *but better than me going a bit overboard when no one was looking*).

Four days later, I was back in Auckland. During the return journey, I had turned off my Blackberry and ignored my laptop. I needed some peace. Prior to getting into my office on Friday lunchtime, good old Evan intercepted me and dragged me to the pub. *"Oh dear, here we go*, I thought, *the proverbial has really hit the fan.* However, to my astonishment, Evan told me that Pete had desperately been trying to get hold of me to tell me that something fundamental on the island had changed.

After some serious soul searching, the good guys and bad guys on Pitcairn had decided that, after over 200 years of fighting HMG at each turn, now might be a good time to try a more conciliatory approach – lest we forget, there were 2.4 million reasons why they should take this new approach. And so, now that more goats were being culled by the Pitcairners' own guns and a proper goat management regime was in place, the environment was being protected and a much more harmonious, collaborative relationship was in place between the Island and Auckland and London, we all agreed to reinstate the alternative harbour. And, as if to wish us all well, 2015 was, unbelievably, the Chinese Year of the Goat. And, of course, a full report was sent back to the FCO and to anyone in Whitehall who cared (which in hindsight, was not many, I suspect).

But perspective is everything. Some months after the 'Goat Wars', I was in London and someone asked me if I knew about the goat issue. I bored them for a while before my interlocutor told me a little story. The Head of the Syrian Section in the FCO had seen the report on the affair of the Pitcairn goats. This gentleman at the time was the team-leader dealing with Syria. A matter that included a massive civil war, which included barrel bombings, massive abuses of Human Rights, the use of illegal chemicals on civilians, refugees everywhere and Russian interference in the peace efforts. But, kindly, the team leader circulated the Pitcairn goat report to his vast Syrian team with the immortal words: "And you think we have problems?!"

And finally, on my last visit to Pitcairn (which was combined with the incarceration of the former Mayor, which hopefully ended, once and for all, that dark side of Pitcairn's history), a tour of the island immediately indicated a lot more greenery in areas where the goats could no longer decimate the vegetation, and even those goats kept for food, or whatever, were in pens and well managed. I was also due to open the alternative harbour. That was not to be.

After a very pleasant afternoon high up on Pitcairn, I ended up upside down in a ditch, pinned down by a converted quad bike, with a broken arm and petrol dripping. The Head of Tourism was bleeding badly, as was I, although my blood was probably more white wine than blood, and it was getting dark. To cut a long story short, we were saved by two people, who in their past lives, had been the most vehement anti-HMG people on Pitcairn and who, more recently, were anti-cull generals orchestrating the undermining of the goat cull. Years earlier, these two souls might, very conveniently, have not noticed the quad bike and Deputy Governor in the ditch, and who knows what would have happened then?

Times had indeed very much changed. I thank them for their help that day and I hope they are both well.

Chapter 35

Pitcairn Postscript

For me personally, the chance to live on Pitcairn for three months was the chance of a lifetime, and an amazing experience. It is one of the few great adventures left in the world – or at least left to us in the Foreign Office.

Dealing with its trials, tribulations, successes and people was challenging to say the least! I have learnt an enormous amount about legal process, the witness stand, courts, EU funding, problem-solving, harbours, shipping, Freedom of Information, Marine Protected Areas, DFID, NGOs, council work and, of course, goats. I never ever want to see, meet or eat a goat ever again.

During the seven years between 2010 and 2018, Pitcairn was once again rudely reminded of its dark past because of one man. His pointless arguments against what he knew to be the truth (he was convicted of serious child pornography crimes) meant the waste of over a million pounds on proceedings which gave rise to twenty-one defence applications, over 2,000 pages of written legal submissions, sixty days of oral hearings, 320 judgements and me in the witness box, and Her Majesty's Government completely vindicated. England's highest court threw everything out. And now the case has been closed.

I left Pitcairn in September 2016, when the island was in, in my humble opinion, in a much better place than it had been in 2011, and the subsequent years leading up to the Year of the Goat.

I write in 2018, and the island might have changed since 2016. If it has, I would hazard a guess that it will have been for the better. The people know that the dark side of the legacy of child abuse cannot be erased. But they are working hard – at least, most of them are – for a better brighter future. I wish them well – not all of them, but most of them. It is one of the most unique islands and mini-communities in the world. Its history can show us how man and woman can deteriorate to a *Lord of the Flies* level, but then redirect themselves and hopefully propel themselves into a bright long-lasting future.

And I for one think and hope that they make it.

Part Twelve

Auckland (New Zealand)

January 2012 – December 2016

Chapter 36

A Rogue, a Rogue, my Consulate is a Rogue

And so, alongside dealing with Pitcairn (no more Pitcairn please, I hear you cry), I had the other job of being Consul General in Auckland. My Last Diplomatic Crusade. It was January 2012.

The job was Consul General in charge (but that was not to be) of the Consulate General in Auckland – one of best cities in the world in which to live. After four years in Denver, similarly one of the best cities in the world, this was the life.

We, the whole family, flew out Business Class on Korean Airlines via Seoul. Getting closer to the Korean peninsula, I kept a good eye out the window to ensure that we were not going to enter North Korean airspace – something any non-North Korean plane would do at its peril. It was particularly important for me as I am sure that they had not forgiven me for, to them, escaping across the Demilitarised Zone way back in 2005. And if I ended up back in North Korea because of some unknown flight difficulty, I feared that my health might suffer irreparably. How would I know that we had not accidentally entered the dastardly dictator's atmosphere? I think being shot at or shot down would have been the giveaway. As that did not happen, and we arrived safely in Seoul, logic dictated that we had not entered the Devil's airspace.

From Seoul, there was another twelve-hour flight to our new life in Auckland. Whilst living the leisure life in Denver, I seemed to have missed out on certain economic realities that were happening back in the UK. The big one being Austerity with a capital A. This soon hit home on our arrival in Auckland – an attempt to put us in a second-rate (cheap) hotel in a strange part of the city was thwarted by yours truly when I threatened to go straight back to Blighty, even if that meant the hotel keeping HMG's room deposit. So there! We managed a short stay in a nice hotel in downtown Auckland. We moved into our Residence shortly thereafter.

Our home (Residence) was situated in a very nice area but it was about the quarter of the size of the one in Denver. But that had a very good upside – it basically meant that any diplomatic entertaining I had to do would have to be done in very nice, upmarket downtown restaurants – where was the austerity in that? On moving into our new home, I searched desperately for my officially provided car and driver. Years ago, the Auckland Consul General had had a Jaguar, driver and a big mansion on the hill with a flagpole. The mansion and flagpole had long been sold and dug up by Her Majesty's Treasury. But surely they had not dispensed with the Jag and driver. However, they had, many years earlier. No one told me – but that was probably because I had recently been enjoying life in Denver and had given up reading any corporate budget stuff (except my payslip) and, more recently, had been existing on Pitcairn, where reading any corporate stuff would have just added to the desire to swim for Tahiti.

Even without reading how desperate the government was to save money, I think the sad home-based civil servants in the Treasury and the FCO Finance departments (who all were keen readers and practitioners of anything to do with austerity) had been carefully and enviously watching the latter part of my career. They had watched it soar from the icy depths of Siberia, via the snow-clad peaks of the Rocky Mountains and the sun-baked shores of Tahiti, to the city of Auckland, where the number on the quality of life and quality of lifestyle scale was nine out of ten (ten being reserved for Deal in Kent in England). In watching my career and travels, they had plotted to relieve me and my family of the little things in life – a chauffeur-driven Jaguar. I should have noticed the salami slicing changes: Yekaterinburg – an official car plus driver (although he was a Russian spy); Denver – an official self-drive car, no one spying on me but myself; Auckland – a fifty-two seat, five-ton, number fifteen bus with a driver who did not spy on me but spied on my ticket on a daily basis.

And so it came to pass that I bussed into the Consulate General feeling slightly (make that totally) jet-lagged to meet the team. In the usual FCO style, the eleven of us (the magnificent eleven) gathered in the boardroom for the usual self-effacing, self-deprecating but wholly untrue self-introductions. These brief introductions were followed closely by even briefer descriptions of objectives and targets (that were mostly fiction). The team were looking at me and I was looking at them. This went on for an eternity until one amongst them asked the usual question, "What are you going to change?"

Diplomatically, I replied that, "If it ain't broke, don't try to fix it, but if Friday afternoon drinks are not already part of the working week, they soon will be."

This broke the ice and in a few months' time, it also looked set to break our livers. Everyone agreed with this new innovation (at least, newish for Auckland) and we celebrated there and then with a couple of bottles of New Zealand Sauvignon Blanc. As it was only 1030, we took the collective decision to return to work for ninety minutes and resume our getting to know each other symposium over a long lunch prior to me heading off to the High Commission in Wellington. *This first working day went well*, I thought.

The High Commission in Wellington seemed much more serious. At my first roundtable with the staff (there were about twenty or thirty – I forget) the usual question came up – what was I going to change in Auckland? I gave the usual reply about things not being broken. I also alluded to my new Friday afternoon meetings over drinks. This caused much hilarity, but when I explained that I was serious, they became very quiet and very serious, and the High Commissioner gave me a look which would ensure that any Sauvignon Blanc within 500 yards would not need chilling in the fridge. I was to get that look once again.

It happened when I was still fairly new and giving a presentation on the benefits of trading with and investing in London and the whole of the United Kingdom. Being diplomatic, I referenced the commercial powerhouse that was Auckland, calling it: "the great capital of New Zealand". This drew much spontaneous applause from the Aucklanders, whilst others just drew their breath and wondered how on earth the FCO had sent someone to New Zealand who did not even know that the capital city had been moved from Auckland to Wellington some 147 years ago. Oops! I quickly corrected my geographical incompetence by explaining that I had been on Pitcairn for the last three months. This seemed to absolve me from my capital cardinal sin. I learnt from this – every time I erred diplomatically, socially, sartorially, professionally, unprofessionally and geographically, I blamed my three months on Pitcairn. It worked a treat – sympathy from all corners.

Back to the matters at hand. After the all-staff meeting, I with met the Wellington Heads of Sections. This was, with hindsight, the proverbial ambush. To a man and a woman, they were fiercely critical of the Auckland team, the very existence of the Consulate General and, by default, they must not have liked my very existence. But I was there and not going anywhere for five years. In good old-fashioned management style, I asked to hear their grievances. That was a mistake. On and on it went and my offers of adjourning to the pub (always a great tranquiliser, equaliser and sanitizer, or do I mean a bringer of sanity?) were roundly rejected. I nevertheless found a fridge, a glass and a half-open bottle of Pinot Gris, and gently sipped that as a New Zealand volcano slowly erupted around me.

Now the interesting thing about all this was that the wine was 2009, supposedly not a good year for the NZ white, but I found it perfectly palatable. The other two good, interesting things I realised were that, firstly, I outranked all of them and secondly (as I had been briefed in London), I did not manage the vast majority of staff in Auckland. In fact, I only managed my part-time Executive Assistant (we shall come to the inestimable Salote Koto – Fijian Royalty). I did not manage any of the Trade and Investment team, not even the Deputy Consul General and Vice-Consul, the infinitely tremendous Barbara Harris (we shall come to Barbara – Matakana Royalty) and I could not, with all my Consular experience, partly manage the Consular Assistant, the remarkable former international rock star Derek Foster (we shall come to Derek – Crystal Palace Royalty). The three musketeers to my d'Artagnan. Or perhaps, and more likely, the Four Horsepersons of the Belgian Bar.

But back to the ambush. As I sipped and took in the wonderment of the 2009 Marlborough Pinot Gris, I occasionally gave ten per cent of my thoughts to the incessant criticism of Auckland that was enveloping the room in a dark cloud, the likes of which I had only seen while talking to the North Koreans about human rights. Time to put things right. I asked what was to be done, what had they done thus far, and the number of the local taxi firm so that I could get back to my hotel and listen to the banality at the bar rather than this unproductive invective (of course, I did not mention aloud this last thought).

The answers to my questions were that, as I was now here, I had to sort things out (even though most of the teams were managed out of Sydney or, believe it or not, Wellington). And, of course, they themselves had done nothing thus far – which, I deduced was a good thing. This was simply because the reports I had seen were that the Trade and Investment team were overachieving their targets and objectives and were globally a high-performing crew, and Derek, the Consular guru, had regularly received very high praise – and later on, especially from me, when it was his round. So, logically speaking, any possible interventions from Wellington might have been counter-productive. Of course, again, I did not say this out loud. But the expectation was that the Messiah had arrived and He would tame this 'rogue' post. As I outranked them all, I closed the meeting, promising to take note and act upon all their invective (sorry, 'points') and how I looked forward to a wonderful, productive and friendly non-rogue relationship between the two cities. They almost cheered. How little did they know this rogue Messiah; even my private mobile ended in 666.

In the very unlikely event that someone from New Zealand is reading this book and has actually gotten this far (and I hope they have not cheated and jumped straight to the NZ bit) and is wondering if they can sue me, suffice to say, I might be making all this up. This will be my defence in any court of law. Then I might be charged with perjury, but I do have the presumption of innocence and, after the experience of a certain remote island in the South Pacific, I know how to drag out a trial. However, at the moment, I am dragging this out.

Just a bit more on management. I was managed by two High Commissioners over the 2012 – 2016 period. Both brilliantly and wisely left me to my own devices. Both were excellent and they deserve further honours for trying to keep me on the straight and narrow.

The hour-long flight back to Auckland gave me time to reflect on my visit to Wellington. After that, and still with fifty-five minutes to go, I read the in-flight magazine and mentally achieved a hundred per cent in the quiz, which appeared on the drop-down safety video screens above our heads. On one occasion, the drop-down screen did literally that, during the safety video. It dropped down on a passengers head. I did laugh, but no one else seemed to see the irony or the humour.

The following day in Auckland – in view of the invective – I called a meeting in the boardroom at 1200 prompt. At 1200 no one was there, nor at 1205 nor at 1215. Actually, no one was in the Consulate. Fortunately, my trusty sidekick Barbara found me wandering as lonely as the long white cloud which the Maori named New Zealand after. (The Maori did not name New Zealand, that might have been Able Tasman – or more correctly, Unable Tasman. He was unable to land and later we British did, and now it is a Realm of Her Majesty the Queen rather than a Dutch elm). But again, and hopefully, for the last time, I digress.

Barbara delicately took me by the hand and led me to the real Boardroom – not some secret room tucked away behind lead-lined walls and ceilings, only accessed by iris recognition electronically operated doors. No, the real Boardroom was the Belgian Bar opposite the Consulate building. Who knew? And life again was coming full circle. Brussels, my first Posting, was, unsurprisingly, full of Belgian bars and beers. And now thirty-one years later, here I was in a Belgian bar full of Belgian beer, some 11,305 miles from Brussels. Stella Artois all round.

And so, at our first 'board' meeting (there were to be many), I acquainted the team with the Wellington view (not the one of the harbour, but the office one), but before the riot really got out of control, I calmed the many-headed beast that was in an unseemly rush to burn down their capital city, or at least the part of it that was British sovereign territory. I explained that I knew all about the wonderful good work they were doing, enlightened them to the fact that I quite enjoyed the moniker 'Rogue Post'. And that we would work hard and play hard. And that was that; the tone was set for the coming years.

Chapter 37

The Swamp

And so began the Consul General 'diplomatic' work. As with Denver, I considered it my duty to get out and about and to get to know the major political figures, the business community, my fellow Consuls General and Consuls, anyone of influence and, of course, the ideal places (bars, restaurants and clubs) wherein to meet these people. It is hard to believe how difficult it is to regularly frequent bars, restaurants and clubs in order to meet and entertain those people who might in some small way contribute to Her Majesty's Government's foreign policy and trade targets. A tough job, I know, but someone had to do it.

My first port of call was on the Mayor of the great city of Auckland. A great man, but unbeknownst to him, he had the same name as a convicted rapist on Pitcairn. Being the ultimate professional, this did not deter me. But I did have to ensure that, in Auckland, I did not mix up the Mayor with the convict, and once in Pitcairn, I did not mix up the convict with the Mayor of Auckland. A difficult task, I know, but I think I succeeded.

During my time in Auckland, I attended many meetings with the Mayor and, hopefully, further strengthened and deepened UK/Auckland relations. But I could not help noticing (and not just me) that Auckland/New Zealand was pivoting on its Southern Hemisphere axis and tilting towards the growing economies of India and China. And who could blame them? The United Kingdom had had its day in the eighteenth and nineteenth centuries. The Americans had had the lion's share of money and geopolitical power in the twentieth century and now China and India were growing in influence. New Zealand wanted and wants some of that action. Of course, part of my role was to try to ensure that Auckland did not totally forget their old friend from the other side of the globe – even after we shafted their lamb exports and other bilateral agreements when we joined the EU in 1973. Brexit has ensured that the tables are now turned. New Zealand now has the ability to shaft us in any bilateral trade agreement we might try to negotiate.

Of course, with the exception – naturally – of my Asian colleagues, every other Consul General and Consul was trying to safeguard their own national interests. But my role was somewhat undermined by the big A – Austerity. Even though the UK had the world's fifth largest economy, we were (then) a major influence in the world's largest trading block (the EU, in case you did not know), we were (still are) at the top table of the United Nations Security Council and a major player in NATO. Even though we had all this influence, I was the only Consul General who took the bus to work and to official engagements. My residence was the smallest amongst all my diplomatic colleagues and my entertainment budget was, in my humble opinion, limited. Some would say "good", and I would not blame them. So I will not dwell on the miserable, miserly, stingy, penurious, penny-pinching peasantry sitting in Her Majesty's Treasury in Whitehall. They should come and try living in one of the world's nicest cities for a few years. That would show them (or maybe it is not a good idea).

My consular colleagues were an amiable bunch. At least most of the time. Like any group of human beings, there were those who had views, opinions and actions that might not endear themselves to other members of the group. I think it is called in-fighting. Now, in most cases, this in-fighting can, at worst, rob groups of their effectiveness, and result in barbed comments over a beer. But not the Auckland Consular Corps. No, we were determined to outdo any other Consular Corps on the planet and even our extra-terrestrial Consular and Diplomatic colleagues.

We decided to invite the really important people from politics and business to our annual dinner. And then, just for entertainment, of course, we decided that two of our esteemed Corps should have a fight. During the fight, a singularly brave peace-making Consul would be knocked to the ground. It was like something out of the Wild West. All thoroughly enjoyable, if one was at the rodeo or a boxing match, or was a fully paid-up member of *Fight Club*, but not really the ideal advert for a Service steeped in the tradition of deal-making and peace-making. As with all fights, it eventually ended. I think it was a draw – it certainly drew in our VIP guests who seemed to thoroughly enjoy this unexpected and unprecedented entertainment. If memory serves me correctly, the two protagonists have never uttered another word to each other. The peace-making Consul lived to tell the tale and has delighted in telling the tale far and wide – I heard a rumour that the then-New Zealand Prime

Minister was seized of the entertainment and found it very amusing – probably wished he had bought ringside seats.

But not every day was filled with such excitement. Other days were filled with Black Velvets (not the fabric, but the drink – Guinness and Champagne) and Bluff oysters (not oysters that call your bluff at five-card poker, but the world-famous oysters from the Foveaux Strait, just off the coast from the town of Bluff in the South Island of New Zealand). Black Velvets and Bluff Oysters, a magnificent mix served up with true style, bonhomie and much laughter by my great friend the Irish Consul General. Still, he has never forgiven me for the evening when I took him home in my official vehicle. He was not used to having to get a ticket to get into a diplomatic vehicle, or my automatic doors, which were controlled by a complete stranger sitting several yards away, and so, not being used to the austerity machine, he became trapped in the doors and was lucky to escape with life and limb intact.

Other days were as equally stressful: there were the never-ending fishing trips, the visits to various towns and indeed islands. On one occasion, I and my darling wife had to have dinner on The World – the largest private residential ship on the planet. Another tough evening out. As with most diplomatic postings, there was the inevitable and inescapable round of national day receptions, business-related receptions, visiting VIP-related receptions and, finally, reception-related receptions. There were working breakfasts, lunches and dinners – I did not go to many breakfasts, as there was a tendency not to serve the outstanding New Zealand Sauvignon Blanc. Not sure why; and when I did request it instead of coffee, people (for reasons I am still unable to fathom) looked at me in a rather peculiar way.

I was not alone in taking on all this hard work. The delightful Barbara J Harris (Deputy Consul General and Vice-Consul) was invariably at my side. She provided inestimable introductions to the great and the good of Auckland society, provided sound advice (Barbara was our unequalled, politically well-connected, trade and investment expert) on the politics and economics of Auckland, she provided sound counsel on my speeches and pontificating and, most importantly, provided me with a never-ending supply of Sauvignon Blanc. We were a good team and we took our work very seriously. Prior to any major outing, be it a lunch, dinner, reception or whatever, or even occasionally just for nothing, we would have briefing meetings in Barbara's office.

Barbara's office was a wonderment of exotic statues and plants. And a hidden supply of red and white grape juice. I nicknamed it 'The Swamp' after the tent in the brilliant *M*A*S*H*.

BJ Harris was the BJ Hunnicutt to my Hawkeye Pearce. I know that Barbara is a woman (still is, as far as I am aware – you never know in this ever-changing world) and that BJ Hunnicutt was a man. And that I am not as tall or as hirsute as Hawkeye Pearce, but it's my story and I am allowed some licence in my own musings. Anyway, I digress slightly. In the Swamp, over the years, many briefings were briefed, many projects were projected, many plots plotted, many plans were planned and many wines were wined. And many happy, funny conversations conversed. As if that was not enough, I think we did some work.

In addition to the trade work, there were the usual visits to be arranged. The key to getting a senior British minister, businessperson or official to New Zealand was to find out if they were going to see Big Brother (Australia) across the Tasman Sea. If they were, then the old ruse was to say to their handlers – "Look they've come all the way to Australia, why not tag a couple of days onto New Zealand?" It worked on quite a few occasions. Amongst many others, we hosted William Hague (Foreign Secretary), the Lord Mayor of the City of London, the Speaker of the House of Commons and the Chairman of Lloyds of London – the key to that visit was not to confuse this eminent corporate body with Lloyd's bank: to plagiarise Basil Fawlty, I think I mentioned the bank once, but got away with it.

I have to admit that it was not all hard industrious trade, investment and visit work. I am not sure what the non-trade and investment work there was (excluding Pitcairn) but I am sure it was out there. I am sure because I had the wonderful Salote Koto as an Executive Assistant helping me with all that. One element of the work was being a full-blown member of the Consular Corps of Auckland – more receptions and cocktail parties, I am afraid. And, as time went by, in 2015/2016, I eventually became the Dean of the Auckland Consular Corps. One would have thought that job would have been a nice cushy number. Not so.

There was the big thorny issue of entertainment at the annual Christmas Consular dinner. We needed to find a way to stop one of our esteemed members taking over the microphone and singing as though all our lives depended on it. The reality was that, by the time he was halfway through his repertoire, the majority of us were close to taking our own lives, if not his. As the Dean, I had a cunning plan.

As soon as our esteemed colleague momentarily paused after the second verse of his first song, I stood up and applauded with all my might and (as I had suspected) the herd followed suit. After a two-minute standing ovation and, we thought, a return to the civilised post-dinner idle chatter, I would be the hero of the evening. That was not to be. Our entertainer took the ovation as a sign that we wanted more, much more. Alas, his encore lasted longer than the intended original performance. A miserable failure and a lot of my colleagues avoided me for a very long time after that.

Another key representational role was to be the 'Giver of Speeches'. A so-called easy way to extoll the virtues of how wonderful the UK is. And, even more than that, the speech can explain how it would be in the best interests of every living being and organism in New Zealand to buy British goods and services and invest their very last cent into improving the British economy. The FCO in London regularly sent out core scripts for one to use in one's own style. I had my own views on speeches:

- Make them long and boring.
- No humour.
- If you wear glasses, fiddle with them and occasionally (accidentally) drop them in your glass of water.
- Do not practice your speech – anywhere, anytime – just go for it.
- Lose your thread.
- Use loads and loads of statistics and mention things like the Indifference Curve, Price Equilibrium and (my favourite) Equity Risk Premium.

Try to make your speech when England have been thoroughly thrashed at football, cricket or rugby. This enables the audience to seriously indulge in mocking you rather than listening to your key pro-UK messages.

Now some public speaking experts might find all this a tad confusing. Well, let me explain. Giving speeches presenting HMG's policies is work, hard work. And, if possible, it is to be avoided at all costs. Alas, early on in last two postings, I forgot these basics and was much in demand on the speaking circuit in both Denver and now Auckland. That meant rigorously following the six Ps – Prior Preparation Prevents Piss Poor Performance. Lots of work but sound advice for effective public speaking.

And also, in 2015/2016, I had somehow become a much titled individual – Her Majesty's Consul General of Auckland, Deputy Governor of the Pitcairn Islands and Dean of the Auckland Consular Corps. I did not get any more pay but the representational burden (code for freeloading at lots and lots of official events) was taking its toll. Something had to give. I made a decision – very unusual for us Foreign Office chappies. I decided that I would work less. I did not tell anyone (except Salote who fully agreed that I should work less and we should spend more time discussing the service sectors – the usual excuse for visits to local hostelries). But the strange thing about cutting down on real work was that no one noticed. To this day, I am not sure if that was a good thing or a bad thing. But I do not lose sleep over it.

Alongside Salote was the equally superb Derek. Between the three of us, we handled anything out of the ordinary and, with Derek's expert hand, handled all the consular cases involving British nationals. We were always innovating new ways of working, one of which was Friday afternoon briefing meetings – discussions relating to the events of the past week (if anyone could remember) and discussions covering work coming up the following week. (If anyone could be bothered to bring their electronic diaries – too heavy to carry was the usual excuse, but I did notice that the drink and nibbles tray was never too heavy to carry.) However, these meetings stopped because someone undiplomatically informed Wellington about them. And Wellington then decided they wanted to video in. Not a good idea, I thought, and so I brilliantly came up with the latest management consultancy speak that there was 'meeting overload' and I would be the first to take the initiative and abolish the Friday afternoon meeting. At least, that was the overt plan of action.

Spitting feathers (in the sense of anger rather than thirst – at least I think so, subliminally it might have been the latter) that my Friday post-lunch meetings had been rumbled, I brought in my two musketeers and sought their advice about reinstating, covertly, our favourite Friday afternoon pastime. I told them I was spitting feathers and, as one, they cheered, danced, applauded, and called me a genius and agreed. *What strange behaviour*, I thought. *And to what had they agreed?* It turned out, unbeknownst to me – a world-renowned barfly – that a traditional English pub called the 'Spitting Feathers' was located opposite the side entrance to the Consulate, wherein a bottle of Heineken was only NZ$ 3.00. And so the briefing meetings were reinstated, careers ruined and beers drank.

It was during one of these Friday afternoon working sessions (all work and no play for me), that a British friend of a friend from Denver days, who was now living in Auckland (small world), explained to me a syndrome that enlightened me somewhat about working in New Zealand. It is not all-pervasive. But, like *The Mist* in Stephen King's novel of the same name, it is out there. It seems to me to be peculiar to the antipodes. In my simple words, it is a culture that tries to undermine success. It is called the 'Tall Poppy Syndrome'. Try not to catch this syndrome. It is not good. But when I was made aware of it, it dawned on me that our colleagues in Wellington might have had a bad case of the syndrome. The Auckland Consulate worked hard and played hard and I think that caused some resentment – hence, the 'rogue' post designation. Tall Poppy Syndrome was probably in play. Of course, I may be wrong (ever the diplomat trying not to offend people).

Chapter 38

The Earth Moved and so Did We

There is a lot to be said for humankind's incessant search for new knowledge, new lands, new civilisations, new bars and restaurants. But surely, God had planned that New Zealand should be left alone by us humans. 'Why?' I hear you cry. Because it is very far away from anywhere (but the Kiwis might argue that anywhere is very far away from them). But no, that is not the answer. It is because (according to me, anyway) New Zealand – both its big islands and all of its little islands – is part of the Pacific Ring of Fire. Actually, to be completely accurate, it sits right in the middle of the lower end of one of the rings (this is not really a ring, it's more of an upside horseshoe – that in itself should be a clue; all the luck falls out). This Ring of Fire is not a Johnny Cash song. This Ring of Fire is a very large area of the Pacific in which one can guarantee earthquakes and volcanic eruptions. Why would one want to live in such a dangerous place when life and property insurance must be stratospheric? When you add to that New Zealand's location – it almost exactly straddles two tectonic plates, the Australian plate and the Pacific plate – life becomes much more interesting

Now hear this! Now hear this! Tectonic plates are not to be messed with. It is not good when they grind against each other. Years ago, they created the Himalayan Mountain range. I am not saying that the plates knocked them up overnight, just that the Himalayan mountains would not exist had it not been for tectonic shifts (to use the scientific jargon) and there probably would be, instead, a large ocean. So when they are dormant, tectonic plates are ok, but when they move, that is not OK. It is a bit like being six feet away from a sleeping grizzly bear who, unbeknownst to you, is going to wake up hungry and angry. Why is he or she angry? I do not know. Probably attending too many receptions.

Anyway, my theory is that we might have chosen a better piece of real estate to colonise had we humans known all about Rings of Fire, the tectonic shifts and (it gets worse) the seven major Volcanoes on the North Island. I think Wales might have been a safer bet. But perversely,

I am glad that it is populated because, otherwise, I would not have ended up there nor met some great people who called it home.

Having now expressed my somewhat limited views on the natural hazards of New Zealand (there were other man-made hazards equally as dangerous – Asian tourists driving on the wrong side of the road, for example, something to be avoided at all costs), it has to be said that New Zealand is a great country to visit (and live in, if you are so minded). And so it came to pass that our good friends Steve and Tracy came to visit. And we happy campers travelled far and wide.

Once, as we were indulging in wine and beer (separate – not mixed) on the South Island, the building began to vibrate and then shake. Yep, those old tectonic plates had decided to stretch their limbs (not sure that plates have limbs, but humour me and live with the metaphor for the moment). At first, we all looked at each other and then at our drinks – could they be so strong that the building was, in fact, static and the alcohol had caused us to lose control of our nervous system so that our limbs were taking on lives of their own. That would have been half OK, but no, it was not the fine New Zealand wine. Instead, it was New Zealand's fine decision to perch itself on where the Pacific and Australian tectonic plates meet and occasionally annoy each other. We had been part of a minor earthquake. We survived. And so that was that box ticked.

Onwards and southwards we travelled to the magnificent Queenstown, on the way traversing mountains and rivers, passing through towns and hamlets and crossing plateaus and valleys. I do believe that I once spotted Gandalf and the Hobbits in the distance. They were having a brew (or more likely, in this part of the world, having a joint). Once in Queenstown, we sat marvelling at the remarkable Remarkables before heading back to Auckland. The trip of a lifetime.

Back in Auckland, there was the email letting me, Leone and Benny and Adele know that our five years in Auckland were coming to an end. The timing was good. Benny was in University in Wales, Adele was finishing her A-levels, Leone wanted to be closer to her Mum and, after the New Zealand/Pitcairn jobs (no other jobs could ever compare), I could not see a better way of bowing out of the wonderful FCO. Christmas 2016 would be spent with family and friends back in Deal in Kent, in England.

Other factors helped to ease my transition back to England; Barbara (BJ Hunnicutt) had, after seventeen years in the Consulate (five in the 'Swamp'), moved on to pastures new. And so that avenue of laughs had disappeared from my working days. Once I left, the powers that were – and many in Wellington – considered the Swamp to be proverbially drained. It will be reconvened in 2020.

In late 2016, the Auckland and Wellington inter-post relations had become very cordial; likewise with Pitcairn. However, with Wellington, I did not need to shoot lots of goats, I merely needed to understand that some poppies naturally grew taller than others.

Whilst I think the Pitcairn Island Office was sad to see me go, Evan indicated that 2017 would be spent rebuilding his liver and Shirley gave me the best compliment – she would miss me. A biggie from Shirley. During a farewell teleconference with the Pitcairn community, I received a round of applause – something that would have been unheard for most of the previous 225 years. The last time they applauded a British official was when they set Captain Bligh adrift in the South Pacific Ocean. Make of that what you will.

Derek and Salote waved goodbye and just went to the bar. I had trained them well!

Barbara did not answer her phone.

Leone was feted by her many many friends and, as usual, will be sadly missed. Adele just went to parties and Benny would meet us back in Blighty.

So almost forty years after walking out of the gates of HM Prison Canterbury to join Her Majesty's Diplomatic Service, the time had come to hang up Her Britannic Majesty's Diplomatic Bag.

I have lived in eight separate countries, spent long periods in another six, and by my count, have visited sixty-six different nations, over 1,000 cities and towns, and visited half the states in the USA. During this time, I've probably used every form of transport bar a balloon. By my own calculations (probably inaccurate), I have travelled close to half a million air miles.

I have visited Times Square, Trafalgar Square, Red Square and Tiananmen Square: there are many squares in the FCO, but the best is the little Grande Place in Brussels.

I have crossed London Bridge, Brooklyn Bridge, Golden Gate Bridge, Sydney Harbour Bridge, Auckland Bridge and, a bridge too far, crashed into a small one on Pitcairn.

Lakes, I have seen a few – Windermere, Geneva, Rose (Senegal), Volta, and Taupo in New Zealand. Rivers I have crossed – the Thames, the Seine, the Danube, the Rhine, the Moscow, the Iset, the Ganges, the Brahmaputra, the Colorado and the Mississippi.

Significant birthdays, we all have them. Mine: 21st – Deal; 25th – Brussels; 30th – Geneva; 35th – Dakar; 40th – Riyadh; 45th – Capetown; 50th – Denver; 55th Auckland; 60th Deal Pier!

I could go on, but most importantly, I met and married Leone, have two great kids and, again very importantly: made many life-long friends from all parts of the globe.

And so, we near the final sentence (not before time, you are thinking). I suppose I could try to end it all (not literally) with something profound. But I have run out of thoughts. And so I will leave it to plagiarising a line from Bob Seger's *Travellin' Man*:

"And these are the memories that make me a wealthy soul."

Epilogue

And so, in 2018, I now find myself not only back in my hometown of Deal, but back in the house of my teenage years. We have bought my Mum and Dad's house. After all my travels, foreign adventures, different cities, countries and culture, wonderful people, and a great family, I was back in the original bedroom of my youth – I am sure that a psychologist (forensic or otherwise) would have a field day with that.

When I left Deal in 1978, we were on the verge of electing our first female Prime Minister. In the FCO, Iran was in turmoil, as was the Middle East; Israel and Palestine were at each other's throats, the Argentines were sabre rattling over the Falklands and the Spanish were making similar noises about Gibraltar. Libya was a mess and on the verge of civil war. The Soviet Union (now aka Russia) was invading sovereign states and basically annoying everyone where she could.

The Aussies were making noises about the monarchy, the UN was toothless, we had doubts about the EU, but were hanging in there; the military (and most other government departments) were whingeing about government cuts. We were fawning to the Saudis because of oil and gas; immigration was a problem (but no one was willing to raise it for fear of being dubbed a racist), Zimbabwe was in the news, the Foreign Secretary was an Old Etonian and the Soviets were in Afghanistan wondering how they could get out – now we are. I could go on, but in a nutshell, I am not sure that I have achieved much in my many years with the fantastic FCO. On the foreign policy fronts, nothing much has changed really. But at least I tried! And had a lot of laughs trying!

I think we have settled back into life in Deal. We have had to adapt to our more sedentary and less public life. To blend in, we tend to minimise our past (and perhaps my fellow diplomatic travellers do likewise). The eyes of some of our interlocutors tend to glaze over if we start to reminisce about servants, drivers, big houses, business (occasionally first) class travel, royalty, different countries and different cultures. That is not to say that we are any better than any of our friends and families – far from it. We have just travelled a different road (literally!). Our friends and families in England and Lithuania have been our reality anchors. And they too have had just as exciting lives. We were doing just the same, but not in England or Lithuania!

Acknowledgements

Trying to get everyone into a book that tries to condense some forty years into a book of this size is an impossible task. Some friends (and, of course, family) are already mentioned in the hallowed pages above – hopefully, they will not sue me. And, hopefully, they are still friends and family.

My Mum is not mentioned in the book, but she has always been there and for that, everlasting thanks.

My brothers and sisters (Chris, Paul, Angela and Debbie) too are not mentioned. Neither are there partners and children. But they too have always been there (mainly in the pub) whenever I (and, subsequently, we) came back on leave or to live in Deal.

Leone's family have always been there for us in Lithuania – Donatas and his family (and Gediminas and his family in Hainesville, Illinois). Many thanks to all of them for their kindness. And many thanks for their understanding when I dragged one of their own out of Lithuania to follow me on, what at the time, was a completely unknown path for us both – marriage, kids and many foreign lands and adventures. We made it!

To long-time great friends, the Jarrett family, the Murtons and to Vince G.

And, of course, there are many FCO-related friends who deserve their own paragraphs or even chapters. Space and time have meant that they do not get a mention in the main body of the book. Many are still life-long friends and we are still in touch. As is the way of the world, we have lost touch with many others, but writing this book has brought them back into our minds. Below, in chronological and posting order, I try to acknowledge them. Shame on me, if I have missed someone. It is not deliberate. There is neither rhyme nor reason to the order of the names.

London: 1978–1981
Adrian B, Joe B, John W, Edward B, Liz D, Pete H, Dave and Janice M, Gill W, the other Kevin J Lynch and family (sorry about the chequebook), Ian S, Jamie B, Bridget B, Mags N, Rod L, Paul L, Katie W, John H, John T, Kevin B, Christine G, Anne C, Karen S, the ladies

from W50 – Barbara P, Carol S (and later on Pitcairn), Mary C, Verity M and Pat R; Miles F, Mags W, Carole E, Tim B, John R, Tom B.

Belgium: 1981–1983
Carolyn and Sheilah, Phil and Gail E, Paul and Carey R, Ian N, Julie B, Janine R, Marie S, Val M, the whole British Missions football team, Mandy H-J, Mike M, Trevor L, Sam H, the NATO UK-based security team (especially Peter B for the cigarettes and Joe for his tales about Rudolf Hess in Spandau Prison), Jan and Den, Kevin M.

Bangladesh: 1984–1986
Gerry and Lesley L, Paul and Trish B, Simon R, Ric L, Richard M, all of the Harvey family (forgive me for gatecrashing all your excellent parties), Coby V-D-L, all our interpreters, Hamish and Marie-L C, big Paul W, Richard F, Tony and Viv M, all the staff at the club who served me too many beers, Abdul Rahman (manservant of the century), Bobbie the dog, Tony S, I and Jan A, Pete and Cyn Smith (and later Pitcairn).

Jeddah: 1986
Richard and Linda B and Noel G.

Baghdad: 1986
Shame on me; I cannot remember the names of my travelling companions.

London: 1987-1990
Liz and Tony K, Millie and Carol, Peter and Elaine J, Marie F, Celia H, Julie O, Graham S, Andy S, Tony K.

Geneva: 1988
All the great Consulate staff.

Senegal: 1990-1993
CW, Claudinette D, Sarou, El Hadj K, Sophie J, Daba, Alan H, Mike W, Harriet F, Mike H, Bob D, Anne M-T, Rover the cat, Dave and Gisele A.

Lithuania: 1994–1997
Remigijius P, Jolanta B, Linas D, Ieva B, all the Embassy guards who opened the gates at all sorts of wonderful times in the early hours, all

the other Lithuanian Embassy staff, Ina and Gedas and their family, Oliver O, Mida and Darius (already mentioned), two Ambassadors and their wives.

Saudi Arabia: 1997–2000
Steve M, Ruth and Andy S, Philip P, Jamie B, Ted C, Andrea and K Mc, John and Jane C, William P, Tony M, Simon and Olivia M, Andrew G, Mike and Libby N, Heather and Basil S, Ismail F, Chris and Zara, Colin and A L.

Ghana: 2001–2004
Carol T and her partner, Ruby A and the whole UKTI team, the Simpson family, Farida and Emile S, Jazz and Tracey and Family, Gillian E and family.

London: 2004–2006
Geoff C, all those from the Friday afternoon club in the Old Shades.

Russia: 2006
Natalie G, Tony B, Galina, the FSB.

USA: 2007–2011
Terry M, Everybody from Churchill's Cigar Bar in the Brown Palace, the poker players from the Celtic Tavern Poker School, all of the Daughters of the British Empire (especially Phil and Olive), Gary and Hilary S, all our neighbours in Cherry Creek, Walter and Nijole R, all the Honorary Consuls, Governor Bill Ritter, Governor John Hickenlooper, Senator Mark Udall.

Pitcairn/Auckland: 2012–2016
Heather M, Kerry Y, Mary T, Leslie J, Lesley T, all the policemen, social workers, doctors (especially Kevin and his lovely wife) and teachers (especially partner 'Big' Roger). The magnificent Sam Smith. All the other GovReps and Administrators, Vicki T, Johnathan S, Paul W, Paul T, Deidre B, John and Angela B, all the career Consuls and all the Honorary Consuls, the Northern Club, Simon M (QC), Danielle K, Paul R, Kieron R, all the judges.

Note: For some ladies, I used either their maiden initials, their married initials or both. And some couples are no longer couples, but they were at the time, so I have left them attached to each other!

In Memoriam

Firstly, to my Dad, Kevin Lynch, and to Leone's Dad, Benediktas Podenas. If there is a bookshop in Heaven, I hope they are reading this.
To FCO colleagues who have gone to that Big Embassy in the sky – all of them taken from us far too early.

Dave Goodall
Phil Ambrose
Roger Clarke
Michael Peart
Roger Beetham
John Atkinson
Doug Grey
Graham Gibson
Graham Watkins
Tim Parsons
Ian and Caroline Blake
Frank Schuchat
Ken and Karen Simpson
And sadly, during the writing of this book
Lord Carrington
And far too young, my good friend
Mike Moon

Printed in Great Britain
by Amazon

14962732R00192